T0345275

Applications of 5G and Beyond in Smart Cities

This book explores the potential of 5G technologies and beyond in smart city set-ups, with the availability of high bandwidths and performance, and low latency. The book starts with an introduction to 5G, along with the challenges, limitations, and research areas in future wireless communication, including the related requirements for transformation of societal paradigms and infrastructure. Applications related to visible light communication, network management in smart cities, the role of 5G in public healthcare, safety, security, and transportation, and existing and planned 6G research frameworks are included.

The features of the book include:

- A broad perspective on 5G communications with a focus on smart cities.
- Discussion of artificial intelligence in future wireless communication and its applications.
- A systemic and comprehensive coverage of 6G technologies, challenges, and uses.
- The role of future wireless communications in safety, health, and transport in smart cities.
- Case studies of future wireless communication.

This book is aimed at researchers and professionals in communications, signal processing, cyber-physical systems, and smart cities.

Computational Intelligence Techniques

Series Editor: Vishal Jain

The objective of this series is to provide researchers a platform to present state of the art innovations, research, and design, and to implement methodological and algorithmic solutions to data processing problems, designing, and analyzing evolving trends in health informatics and computer-aided diagnosis. This series provides support and aid to researchers involved in designing decision support systems that will permit societal acceptance of ambient intelligence. The overall goal of this series is to present the latest snapshot of ongoing research as well as to shed further light on future directions in this space. The series presents novel technical studies as well as position and vision papers comprising hypothetical/speculative scenarios. The book series seeks to compile all aspects of computational intelligence techniques from fundamental principles to current advanced concepts. For this series, we invite researchers, academicians, and professionals to contribute, expressing their ideas and research in the application of intelligent techniques to the field of engineering in handbook, reference, or monograph volumes.

For more information about this series, please visit: www.routledge.com/Computational-Intelligence-Techniques/book-series/CIT

Applications of 5G and Beyond in Smart Cities

Edited by
Ambar Bajpai and Arun Balodi

CRC Press
Taylor & Francis Group
Boca Raton London New York

CRC Press is an imprint of the
Taylor & Francis Group, an **informa** business

Designed cover image: © Shutterstock

First edition published 2023
by CRC Press
6000 Broken Sound Parkway NW, Suite 300, Boca Raton, FL 33487-2742

and by CRC Press
4 Park Square, Milton Park, Abingdon, Oxon, OX14 4RN
CRC Press is an imprint of Taylor & Francis Group, LLC

ISBN: 978-1-032-13142-9 (hbk)
ISBN: 978-1-032-13144-3 (pbk)
ISBN: 978-1-003-22786-1 (ebk)

DOI: 10.1201/9781003227861

Typeset in Times
by Deanta Global Publishing Services, Chennai, India

Contents

Editor Biographies

Dr. Ambar Bajpai, SM'IEEE, F'IETE, L'ISTE, is currently working as a research associate professor at Atria Institute of Technology in Bangalore, India. His alma mater are Chulalongkorn University, Thailand (Ph.D. 2016) and Birla Institute of Technology and Science, Pilani, India (M. Eng., 2008). Dr. Ambar has more than 14 years of teaching and research experience in various institutions in India and abroad. Dr. Bajpai also received various scholarships mainly prestigious graduate school scholarships, 90th-year Research Scholarship, GATE, and Overseas academic presentation scholarship during his Ph.D. and M.Eng.

His areas of interest are iterative channel coding in 5G and beyond and visible light communication. He has published more than 42 papers in peer-reviewed journals and international conferences including invited talks in India and abroad related to the broad domain of Wireless Communication. He has been volunteering in IEEE Bangalore section as a Branch Counsellor, Founder Secretary in the Information Theory Society Chapter, treasurer and execom role of various technical society chapters.

Dr. Arun Balodi, Senior Member IEEE, Fellow IETE, Life Member ISTE, is currently working as Professor and Head at Atria Institute of Technology in Bangalore, India. He is an IEEE student branch advisor at the Atria Institute of Technology. Dr. Arun attained his Ph.D. Electrical Engineering, from the Indian Institute of Technology, Roorkee, India, 2018, his M. Tech., Digital Signal Processing, from Govind Ballabh Pant Engineering College, Pauri, India, 2010, and a B.Tech. in Electronics and Communication Engineering from Uttar Pradesh Technical University, Lucknow, India, 2005. He was awarded Gold Medal in M. Tech., and the Academic Excellence award in the years 2010 and 2011. His research areas are Biomedical Signal and Artificial Intelligence, Digital Signal and Image Processing, Medical Image Analysis, Machine Learning, and Pattern Recognition. Dr. Arun has more than 15 years of teaching and research experience in various institutions in India. He has published more than 28 papers in peer-reviewed journals, international conferences, and book chapters, and has 3 patents. He is an active researcher and reviewer for various indexed journals and conferences and has given various technical talks. He has actively participated in more than 37 FDPs and more than 100 webinars and conducted workshops in the domain of Signal and Image Processing. He has delivered expert talks at more than 30 STPs, conferences, and webinars.

Contributors

R. Amrit
PES University, Bangalore, India

Htain Lynn Aung
Chulalongkorn University, Thailand

Ambar Bajpai
Atria Institute of Technology,
  Bangalore, India

Arun Balodi
Atria Institute of Technology,
  Bangalore, India

Hargovind Bansal
Qualcomm India Pvt Ltd., Hyderabad,
  India

Vidhya Banu
KNS Institute of Technology,
  Bangalore, India

A. Angel Cerli
St. Annes Arts and Science College,
  Chennai, Tamil Nadu, India

Sushank Chaudhary
Chulalongkorn University, Thailand

M. Deepika
B.S. Abdur Rahman Crescent Institute
  of Science and Technology, Chennai,
  Tamil Nadu, India

Philip Eappen
University of Toronto Scarborough,
  Canada

Yatish Joshi
MNNIT Allahabad, India

Gaurav Kabra
OP Jindal Global University Sonipat,
  India

Sunita Khichar
Chulalongkorn University, Thailand

Payal Mukherjee
Indian Institute of Technology,
  Guwahati, Assam, India

M. S. Pramod
PES University, Bangalore, India

Aditya Pratik
PES University, Bangalore, India

S. Pravinth Raja
Presidency University, Bangalore,
  India

Demóstenes Zegarra Rodríguez
Federal University of Lavras, Brazil

Muhammad Saadi
University of Central Punjab, Lahore,
  Pakistan

G. Satya Sankalp
PES University, Bangalore, India

Wiroonsak Santipach
Kasetsart University, Thailand

R. Sapna
Presidency University, Bangalore,
  India

Pruk Sasithong
Chulalongkorn University, Thailand

Satyam
Indian Institute of Technology,
 Guwahati, Assam, India

Abhishek Sharma
Guru Nanak Dev University, Amritsar,
 Punjab, India

Sunny Sharma
IIIT, Allahabad, India

Mansha Swami
DIT University, Dehradun, India

Sankalp Swami
WSP, Indianapolis, USA

Manoj Tolani
Manipal Institute of Technology,
 Manipal, India

Abhishek Tripathi
MNNIT Allahabad, India

Narasimha Rao Vajjhala
University of New York Tirana, Albania

B. Varshita
PES University, Bangalore, India

Lunchakorn Wuttisittikulkij
Chulalongkorn University, Thailand

Preface

This book is designed for everyone interested in modern mobile communications, including non-technical people as well as telecom and marketing students, specialists, and managers. The book explains, in a compact form, a variety of 5G-related topics such as the introduction of 5G and its relevance to smart cities, network management, data science aspects of 5G, and the applications of 5G in smart cities in relation to health care, smart grids, railway transportation, and the environment. The book also discusses current understandings of mmWave transmission and visible light communication localization techniques as potential candidates for 6G technology. In addition, the most important 5G and beyond terminology is summarized.

Acknowledgement

We would like to thank those who supported us during the editing of this book. Editing a book is harder than we thought and more rewarding than we could have ever imagined. This would have not been possible without the support of all our friends and family members. They have cooperated a lot and given their continuous emotional support during this journey.

We are eternally grateful to our parents, who taught us discipline, love, manners, respect, and so much more, which have helped us to succeed in life. They always encouraged us to work hard. We would like to thank all our family members and friends for their direct and indirect support. Thank you to all the contributors who added their research in the form of chapters in this book. Finally, we would also like to pay tribute to our advisors Dr. Lunchakorn Wuttisittikulkij and Dr. R.S. Anand for their suggestions and contributions.

Thanks to everyone in our publishing team.

Editors

Dr. Ambar Bajpai

Dr. Arun Balodi

1 Introduction to 5G and Beyond

Hargovind Bansal

CONTENTS

DOI: 10.1201/9781003227861-1

1

1.1 INTRODUCTION TO 5G NETWORK AND APPLICATIONS

5G is extended as a 5th-generation mobile technology that refers to the next version of mobile telecommunication standards beyond the existing 4G standard. The 5G network has been deployed worldwide in most locations and, further, is being enhanced to provide decent package services combined with advanced features. This technology is known for highly flexible and scalable network configurations, enabling new levels of experience through support for advanced services based on three major application domains, namely enhanced mobile broadband (eMBB), ultra-reliable low latency communication (URLLC), and massive machine-type communications (mMTC).

As a technological advancement, 5G offers better data transfer speeds, accuracy, latency, capacity, and greater and more flexible bandwidth to fulfill the requirements of different economic sectors for various uses and applications, while ensuring a new level of performance never before experienced. When we talk about download speed, a more interesting topic to the everyday user, this can reach 20 Gbps using a high level of New Radio (NR) carrier aggregation and high modulation techniques. Another exciting feature of this technology is that it can support one million devices per square km, unlike 4G which supports only ten percent of that capacity. This connection density feature of the technology is the most critical requirement for smart city development, where a huge number of devices or objects need seamless connectivity.

In the smart city concept, city infrastructure resources are connected through multiple devices, objects, or machines to allow real-time information exchange with superfast data processing, which is possible with 5G network characteristics. Furthermore, many applications in different areas are being transformed on 5G smart platforms, including agriculture, public transportation, healthcare, media, entertainment, the internet of things (IoT), manufacturing, energy and utilities, public safety, and financial services. This breakthrough technology is smartly enhancing our connected lives and defining the scope for innovation.

4G networks were mostly designed for mobile devices only and severely limited to a section of applications, while 5G networks target much more flexible use cases in broad domains touching almost all sectors of the economy. 5G technology offers a network slicing feature which functioning as different networks for different services at the same time. It provides a resilient cloud-based core network with end-to-end support for network slicing. Slices of the network can be defined for a specific purpose and act as independent network layers for various applications.

In brief, the need for 5G networks has been recognized in almost all sectors due to the following requirements being satisfied by this breakthrough technology.

*   High mobile data requirement – Mobile data traffic is rising exponentially with increased video streaming.

- Connection capacity – A growing number of connections with the user having multiple devices.
- Smart device connectivity – IoT applications necessitate networks being able to handle a huge number of devices.

The initial commercial uses of 5G NR focused on eMBB using the Release 15 version of the 3GPP specifications (the first 3GPP specification for 5G standards), which was followed by URLLC and mMTC NR capabilities. The capabilities for URLLC are key factors for the applications targeted in 5G NR. For the mMTC component, 5G NR is complemented by machine-type communication technologies known as LTE-M and narrow band IoT (NB-IoT), already developed by 3GPP specification Release 13, which contribute unrivaled low-power wide-area performance covering a wide range of data rates and possible uses. Subsequent releases of the 3GPP specifications are being built in phases on the foundation provided by 3GPP Release 15. In this way, the second phase of 5G has been standardized as Release 16, with new features focused on mMTC.

Unlike 4G, 5G deployment happens in two ways, namely NSA (non-standalone operation) and SA (standalone operation). In the NSA mode of operation, the 5G carrier is added as a secondary carrier with a dual connectivity (DC) mechanism with a primary 4G carrier. Here, all control operations are done by the primary 4G carrier, and the 5G carrier is used as a secondary carrier to boost the data rate. The SA mode of operation, where the 5G carrier is the primary carrier and secondary carriers are also 5G based, needs additional software capability at the UE and network base station.

1.2   5G NR TERMINOLOGIES IN THE PHYSICAL LAYER

Data transmission in the physical layer of any technology is the simplest way to understand data packaging in physical blocks to transmission on radio frequency. Similar to 4G, data packet transmission in 5G happens at the radio frame level, which is further divided into subframes and slots. The key difference in 5G packet data transmission is slot-level scheduling, where 4G data scheduling happens at a subframe level.

As indicated in Figure 1.1, 5G NR downlink and uplink transmissions are divided into frames, with each frame having a duration of 10 ms consisting of ten subframes, each of 1 ms.

Subcarrier Spacing – Subcarrier spacing is fundamental terminology to define subcarrier size, for orthogonal frequency-division multiplexing (OFDM), where the frequency domain spacing between two subcarriers that carry data is indicated. In NR, subcarrier spacing of 15, 30, 60, 120, and 240 KHz is possible, unlike subcarrier spacing fixed at 15 KHz in LTE technology.

In Table 1.1, each number is labeled as a parameter of μ (mu in Greek). When $\mu =$ 0, this represents subcarrier spacing of 15 kHz, which is the same as LTE.

Frame and subframe – Like 4G LTE, 5G NR downlink and uplink transmissions are divided into frames of 10 ms each. Each frame is further divided into ten equally sized subframes of 1 ms each. In total, there are ten subframes in one frame.

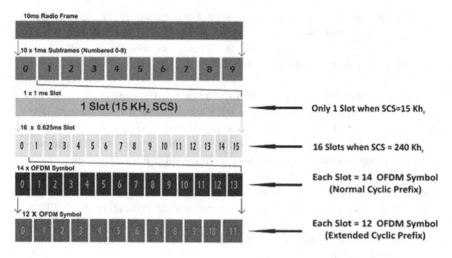

FIGURE 1.1   5G NR numerologies

TABLE 1.1

Subcarrier Spacing to Slot Mapping

μ	Subcarrier spacing in KHz	Slots count per subframe = 2^μ	Slot count per radio frame = 10 * 2^μ	Duration of slot (ms)
0	15	1	10	1
1	30	2	20	0.5
2	60	4	40	0.25
3	120	8	80	0.125
4	240	16	160	0.0625

Slot – A slot is the smallest scheduling unit in 5G NR. A subframe is divided into a number of slots (1 to as many as 16) depending on the subcarrier spacing, which is unlike the two fixed slots in the LTE subframe. The slot length may vary depending on subcarrier spacing. As per the nature of OFDM, the slot length gets shorter as the subcarrier spacing gets wider. Table 1.1 shows the mapping of subcarrier spacing according to the number of slots in a frame and subframe [2]

OFDM symbol – This is defined as the smallest sampling time of the data for the given bandwidth. The number of symbols in a slot is fixed with the subcarrier spacing. OFDM symbols in a slot can be represented as "downlink" (represented here as "D"), "flexible" (represented here as "F"), or "uplink" (represented here as "U") as specified in the 3GPP specification of NR. In a slot in a downlink frame, the UE assumes that downlink transmissions only occur in "downlink" or "flexible" symbols. In a slot in an uplink frame, the UE only transmits in the "uplink" or "flexible" symbols. The number of symbols per slot is 14 in the case of a normal cyclic prefix, and the number of symbols per slot is 12 in the case of an extended CP [2].

1.3 5G NR REQUIREMENTS – IMT2020

International mobile telecommunications (IMT) is the generic term used by the ITU community to define broadband mobile systems. It encompasses IMT-2000, IMT-Advanced, and IMT-2020 collectively. The initial version of IMT standards was approved by ITU in the year 2000 and named IMT-2000. In January 2012, ITU defined LTE-4G wireless cellular technology and named it IMT-Advanced, and this has been deployed worldwide.

The standards development for the next generation 5G NR, IMT-2020, is progressing quickly towards ITU adoption and deployment of 5G technology in trials. Many countries have implemented its use since 2018.

Following usage scenarios under 5G NR for IMT 2020 and beyond with ITU-R M.2083, it can be seen that each scenario meets different wireless technology needs.

A. **eMBB** (enhanced mobile broadband)
B. **URLLC** (ultra-reliable low latency communication)
C. **mMTC** (massive machine-type communication)

Enhanced mobile broadband (eMBB) can simply be seen as the next version of the services first enabled by 4G networks, which ensure mainly high data throughput that leverages a new and much higher 5G spectrum bandwidth. This is an important aspect for the next wave of consumer devices to deal with smartphones' augmented virtual reality, industrial routers, and gateways that need high-level connectivity. This feature provides the greater capacity required to support peak data rates both for large groups of users and for mobile end users to ensure a transformative user experience and revolutionize gaming applications with AR/VR cloud gaming technology.

Ultra-reliable low latency communication (URLLC) is one of the important aspects of 5G, which is the primary requirement in multiple areas, including healthcare, transportation, energy transmission, and manufacturing, to ensure operational efficiency where latency is an important tool. The main applications requiring this feature are mission-critical control, emergency services that require reliable services such as emergency call services, vehicle-to-vehicle communication, remote surgeries, factory automation, autonomous vehicles with drones, industrial IoT, and robotics.

Massive machine-type communication (mMTC) is an extension of MTC communication enabled by a 4G-technology network. It is a type of communication between machines on networks where data generation, information samples exchange, and processing take place with minimal or without human interface. This provides connections to huge numbers of devices that intermittently exchange small amounts of data traffic with the help of a broad array of wireless communication. This capability is suitable for a huge number of IoT-connected devices with low power consumption and low data rates, applications like smart meters and track-and-trace

TABLE 1.2

IMT 2020 5G vs IMT Advanced 4G Requirements Key Comparison

Capability	Description	5G requirement (IMT 2020)	5G usage application	4G requirement (IMT advanced)
Peak data rate (DL)	Maximum data rate supported	20 Gbit/s	eMBB	1 Gbit/s
Latency	Data packet travel time	4 ms	eMBB	10 ms
Latency	Data packet travel time	1 ms	URLLC	10 ms
Mobility	Maximum handoff speed and QoS requirements	500 km/h	eMBB/URLLC	350 km/h
Connection density	Number of devices per unit area	10^6/km^2	mMTC	10^5/km^2
Area traffic capacity	Aggregated traffic across coverage area	10 Mbps/m^2	eMBB	0.1 Mbps/m^2
Peak downlink spectrum efficiency	Spectrum efficiency in downlink	30 bit/s/Hz	eMBB	10 bit/s/Hz
Data rate (user experience)	Data rate in dense urban areas	100 Mbps	eMBB	10 Mbps

apps that are independent in terms of speed and latency but with optimal power efficiency. Its focus is on efficiently transmitting/receiving low data volume to and from devices that need broad area coverage and longer battery life [8].

1.4 5G NR SPECTRUM

Frequency spectrum refers to the radio frequencies carrying data from user devices to cellular base stations and vice versa. Since the addition of first-generation telecommunication standards, network operators use radio waves to transmit and receive information. The frequency spectrum includes frequencies from 3 kHz to 300 GHz.

The 5G spectrum radio frequencies in the sub-6 GHz range categorized as FR 1 and the millimeter-wave (mm-Wave) frequency fall under the range from 24.25 GHz and above, are categorized as FR2. Table 1.3 shows the frequency range of FR1 and FR2 for 5G standards. There are more than 80 active frequency bands in sub-6 GHz spectrum, and more new bands are yet to be allocated in the millimeter wave spectrum.

In FDD mode (frequency division duplex), a separate frequency range of the bands is used for uplink and downlink, while in TDD mode (time division duplex) it is the same frequency range for uplink and downlink with different time slots depending on the TDD configuration.

TABLE 1.3
FR1 and FR2 Frequency Ranges

Frequency range	Frequency range in MHz
FR1	410–7125
FR2	24250–52600

1.4.1 FREQUENCY RANGE 1 (FR1)

This range of frequency is known as the sub-6 GHz spectrum for 5G NR. FR1 was planned to define bands below the 6 GHz radio range, but the FR1 range has been extended to 7.125 GHz with additional spectrum allocation.

FR1 frequency spectrum occupies the 100 MHz maximum channel bandwidth. There is less availability of a continuous spectrum in this crowded frequency range. The most widely used bands in 5G in the FR ranges fall between 3.3 GHz and 4.2 GHz. The FR1 frequency bands mostly utilize the same frequency bands, which are used for LTE.

1.4.2 FREQUENCY RANGE 2 (FR2)

This range of frequency is known as the millimeter-wave (mm-Wave) spectrum for 5G NR. The minimum and maximum bandwidths defined for FR2 are 50 MHz and 400 MHz, respectively. The most exciting feature of FR2 is the larger bandwidth availability, but the flip side is the low coverage area because a higher frequency signal is limited in long distances (more than a few hundred meters) travel.

The millimeter-wave 5G signals have problems penetrating solid objects such as buildings, moving vehicles, and trees because of the nature of electromagnetic waves in higher frequencies in FR2. The frequency range ensures a very high data rate, as a larger bandwidth availability provides coverage limitations.

5G NR supports carrier aggregation (CA) to provide thigh aggregated bandwidth for more data transfer. The current 3GPP specification permits an aggregation of up to 16 component carriers with a combination of inter- and intra-band carrier aggregation (Table 1.4).

1.5 5G NR NETWORK ARCHITECTURE

The network architecture of a technology consists of the essential functional building blocks responsible for end-to-end information flow. 5G NR network architecture blocks are depicted in Figure 1.2, where they consist of the air access nodes and core network nodes in the control and user plane, and can be represented as follows:

- UE – user equipment (user handset or device)
- Network base station – gNB (gNodeB) – radio access network

TABLE 1.4
FR1 and FR2 Parameters

5G NR Parameters	FR1	FR2
Bandwidth option per carrier (MHz)	5, 10, 15, 20, 25, 30, 40, 50, 60, 70, 80, 90, 100	50, 100, 200, 400
Subcarrier spacing	15, 30, 60 (kHz)	60, 120, 240 (kHz)
Duplex mode	FDD, TDD	TDD
Multiple access scheme	Downlink: CP-OFDMUplink: CP-OFDM; DFT-s-OFDM	Downlink: CP-OFDMUplink: CP-OFDM; DFT-s-OFDM
Modulation schemes	QPSK, 16QAM, 64QAM, 256QAM, uplink also allows π/2-BPSK	QPSK, 16QAM, 64QAM, 256QAM, uplink also allows π/2-BPSK

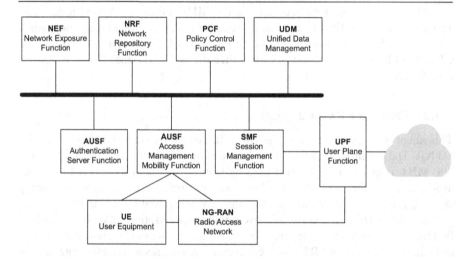

FIGURE 1.2 5G NR network architecture blocks

- 5G core network control plane – consisting of multiple nodes with different functionalities in the control plane
- 5G core network user plane – consisting of multiple nodes with different functionalities in the user plane

1.5.1 5G Access Network

The new radio access nodes are an integral part of the 5th generation mobile system and facilitate an enhanced broadband and ultra-reliable low latency network over air. This part of end-to-end network architecture broadly deals with user equipment and network base station (gNB) access nodes.

The 5G NG-RAN, referred to as the next-generation radio access technology, can have a gNB or ng-eNB node (here ng stands for "next generation"). The ng-eNB is

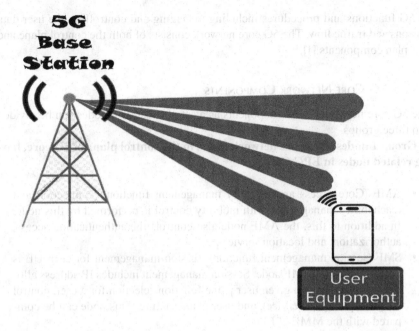

FIGURE 1.3 5G NR base station downlink beams to UE

an enhanced version of 4G eNodeB. The 5G-RAN node uses new NG interfaces for the 5G core but uses different radio interfaces for the UE.

This UE and NG-RAN interface defines the radio frequency communication path between the 5G device and the base station. When a 5G device moves (in the case of a movable device), base stations keep changing based on the signal strength and other criteria, and this process is called handover. Both UE and base station deal here with the beams, unlike the isotropic radiation in LTE. These beams depend on the frequency spectrum and number of Tx/Rx antennas at the UE and base station sides. Figure 1.3 shows the beam communication of the UE.

RAN architecture has evolved as a wireless technology advancement in 5G NR. Here, NG-RAN is responsible for various functions such as radio and baseband signal processing at the lower layer and packet processing at the upper layer with the radio resource control function. Signaling and data transport entities are logically separated within NG-RAN and referred to as the control and user plane respectively. As a flexible next generation RAN architecture, RAN nodes are deployed based on spectrum efficiency and network performance requirements.

1.5.2 5G CORE NETWORK

The 5th generation core is the backbone of the end-to-end 5G network and offers a variety of services to the users who are interconnected by the access network [11]. It enables increased data transfer demand supported by 5G. As per the definition of 3GPP, the 5th generation core uses cloud-aligned and service-based architecture for all 5G functions and procedures including managing and controlling the user data sessions and traffic flow. The 5G core network consists of both the control plane and user plan components [1].

1.5.3   5G CORE NETWORK COMPONENTS

The 5G core network block components as a set of functional nodes can be divided into three groups.

Group 1 nodes: these are network nodes in the control plane of 5G core, having related nodes in EPC Core.

- AMF (Core access and mobility management function): connection and reachability management with mobility control is performed by this node. In addition to this, the AMF node also controls the authentication access, authorization, and location services.
- SMF (session management function): session management for each UE is performed by the SMF node. Session management includes IP address allocation, selection of a given user plane function selection for a user, control of QoS (quality of service), and user plane routing. This node can be compared with the MME of EPC.
- PCF (policy control function): the PCF component manages policy rules of the control plane functions. This can be compared with the PCRF (policy and charging rule function) in the EPC.
- UDM (unified data management): this component of the core network manages user identity and the generation of authentication credentials. This node can be compared with the HSS node in EPC.
- AUSF (authentication server function): as the name indicates, this is an authentication server to authenticate the user for various services. This node can be compared with the HSS node in EPC.

Group 2 nodes: this group of nodes consists of network nodes in the control plane 5G core and having no related nodes in the EPC core.

Network exposure function (NEF): this node of the core network is responsible for making specific capabilities visible to third-party services, including internal and external data representation translation.

- NF repository function (NRF): this node is responsible for searching available services. It is implemented by a "discovery service" in a micro-services-based system.
- Network slicing selector function (NSSF): this core network node helps in the selection of network slices to provide the required service to a UE. Network slices are a new concept in the 5G network providing an essential interface to divide resources of the network into different services requested by different users. It is a critical feature of the 5th-generation core network and is responsible for creating a high-level enhanced service experience for users.

Group 3 nodes: this group includes the UPF component that is responsible for user plane traffic.

- User plane function (UPF): this component ensures the internet traffic movement from and to RAN, corresponding to the SGW/PGW combination in EPC. UPF provides a user plan connectivity to forward the data packets and store and report the traffic usage as a prime responsibility. In addition to this, it controls and manages the user data policy to ensure lawful intercept and QoS.

In another major difference from the 4G LTE core, the 4G EPC group is considerably different from 5th-generation core network nodes. RAN virtualization and cloud-based software design are redefined in the 5th-generation core network. Some core-level differences between the 4th generation and the 5th generation networks are significant, such as the new additions of massive MIMO, network slicing, and new discrete elements added to offer a high-level experience.

1.6   5TH GENERATION NETWORK APPLICATIONS

5G network refers to a new interface of an internet-enabled brain, almost used in all kinds of products and industries, creating improvements to numerous applications across the economic sectors, with high speed, capacity, and ultra-low latency features. There have been multiple areas where 5G applications are showing a stable presence, leading to dramatic changes to economies and lifestyles around the world.

Some of the high-level application areas are as follows:

- Smart city – next vision of living
- Manufacturing
- Agriculture
- Media and entertainment
- Healthcare: advanced OPD/hospital and robotic remote surgeries
- Engineering Applications
- Financial services
- Public safety
- Energy and utilities
- Public transport

1.6.1   Smart City – Next Vision of Living

Urbanization is an important social and economic factor. More than half the population of the world lives in cities, and this number is rising year by year as urbanization increases and is expected to exceed 70% by 2050. As more people move towards cities, numerous challenges, such as the handling of traffic, crime, pollution, resource scarcity, and lower quality of life, become more prominent. A future vision of a city is where all such challenges can be handled effectively, efficiently, and smartly to make citizens' lives easier. Smart cities are envisioned as entirely interconnected to regulate traffic, use energy resources efficiently, and report crimes, all assisted by data exchange and processing in real time.

Smart cities can be conceptualized as an intelligent framework using technology that enables a high standard of quality of living using high-speed and efficient real-time data information flow and collection using different types of electronic methods (smart sensors and networks) to ensure highly efficient communication between the various objects and machines in the city. The data collected here are used to manage the assets and resources of various public departments to improve operations across the city. Data transmission using wireless technology and the cloud is highly digitally processed and ensures super-fast real-time data transmission.

Citizens can connect with smart city ecosystems in multiple ways using smartphone devices, connected smart cars, connected smart homes, and smart city infrastructure such as utility providers, water supply networks, hospitals, libraries, schools, waste management, traffic lights, vehicle traffic, and other community services. Multiple objects/machines can communicate in real time with super-fast data processing to ensure instant reactions [3].

Overall, the smart city concept will ensure high-quality living standards. Pairing devices and data with the physical infrastructure of the city leads to high-level services with reduced costs and enhanced sustainability. 5G connectivity, with the help of IoT, ensures improved energy distribution and savings, streamlines trash collection, decreases traffic congestion with enhanced driving supports, and improves air quality.

1.6.2   How is 5G a Game-Changer in the Concept of the Smart City?

The concept of the smart city is transforming due to the 5G network's advanced features, 5G will enable a new wave of smart city development due to the following new essential features delivered by 5G:

- Higher data rates due to its greater bandwidth availability
- Increased traffic capacity to handle a greater number of users at the same time
- Ultra-low latency feature to ensure real-time data sampling and processing time
- High connection density to ensure a greater number of devices per square km area.

Three major steps to develop a smart city are:
   Connected devices with smart sensors/devices across the city

- Efficient collection and analysis of data with ultra-low latency
- Based on analyzed data, the development of solutions for the citizen in a seamless fashion.

The smart city is a digital concept that offers novel methods of planning city functions to make citizens' lives easier for all daily activities and for environmental purposes as well. 5G technology delivers solid network connectivity with a massive number of connections at the same time, which will transform urban life.

1.6.3 TYPICAL ACTIVITIES IN A SMART CITY

In this section, we outline some typical activities in a smart city

- Regular streetlights replaced by smart power lighting, which connects with other IoT devices and provides broadband.
- Driverless cars
- Robots and drones handling goods, even small items, or serving coffee in cafés.
- Smart harvesting with automated functioning and smart automated drainage and garbage systems
- Rea-time superfast communication with a control center for various emergency situations
- Smart traffic management with the help of the IoT network and an enhanced parking management system
- Energy resources are used more efficiently with the help of connected sensors with the 5G network
- Advanced policing system (police robotic system equipped with high-definition cameras with face recognition capabilities to identify criminals)
- Remote monitoring and data collection of energy consumption utility systems such as smart electric and water meters.
- Interconnected sensors assess air quality, send information to a data center in real time, analyze data, and if necessary, report bad air quality in a real-time information flow.

To develop a smart city, a technical smart network engine is essential, which promises to provide super-fast, reliable, and large capacity to handle more devices. This engine is the internet of things (IoT), which runs efficiently on the 5G network. Further machine-to-machine communication has a critical contribution to emerging IoT capabilities. The emerging IoT-5G uses extend from IoT capabilities which are sensor-based to robots, actuators, and drones for improved distributed coordination and low latency, with a highly reliable execution of tasks.

1.7 MANUFACTURING

Manufacturing is one of the sectors of the economy that always need next version of an advanced technique in faster environment, with machines and robots equipped with a series of sensors connected to engines with high computation power. The 5G network will provide a transformative interface to supplement this high-speed manufacturing environment with high flexibility, and much faster and more accurate timing features. The 5G network's high capacity and faster data rate ensure the handling of more machine and sensor connections, with faster data transfer in real time offering the next level of technology to this industry.

The 5G network offers manufacturers further opportunities to develop advanced factories and ensure the benefits of emerging technologies such as smart neural artificial intelligence with 5G network connectivity for finding faults, and advanced IoT.

5G technology is characterized by low latency and high reliability, which is critical to enable the manufacturing industry to make significant advancements. Further larger bandwidth and high connection capacity are other important aspects to secure widespread connectivity. The 5G network will enable greater connectivity with lower costs and shorter response times for machinery production redesign, layout changes, and alterations [12].

5G connectivity is helping to provide simultaneous product customization and increasing production output by creating a connected machine environment that enables manufacturers to ensure real-time collection, analysis, and distribution of data. Improving connectivity and keeping workers in the loop will help manufacturers to receive and access much larger amounts of data at very high speeds and more efficiently. The unmatched reliability with extremely low latency of the 5G network could revolutionize the way for advanced applications in the industrial environment.

Furthermore, manufacturers faced a serious challenge during the Covid-19 pandemic, which saw the value of advanced automation and smarter work with an efficient supply chain. The unique advantages of 5G in improving factory floor automation and incorporating new services for a variety of products will make it critical post-Covid-19.

1.7.1 SMART FACTORY USES

The future of the 5G smart factory will focus on developing a fully connected experience in a real-time environment, from revolutionary device connectivity and transformative technology experiences to advanced automation and network flexibility. Manufacturers can focus on several key benefits to get the most from their 5G investments and revolutionary technology in a challenging economy. These include greater automation, smarter supply chains, and increased machine activity. 5G network connectivity has created many more options for businesses to enable automation in their operations, boost productivity, and increase agility.

The many uses of 5G technology in the manufacturing industry are transforming methods of production and management as :

- Manufacturing process automation
- Remote monitoring of assets (production and logistics)
- Advanced manufacturing robots with high collaboration in a real-time environment
- Faster data analysis and fault detection (smart prediction of breakdowns and downtimes)
- AR-assisted factory maintenance/troubleshooting
- New business model creation

1.8 AGRICULTURE

Agriculture is one of the largest economic sectors of the world. As the world's population approaches eight billion, this industry requires the technology to fulfill increasing food demand. A major concern for this industry is how to deal with uncertainty in environmental changes, such as temperature and air moisture changes that can cause delays in fault detection necessary to avoid damage. In addition, the automated and fast machinery required in this field is not at the level needed.

The agriculture industry is evolving and is on the path to advanced digital transformation with the invention of 5G technology. The 5G network could enable precision farming and help in optimizing agriculture resource usage with enhanced productivity. The concept of 5G-enabled smart farms is taking shape with enhanced capabilities to harness the value of data. The 5G network is improving standards by supporting a significantly faster data transfer speed, significantly higher than 4G, enabling advanced machine learning and real-time communication between devices, leading to automated farming processes and thereby transforming the concept of 5G technology.

1.8.1 How 5G Can Change the Agriculture Sector: Smart Farming

The smart farming concept can be understood as the administration of precise treatments to crops. Instead of treating an entire field in the same way, each row in a field can be given a specific treatment using a series of sensors connected in a smart order and controlled by a 5G network. This will ensure significant savings in water, food, fertilizer, and herbicides. 5G technology here allows machines to be controlled centrally, and data are returned in real time. Farmers can better understand water consumption and adjust irrigation systems based on accurate data [4].

Further, climate change can be unpredictable, leading to water availability and rainfall predictability being dramatically affected. Cutting-edge technologies can help industrial farmers overcome water shortages and extended dry spells.

IoT sensors embedded in the soil can measure moisture levels, and data captured from drones can help generate heat maps that highlight problem areas that, when further inputted to advanced machine learning algorithms that can process this data intelligently in real time, enable the distribution of water where it is needed most. The speed and throughput of 5G facilitate the transmission of these large data sets.

In IoT-based smart farming, a system is built for monitoring the crop field (for light, humidity, temperature, soil moisture, etc.) with the help of sensors. In terms of environmental issues, smart farming can be very beneficial, including assisting with more efficient water usage and the optimization of inputs and treatments.

In brief, smart farming is developing into an advanced ecosystem with the help of 5G network connectivity elements, such as:

- Advanced farm machinery: 5G connectivity with farm machinery that has sensors will increase data availability. Artificial intelligence can now spot patterns in the data, further ensuring improved yields by generating advanced warnings for possible crop diseases.

- Advanced 5G drones: when connected to the 5G network, autonomous drones, facilitated with weed scanners and crop sprayers, play a critical role in the farming industry by intelligently scanning crops to identify when pesticide is required. After a specific time, the drones return to a field control room to refuel fuel and charge their batteries.
- Enhanced field monitoring: with advanced cameras working autonomously with high-resolution images and using artificial intelligence to identify the differences between crops and weeds, the field monitoring system is transforming. With a 5G connected network, the location of weeds or potential trouble spots can be reported with very fast speed and in real time to enable a solution to be applied before any significant damage occurs.

Much of today's 5G infrastructure is being deployed in dense urban areas. Coverage in rural areas needs to be expanded so that the agricultural sector can realize more benefits and opportunities. Further innovation across the farming sector will be necessary to meet the requirements for quality food for a rising world population. 5G-enabled solutions will help in the digital transformation of the agriculture sector, but much more is needed to be done, such as in the areas of planning, better coordination and tracking, and shipments.

1.9 MEDIA AND ENTERTAINMENT

The media and entertainment industries consistently utilize technological advancements to create content, videos, movies, and other entertainment with high quality. This content is transmitted around the globe and delivered to home consumers and mobile devices with a minimum delay of services. Currently, the capabilities of smartphones are limited, as they are often connected to budget digital data networks that need to be upgraded to the super-fast 5G network so that entertainment experiences are improved.

Referring to the "5G Economics of Entertainment Report," usage is estimated to reach 84.80 Gb per 5G user per month by 2028. Video traffic is estimated to contribute 90% of all 5G data traffic. Future innovation in this industry will ensure the next level of high-quality content in real time at the desired location, with faster speeds on a huge scalable bandwidth and lower network latency.

A major challenge during the Covid-19 pandemic was the limitation of physical contact, and billions of consumers across the globe were highly dependent on mobile phones, with limited network capabilities, for entertainment. 5G deployment has become a game-changer for the media and entertainment industries, where high-speed data, quality transmission, and the simultaneous connectivity of a large number of devices can be enjoyed.

Below are two major applications in the entertainment industry by using the 5G network.

- An advanced real-time entertainment experience – smart devices with 5G capabilities and networks will ensure seamless live entertainment experiences, such as live musical concerts, movie premieres, sporting events, etc. across different time zones.

- High-level gaming experience – advanced gaming needs real-time and super-fast data transmission with very low latency to enrich the user experience. 5G thereby enhances the gaming experience, and fast responses and high-resolution streaming is assured. The revenue of 5G mobile games has increased to new levels and is expected to increase by 100 billion dollars annually up to 2028, indicating the potential profits of this industry.

1.10 HEALTHCARE

5G will define revolutionary advancement in the healthcare ecosystem. It enables mobile networks to handle a high level of healthcare applications as an enhancement in many existing uses such as remote robotic surgeries, online patient examination, handling telemedicine appointments, and smart data centers. This topic has become very relevant recently as the spread of the coronavirus put unprecedented stress on healthcare systems across the globe.

By combining 5G technology with other leading-edge technologies, another level of opportunities can be created to transform many aspects of patient health monitoring and medical procedures.

The possible applications in the healthcare system are increasing, with advancements and connections in robotics, artificial intelligence, and IoT devices all being made possible by 5G technology.

5G NR technology is becoming vital to healthcare transformation, as seen from the following novel 5G network features:

- The 5G new radio capability extends beyond previous mobile generations and has a huge system capacity to cater to a large volume of users with more downlink and uplink data speed.
- The new network slicing feature provides service-based layers to avoid any congestion in the network for services.
- The RAN virtualization and distributed cloud features of the 5G network ensure very low latency, which is a critical requirement in the healthcare sector. Further artificial intelligence and machine learning with 5G connectivity could transform the healthcare sector.

1.10.1 HEALTHCARE APPLICATIONS

5G technology is known for great data transfer speed and ultra-low latency, which are core requirements in critical medical applications, transforming the healthcare system. Some advanced healthcare applications are as follows:

- Remote monitoring
- Advance remote procedures
- Advanced handling of patient data records
- Telemedicine appointments

1.10.1.1   Remote Monitoring

Remote monitoring of patient health through existing wearable devices with the help of advanced 5G networks is becoming a reality, making real-time and efficient remote patient health monitoring possible and updating a central data storage center.

Currently, wearable devices are used widely to prevent health issues, but these are limited in accuracy and less reliable in diagnosis due to connectivity issues with technology that is not up to date. Previous network versions are limited in handling many connections at one time – an aspect that is critical in setting up advanced remote monitoring. The 5G network can resolve this problem, and remote monitoring will transform the healthcare sector.

Healthcare wearables require frequent updates from a health database server with accuracy and real-time information flow, which is possible with 5G radio connectivity. 5G connectivity is not only limited to wearables but also in many medical procedures where the transfer of patient diagnosis data in real time to the doctor is beneficial [6], [7], [9].

1.10.1.2   Advance Remote Procedures with 5G Technology

In the medical field, robotic surgery is not a new concept and is already in place in operation theaters. However, it is limited to the human surgeon and robot being in the theater at the same time.

To perform remote robotic surgeries, an intelligent real-time, fast network is needed, as complicated medical procedures need super-fast data connectivity with real-time information flow. This procedure can only be conducted with feedback in real time for high-definition image capture and streaming to the end user, requiring very low latency and more data inflow speed. The 5G network platform can make advanced remote services possible and could transform the healthcare sector.

China was the first country to conduct remote surgery on a human using 5G technology. The critical requirement of very low latency offered by 5G technology made this process possible and enabled near-instantaneous data transmission.

The key steps of the 5G technology in remote robotic surgery are as follows:

1. 5G connects a surgeon in a remote location to a surgical robot
2. 5G mobile connection is mandatory to perform remote surgery
3. 5G provides 1 ms latency, enabling haptic feedback

1.10.1.3   Handling of Patient Data Records

Data handling can be a major issue because huge data files are generated in many medical and diagnostic procedures, including imaging. Handling and reliable transfer of this data can only be possible with a high-performance network such as 5G. It helps to transfer diagnostic data quickly, allowing access to the doctor when the patient leaves the diagnostic room.

The 5G network ensures fast and reliable transmission of these large files between doctors and hospitals, reducing the time that would otherwise be needed. This reduction in time means more timely diagnoses, second opinions, treatment start dates, and adjustments, as the medical data can be transmitted and analyzed by doctors faster than ever before, whether they are at home or in the hospital.

1.10.1.4   Telemedicine Appointments

A challenge has arisen in the healthcare system, where the technology used in tele-medicine appointments has been unable to handle large volumes of data and provide reliable undisturbed high-quality video calls. Improvements can only be made with a transformative network that has the capacity to handle data load with faster real-time communication.

For a sick person living in a rural area where doctor and hospital availability is very poor, traveling to another town or city can be quite challenging. In addition, time is critical in emergency situations. Furthermore, in pandemic situations such as Covid-19, the need for faster service delivery is great. 5G technology connec-tivity has uncovered ways to resolve these challenges. With 5G network character-istics, doctors can have a high-quality short video call with a patient and provide recommendations to assist the patient more quickly and can even submit prescription requests. The 5G network further ensures faster connectivity and image transmission in real time, making the process much simpler.

1.11   ENGINEERING APPLICATIONS

The engineering sector is all set to reach new levels with the help of the advanced features of 5G technology. Drones inspecting bridges, wind turbines, and tunnels can be envisaged, with the high-speed data transfer and ultra-low latency in 5G pro-viding a new level of engineering experience.

In addition, the 5G network can ensure a larger number of connected drones that will be able to transmit data and high-definition live footage in just milliseconds, making this technology very attractive.

Let's look at an example. A drone connected to the 5G network will allow faster real-time automatic operation using a faster network to inspect the live construction of a bridge so that any actions necessary for smooth operation can be taken in real time. A drone flown close to any structure, whether on top of a building or in a tunnel, will use a high-resolution camera installed with an advanced level of light detection, ranging, and thermal detection instruments to highlight erosion, cracks in walls or pipes, or hidden water leaks. In a manual operation, these checks could be delayed, but with the use of the latest 5G technology, this is a very fast and efficient operation. The efficiency of the 5G network plays a vital role here. Ultra-fast data transfer speeds and reduced latency are critical parts of the technical nature of the 5G system to ensure instantaneous access to data and information, leading to greater collaboration and advanced decision-making.

There could be many improvements in the engineering field with the advance-ment of 5G technology. Some of these are as follows:

1.11.1   Remote Operation

Remote operations are a major challenge in the engineering sector. Sometimes half of the team is in the office and half of the team is at a location offsite. Communication between teams and transferring high levels of data are critical to ensure smooth operation. Files and data can be shared using cloud software or an email system.

Therefore, to achieve complete efficiency, the 5G network plays a critical role with its high data transfer and low latency features.

1.11.2 Advanced Design Decisions

With the help of advanced sensors, advanced artificial intelligence, machine learning, and cloud computing methods, the 5G technology network is committed to improving project delivery and advanced design decisions, ensuring the reduction of potential engineering faults and material wastage. This will further ensure the possibility of next collaboration on, and interaction with, real-time virtual reality models.

1.11.3 Timely Deliveries

Companies have greatly realized the potential of remote working in the unprecedented time of Covid-19. For this reason, the architecture, engineering, and construction sectors must prepare well for the remote-working opportunities that a 5G interface will provide. In the engineering sector, there is still a lot of development going on.

Engineering projects across the globe were delayed due to the Covid-19 pandemic. Now 5G network connectivity can help the unprecedented demand for connectivity placed by millions working from home.

1.12 FINANCIAL SERVICES

5G technological advancement surfaced as a next-generation network and will lead to new opportunities for financial services (FS) institutions in terms of advanced handling of digital work and the automation of many applications with high connectivity.

Let's think of a smart bank concept like a smart city. Yes, here the 5G network will make experiences possible never seen by financial services customers before.

A high level of enhancement in FS applications can be seen with 5G networks

- Advanced version of digital handling
- The recent Covid-19 pandemic has shown us the importance of digitally working with remote tasks. Mobile banking and other financial apps are some of the best examples to understand the importance of digital transactions to provide a convenient way of dealing with finances. The increased usage of online digital financial services with mobile apps etc. has meant an advanced network with high capacity, larger data rates to handle many customers, and advanced security levels are required. The 5G network will play a crucial role to satisfy these requirements.
- Smart branches with 5G network
- Traditionally, branches of financial institutions are built on a local network to serve the requirement of the local community for various services, but the era of modern technological advancement and the need for remote handling has created a challenge for institutions to efficiently satisfy a large number of customers online along with interconnectivity between their branches across the

globe. Here, the 5G network plays a critical role in making branches smarter in terms of interconnectivity and being data-driven. Furthermore, the 5G network ensures the smart connection of in-branch devices such as ATMs, kiosks, and CCTV cameras with superfast information exchange and data processing, ensuring efficient operations in customer and in-house management, and adherence to security and safety protocols.

1.13 PUBLIC TRANSPORT

The transportation industry has entered a new phase, with 5G network connectivity enabling a new experience of traveling. Vehicle-to-vehicle and vehicle-to-infrastructure communication will ensure a new level of road safety and a better driving environment while allowing public transportation to run more efficiently and improving driving efficiency through real-time vehicle monitoring.

Compared to existing network architectures, the 5G network has great scope to facilitate increased visibility and promote control over transportation mechanisms. The three major characteristics of 5G, low latency, high capacity, and reliability, will enhance the transport of goods and passenger travel.

The advanced 5G features of increased bandwidth availability and low latency are driving factors to increase the use of connected and autonomous vehicles with improved and smart logistics. Vehicle diagnostic data processing in real time will be crucial for monitoring and adjusting the vehicles and improving efficiency with real-time updates/alerts for potential maintenance. In addition, the 5G network could bring about well-regulated systems to ensure a preference for public transport over private vehicles.

In summary, smart-connected vehicles can regularize traffic and transport demand. Transport service demand is connected to smart public transport, which is very efficient, cost-effective, and offers a next-level travel experience.

The 5G network is expected to provide end-to-end fast and reliable connectivity across cities and beyond. It will support different types of communications for transport logistics. Two of the most important vehicle communications that greatly benefit from 5G connectivity are as follows [10]:

- **V2V (vehicle-to-vehicle)**: this involves vehicles communicating with other vehicles. There is very low latency, as the processing time of 5G connectivity is significantly low, creating real-time communication between vehicles to ensure optimum safety and offer a new experience of travel.
- **V2I (vehicle-to-infrastructure)**: vehicles communicate with sensors installed on public infrastructure such as bridges, traffic signals, and roads. With the features of 5G, high numbers of devices or objects can communicate and process data in real time, ensuring a new level of service experience.

Figure 1.4 represents the advanced uses of 5G in the transportation industry. Transportation with 5G network connectivity is becoming diverse. Some uses are as follows:

- Remote driving with highly controlled operations
- Passenger information flow

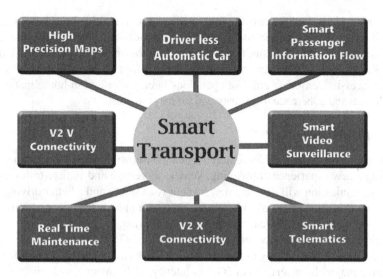

FIGURE 1.4   Smart transport with 5G network

- Smart passenger Wi-Fi
- Telematics
- Video surveillance and accessibility
- Preventive real-time maintenance
- Charging and battery management for vehicles
- High-precision maps with advanced information

1.14   PUBLIC SAFETY

The public safety sector depends on advanced technologies to protect citizens from different kinds of dangers. All public safety operations are critical, and super-fast information exchange with very low latency to provide support to victims with minimum response times is vital. The 5G network can add a new level of value because of its very fast data transmission, high network capacity, and ultra-low latency, which greatly help to improve the response time and efficiency of public operations.

Take a very simple example of an emergency call, where due to network congestion or other network issues, e.g. a slower response time, the call needs more time to connect and could lead to a life-threatening situation. Therefore, the difference between a reliable and unreliable network could be the difference between life and death. This means that an emergency call requires a network where fast and reliable communication in real time is ensured.

The capabilities of the 5G network can promote an improved experience by ensuring high standards of public safety with connectivity to various public emergency services including police and medical services, thereby minimizing the possibilities of life-threatening situations occurring.

There are already designated broadband services provided with a fast LTE network and ready to switch to next-level capabilities. This would create great changes in this sector, with new services using the highly capable 5G network with a shorter response time.

The 5G network, with its capabilities of service provision, could ensure intelligent public safety operations with faster emergency responses. The following aspects could be enabled:

- A new level of service regarding emergency calls, sensors, and cameras together with fast monitoring, high security, and reliability
- Improved data analysis time and faster response to real-time commands, communicating with control centers and ensuring efficient collaboration to deal with any kind of emergency
- High network capacity and real-time responses for any public emergency, including traffic congestion or unexpected crowds at planned or unplanned events

1.15 ENERGY AND UTILITIES

The energy and utilities industries deal with energy that is transmitted and distributed to consumers, including electricity, natural gases, and water, in addition to power grid handling. The 5G network allows a new level of digitization for this utility-driven service.

This sector is one of the most visible sectors to benefit from 5G network services. There are multiple ways in which the technology introduced by the 5G standard of mobile networks will benefit the energy sector, not only in terms of profitability for suppliers but also increasing accessibility for consumers. Here, finally, the most promising and critical advantage is the positive effect on the environment and the planet's resources.

Advanced levels of application in the energy and utility sectors assisted by the 5G network are as follows:

- Distribution of energy within a smart-network channel with minimal or no human intervention
- Smart meters for the home for automatic real-time data collection
- Advanced remote monitoring systems for energy sites such as wind energy stations and solar farms
- Highly efficient energy systems, advanced climate change monitoring and protection warning

Let's have a look at some advancements in this field with 5G empowerment.

1.15.1 SMART GRID

The introduction of the 5G network will open the way for smart grid operations with improved functionality, allowing a huge number of devices to be connected that previously was not possible due to network capacity limitations. 5G will help advance the monitoring of energy use, allow better estimates of energy consumption, forecast energy usage needs, and minimize unnecessary energy wastage to reduce costs.

5G will ensure smart energy distribution by identifying potential energy peaks, help in handling load balancing, and minimize energy wastage, helping suppliers improve smart energy distribution to reduce energy costs.

The possibility of data collection using the 5G network will help in efficient infrastructure planning for larger cities to spend optimally, which will ensure not only energy saving but also less wastage and higher efficiency.

1.15.2 Smart Meters for the Home

The smart meter is now becoming part of daily consumer life in smart energy monitoring and can be placed anywhere in a home or office. It consists of an effective and easy interface for the user to monitor and view energy usage and an indication of usage costs in real time to effectively track and ensure efficient utilization of energy.

The addition of smart meters in many homes and other sites with existing telecommunication infrastructure is not new, but 5G connectivity with these smart meters will optimize the monitoring of data efficiently, ensuring the distribution and management of energy more precisely by establishing a smart interface between the consumer and service provider.

5G connectivity will allow more detailed information to be captured and transferred compared to previous technologies, providing consumers with detailed energy usage for a specific time or day. In addition, tracking and managing energy usage will ensure a significant reduction in energy wastage.

1.15.3 Remote Monitoring of Energy Sites

Remote energy monitoring is already featured in many smart meters of energy suppliers. With new radio 5G services, improvements in service speed and latency will allow more information to be transferred and gathered quickly.

Today, energy-producing sites are developing, and smart meters attached to solar energy stations, wind stations, and other energy sites can monitor energy usage levels. Connectivity between smart meters and the 5G network will assist in providing an advanced experience in the efficient management of energy sites.

1.16 SUMMARY

This chapter has provided an overview of the modern wireless communication network using 5G technology, which is being deployed across the globe and developed for transformative new service packages. 5G networks offer higher spectrum bandwidth, higher connection density, and lower latency than their predecessor, the 4G network, and are helping to define higher industry-leading speeds, next-level reliability, and higher efficiency that will lead to new transformative experiences for various sectors. New advanced features will lead to this radio mobile technology being in demand for sectors such as manufacturing, engineering, agriculture, internet of things devices, energy and utilities, healthcare, transport, artificial intelligence, and media and entertainment, with real-time transmission. The development of the smart city is the most important scenario under the 5G network, allowing a seamless and transformative user experience in day-to-day life and lifestyles.

5G networks are well advanced in deployment around the world, serving multiple sectors with advanced mobile technology, ensuring digital transformation, and the economic success of many countries. There are however some technological challenges, such as infrastructural development, political willingness to create resources, and other geographical factors, concerning implementation in certain locations [5].

Beyond 5G, the 6th generation mobile system (6G) technology lab experiments are also in trials and are expected to be commercially available by 2028 at the earliest. The initial experiments are being performed and interesting lab results have been observed. It is expected that 6G will likely be significantly faster with much more bandwidth. Several countries already have shown interest in 6G networks and have started research in the lab for the proposed 6G-level spectrum and hardware testing and are preparing for a transformed world [7][9].

ACRONYMS

3GPP: 3rd-generation partnership project
5G: 5th generation
AMF: Access and mobility management function
CU: Centralized unit
C-V2X: Cellular vehicle-to-everything
eNB: Evolved node B (LTE)
EPC: Evolved packet core (LTE)
FDD: Frequency division duplex
FDM: Frequency-division multiplexing
FR1: Frequency range 1
FR2: Frequency range 2
FS: Financial services
gNB: 5G NR base station
IIoT: Industrial internet of things
IMT: International mobile telecommunications
IoT: Internet of things
ITU: International Telecommunication Union
km: Kilometer (a measure of distance, 1 mile is equal to 1.60934 km)
LTE: Long-term evolution
MME: Mobility management entity (LTE)
NG-RAN: Next-generation RAN
NR: New radio
TDD: Time division duplex
Tx/Rx: Transmit and receive

UE: User equipment
UPF: User plane function
V2V: Vehicle to vehicle

REFERENCES

1. 3rd Generation Partnership Project; Technical Specification Group Services and System Aspects; System architecture for the 5G System (5GS);Stage 2 (Release 17) 3GPP TS 23.501, V17.1.1, *Technical Specification Group Services and Systems Aspects*, 3GPP, Sept. 2021.
2. "3rd Generation Partnership Project; Technical Specification Group Radio Access Network;NR;Physical channels and modulation," document 3GPP TS 38.211 V 16.7.0 *Technical Specification Group*, 3GPP, Sept.2021.
3. W. Ejaz et al., "Internet of Things (IoT) in 5G Wireless Communications," in *IEEE Access*, vol. 4, pp. 10310–10314, 2016, doi: 10.1109/ACCESS.2016.2646120.
4. T. Li and D. Li, "Prospects for the Application of 5G Technology in Agriculture and Rural Areas," 2020 5th International Conference on Mechanical, Control and Computer Engineering (ICMCCE), 2020, pp. 2176–2179, doi: 10.1109/ICMCCE51767.2020.00472.
5. M. Taheribakhsh, A. Jafari, M. M. Peiro and N. Kazemifard, "5G Implementation: Major Issues and Challenges," 2020 25th International Computer Conference, Computer Society of Iran (CSICC), 2020, pp. 1–5, doi: 10.1109/CSICC49403.2020.9050110.
6. S. Painuly, P. Kohli, P. Matta and S. Sharma, "Advance Applications and Future Challenges of 5G IoT," 2020 3rd International Conference on Intelligent Sustainable Systems (ICISS), 2020, pp. 1381–1384, doi: 10.1109/ICISS49785.2020.9316004.
7. M. A. Uusitalo et al., "6G Vision, Value, Use Cases and Technologies From European 6G Flagship Project Hexa-X," in *IEEE Access*, vol. 9, pp. 160004–160020, 2021, doi: 10.1109/ACCESS.2021.3130030.
8. A. Ghosh, A. Maeder, M. Baker and D. Chandramouli, "5G Evolution: A View on 5G Cellular Technology Beyond 3GPP Release 15," in *IEEE Access*, vol. 7, pp. 127639–127651, 2019, doi: 10.1109/ACCESS.2019.2939938.
9. H. Tataria, M. Shafi, A. F. Molisch, M. Dohler, H. Sjöland and F. Tufvesson, "6G Wireless Systems: Vision, Requirements, Challenges, Insights, and Opportunities," in *Proceedings of the IEEE*, vol. 109, no. 7, pp. 1166–1199, July 2021, doi: 10.1109/JPROC.2021.3061701.
10. E. Dahlman and S. Parkvall, "NR: The New 5G Radio-Access Technology," 2018 IEEE 87th Vehicular Technology Conference (VTC Spring), 2018, pp. 1–6, doi: 10.1109/VTCSpring.2018.8417851.
11. L. Xia, M. Zhao and Z. Tian, "5G Service Based Core Network Design," 2019 IEEE Wireless Communications and Networking Conference Workshop (WCNCW), 2019, pp. 1–6, doi: 10.1109/WCNCW.2019.8902883.
12. J. Montonen, J. Koskinen, J. Mäkelä, S. Ruponen, T. Heikkilä and M. Hentula, "Applying 5G and Edge Processing in Smart Manufacturing," 2021 IFIP Networking Conference (IFIP Networking), 2021, pp. 1–2, doi: 10.23919/IFIPNetworking52078.2021.9472851.

2 The Role of 5G in Smart Transportation

Mansha Swami and Sankalp Swami

CONTENTS

2.1 INTRODUCTION

The world has come a long way since 1993 when 2G networks were first introduced. Now, data transfer can be as fast as 10 GBPS, which is considerably faster than the erstwhile 2G (64 KBPS only) and subsequent versions like 3G (8 MBPS) and 4G (50 MBPS). The ping rate during speed tests has revealed exceptionally high latency in comparison to 4G networks. 4G latency is around 60–98 milliseconds, while the latency of 5G networks is less than 1 millisecond. This translates into considerably less time consumed in data package capturing, transmission of data, multiple device-based processing, and decoding at the destination end. The entire process of data transfer becomes much faster. This would increase processes in transportation systems, with lower latency, greater bandwidth, more capacity to allocate resources to critical functions, a greater number of devices used at once, and faster data sharing, all at an exponentially higher efficiency [6].

The type of data speed required for driverless cars and other intelligent transport applications is just so much better with 5G networks. For gaming applications, typically a 20-40 millisecond range works best, but a latency of less than 1 millisecond is phenomenal as the traffic-related decision-making time slots are much lower. This feature is also imperative in critical situations. With this massive reduction in the round-trip time of the ping, the decision-making for smart transportation applications will become easier. Therefore, 5G seems to have a promising scope in

DOI: 10.1201/9781003227861-2

intelligent transportation applications. Let us have a look at some of the possibilities of 5G networks. Since their inception in 2018, they have been expected to play a transformative role in transportation engineering applications like autonomous vehicles, logistics, and other ITS-ICT (intelligent transport systems-information and communications technology)-based applications [8].

The massive connectivity demand that will arise out of the advent of 5G will also require equally massive financial resources to provide expanded 5G coverage and the telecom infrastructure required for it.

2.2   ROLE OF 5G IN REAL-TIME TRAFFIC OPERATIONS

With 5G networks in place, the real-time vehicle driving experience will be more entertaining, efficient, and manageable than ever. Real-time location tracking will be possible with higher speeds of connectivity, which will enhance the travel experience. Traffic management through GPS would be more organized, hassle-free, and faster. In addition, decisions regarding signalized locations and the signal priority system for automatic signals would now suffer from negligible time delay and other network-related lapses.

Smart traffic management systems would help in increasing the traffic flow in corridors and would reduce congestion by utilizing alternate routes more efficiently. Traffic signals would now change according to real-time ever-changing traffic situations responding more responsively to bottlenecks and halted vehicles. In Pittsburgh, USA, the students of Carnegie Melon University tested a small smart traffic lights system that led to a 40% decrease in the average vehicle's waiting time due to congestion. In addition, 26% of the journey speeds were increased. Vehicle emissions due to these changes were also reduced by 21%. These are significant changes possible only due to faster networks and better connectivity.

App-based cab service providers can also save significant time and pick up more passengers during one working day due to increased traffic flow along with significant savings on fuel. Car platooning with safe distances will also be possible if vehicle-to-vehicle technology (V2V) is merged with high-speed 5G networks, and vehicles will be able to know the appropriate yet optimized distance between each other, thereby avoiding traffic queues and delays caused due to non-uniform gaps on the roads. This platooning would also help in augmenting the existing capacity of highways and, again, will reduce travel times.

Vehicle-to-infrastructure (V2I) will allow vehicles to be able to communicate with sensor systems installed on turnpikes, bridges, tunnels, roadways, traffic lights, parking entry and exit points, and more. The drivers in long traffic queues will now get real-time information on queue length and time that will be reduced by clearing the queue. Additionally, drivers who are yet to join a certain route will get updates and warnings on possible congestion on the route beforehand. Passengers will get information on adverse conditions on the route such as mudslides, accident pile ups, snowstorms, landslides, road infrastructure mishaps, etc. An estimated time of arrival (ETA) can also be provided. With this information, the driver can make better decisions about re-routing the journey. Google Traffic is doing a good job in

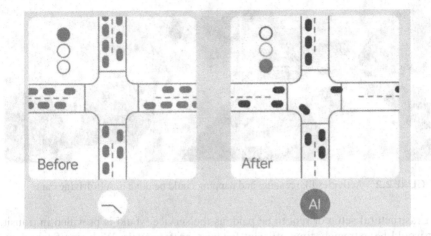

FIGURE 2.1 Intersection diagram based on timer setting and AI-based signal management (Source: Google)

similar information dispersion, and it helps millions of commuters every day across the globe.

Recently, Google has also announced that it is developing artificial intelligence (AI)-based traffic light management, which will not only save precious minutes but also fuel when vehicles are waiting for their turn at intersections. The traffic lights would distribute and disperse traffic through green signals more often and based on volume changes on all approaches more efficiently. Four pilot testing scenarios have been conducted in Israel already. These pilots have already produced a reduction in fuel along with intersection time delays by 10–20%. Figure 2.1 shows the intersection diagram before and after AI implementation on signalized intersections [1].

2.3 ROLE OF 5G IN ENTERTAINMENT SYSTEMS IN VEHICLES

With the advent of 5G network applications in entertainment systems in vehicles, there can be fast streaming of high-resolution movies, media, and even gaming facilities within the vehicle at gigabit speeds. There is the potential for video conferencing on the go at less than 1-millisecond latency with almost no lag time. This facility will help professionals gain much more productivity by being able to attend meetings on the go. Also in driverless cars, the passenger can focus more on the meetings while the vehicle can autonomously take care of itself. The range of activities in which the driver can take part includes video calling on the go, browsing the internet or managing emails, listening to music, streaming videos, gaming, augmented reality/virtual reality (AR/VR), experiencing a salon treatment, taking a nap, etc., which will depend on which level of autonomy the vehicle is functioning. Figure 2.2 shows activities that could be done in driverless vehicles.

These services will be beneficial in two ways. Firstly, the commuter will save on time and hence, eventually, money. Secondly, the service provider will need no

FIGURE 2.2   Activities like reading and napping could be done in self-driving cars

infrastructural setup or rent to be paid, as the service would is provided in transit. It would be extremely time efficient for busy professionals. With significant commuting time saved, these professionals would now be able to learn new skills and spend time on their interests and hobbies more than ever before. Even for passengers commuting on public transport, there would be entertainment, as with 5G on board there would be faster streaming of videos and other multimedia options. Further, live sporting fixtures or major events could be shown on big screens on public transport. Current onboard multimedia is rarely available across public transit, however, even if available, it is usually very expensive. This would change with 5G networks, as it would become very affordable to subscribe to infotainment services while onboard public transit.

2.4   ROLE OF 5G IN DRIVERLESS CARS AND AUTONOMOUS VEHICLES

Connected and autonomous vehicles (CAVs) will reduce the need for very skilled drivers and will rely more on machine learning, AI, and robotics all combined through the common thread of faster network connectivity. This will save trillions of dollars in the road user or passenger's time. The service industry is extremely keen to release the autonomous vehicle's autonomy. Time spent on driving and focusing on the road will be saved by the driver, and this time can be used by the passenger for leisure activities, such as dining, spas, salon services, and shopping. Mobility as a service (MaaS) and e-commerce would become viable business models.

The routines of future professionals because of autonomous cars with assisted services from the service industry would lead to massive time savings per day, which could be spent on learning new skills that could eventually contribute to improving the per capita GDP of nations worldwide.

Tesla's autopilot (now discontinued) was a well-known driver assistance mechanism that offered a fully self-driving experience to passengers (as per Tesla). This self-driving system gave the driver extended margins of safety and relaxation, where the burden of having to stay highly alert behind the wheel was reduced. The installation of eight cameras, twelve ultrasonic sensors, and one powerful onboard computer worked together to guide the journey. They were meant for drivers who were in the driving seat, were attentive, and could take control of the vehicle whenever they desired. Some of the features of the autopilot were autosteer and traffic-aware cruise control [3]. At almost double the cost of the autopilot, Tesla then launched an enhanced autopilot with four cameras, radar, a supercomputer, and improved ultrasonic sensors. The reports of the enhanced autopilot were unsatisfactory as the vehicle behaved unpredictably in some situations. Later, full self-driving was launched at a higher price with no input needed from the driver and worked on a point-to-point driving system. This new technology could also look for parking spaces by itself and park itself when the driver stepped out at the destination. The vehicle was smart enough to sync with a calendar and could take the driver to their destination without the driver having to tell it where to go. Now just imagine all this at an even higher speed.

Tesla vehicle safety reports included two types of accidents, either crashes or fire incidents. Although there have been several incidents of fires and crashes in Tesla cars, they are nevertheless the safest vehicles in the world.

The Toyota research institute [2] also is working on autonomous vehicles. They have already tested two different types. The first is the chauffeured mode where the car drives on the driver's behalf and gives a feeling of a chauffeured trip. This could be used by people who do not know how to drive, people with disabilities, or even people who simply do not wish to drive, especially when traffic is bad. Taxi operators may also make use of this mode. Secondly, there is the guardian mode, where a person wants to drive but as a safety net guardian mode is present to prevent them from crashing. For the testing of the guardian system, a customized vehicle with two brakes, two steering wheels, and two accelerating paddles on both sides of the vehicle were used. One was for the safety driver and the other was for the test driver. They further simulated various scenarios, such as obstructions ahead, lane change emergencies, slow-down situations, drowsy driver situations, and obstructions en route. The guardian system is not designed to parallel the autopilot but rather works with the driver as a teammate so the best input from both can be derived as and when required. Figure 2.3 illustrates the Toyota autonomous vehicle system.

Apart from Tesla, Toyota and Google driverless cars (now known as Waymo) are the main players in the development of driverless cars and autonomous vehicles. Jaguar Land Rover announced a collaboration with Google-Waymo in 2019 for the development of the world's premium driverless self-driving electric car. Waymo has also completed around one billion miles test driving the self-driving vehicles under simulation. Another significant company in the market is Pony.ai, which provides solutions based on artificial intelligence.

Apple has also been working on driverless cars since 2014 under the project name Titan. Kia, another automobile manufacturer which is a subsidiary of Hyundai Motors, has announced that it will launch a fully autonomous vehicle by 2030, whose USP will be its affordability for middle-classes. It is developing cost-effective vehicles to serve this purpose. Ford and Audi are two proactive automobile developers looking to develop a fully autonomous vehicle. Huawei, a telecommunications company, has suggested how mobile network operators could play a key role in connected

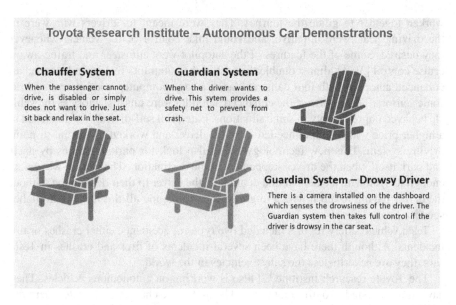

Toyota Research Institute – Autonomous Car Demonstrations

Chauffer System

When the passenger cannot drive, is disabled or simply does not want to drive. Just sit back and relax in the seat.

Guardian System

When the driver wants to drive. This sytem provides a safety net to prevent from crash.

Guardian System – Drowsy Driver

There is a camera installed on the dashboard which senses the drowsiness of the driver. The Guardian system then takes full control if the driver is drowsy in the car seat.

FIGURE 2.3 Toyota demonstration of chauffeur and guided autonomous vehicle system.

automobile systems. Several applications, such as LTE-based emergency services, smart parking, in-car entertainment, and fleet management, can be deployed. They have also collaborated with Audi to develop autonomous technology for China.

At present, autonomous vehicles are not able to detect any obstacles beyond their fields of vision. Also, they cannot process traffic more than 0.5 miles ahead of them. Further, it is also difficult for them to judge the behavior and intention of other drivers, even those that may only be a few feet away. These shortcomings become a challenge when the vehicles are operating in heavily congested urban areas. Due to this, the functioning of autonomous vehicles faces great challenges in urban areas. However, when 5G is combined with artificial intelligence, cybersecurity, and big data, the scenario around the vehicle could be predicted by continuously collecting and interpreting the data collected from the vehicles in the surroundings. In order to provide a constant exchange and flow of information across all IoT devices, 5G technology needs massive machine-type communications (mMTC) along with higher bandwidth and lower latency. These features will enable AVs to connect better to obtain data from traffic streams, traffic lights, pedestrian movements, sensor-based information, road signs, public transit, etc.

The various of levels of automation achieved so far, as determined by SAE International (previously known as the Society of Automotive Engineers) based in USA, are depicted in Figure 2.4. Current technologies have been able to reach level 4. Level 5 vehicles are currently at the experimentation stage in various companies. However, with the advent of 5G communications, the dream of having a fully automated, commercially available car in the near future is possible with the massive exchange of data over the cloud and sensor integration.

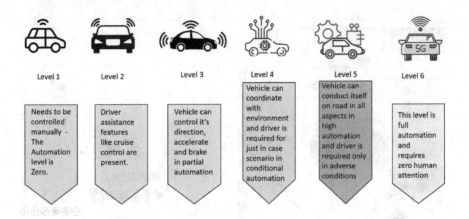

Level 1	Level 2	Level 3	Level 4	Level 5	Level 6
Needs to be controlled manually - The Automation level is Zero.	Driver assistance features like cruise control are present.	Vehicle can control it's direction, accelerate and brake in partial automation	Vehicle can coordinate with environment and driver is required for just in case scenario in conditional automation	Vehicle can conduct itself on road in all aspects in high automation and driver is required only in adverse conditions	This level is full automation and requires zero human attention

FIGURE 2.4   Various levels in automation of vehicles as given by SAE International

2.5   ROLE OF 5G IN SENSOR-BASED INTELLIGENT TRANSPORTATION APPLICATIONS

For road safety hazards and road features like bumps and potholes, real-time information connections using GPS enable faster recognition of deteriorated road patches, and almost instantly the road repair team can reach the identified location and fix the road. Cloud-based ITS services include cooperative adaptive cruise control (C-ACC). This technology uses the V2X communications to locate the vehicle ahead, and using this information, it coordinates the traffic flow. It actively and continuously accommodates the dynamic changes and responds with adaptive cruise control. This activity essentially requires a higher bandwidth with low latency, which can be provided by 5G, as real-time road maneuvers require very fast processing. Vulnerable road users (VRU), such as cyclists, pedestrians, walking senior citizens, small children, and pets, require collision protection from vehicular movement. In order to make sure that VRU mobility is safe, automatic braking systems could be installed in vehicles to avoid collisions. Even at intersections where traffic lights are installed, similar arrangements could be installed for pedestrians crossing the intersection. Further, these technologies could be used for warning-based alerts at intersections, where any erratic driving behavior is detected in the nearby environment; this is known as an advanced intersection collision warning (AICW). 5G will allow for the full automation of such systems and will enhance the efficiency of these systems. 5G features will enable smart connectivity by expanding the coverage in qualitative as well as quantitative dimensions. The 5G features that are applicable to smart connectivity are shown in Figure 2.5.

No-light intersections will allow traffic at intersections without traffic lights to operate smoothly with very fine coordination between vehicular speeds from all directions. Cooperative driving is where the sensors coordinate with vehicle movements and real-time traffic data in order to avoid congestion. Vehicle movements that are coordinated into flow in a platoon, significantly reducing energy consumption

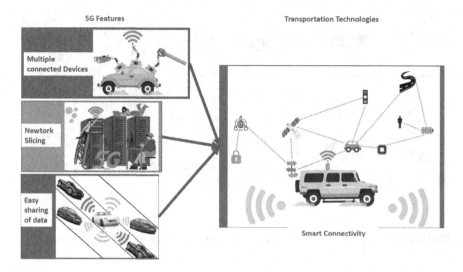

FIGURE 2.5   5G features used for smart connectivity

due to a lower amount of traffic queues, is known as advanced platooning. Trajectory or maneuver sharing is when a vehicle sends a signal whenever it detects another vehicle's intention of performing a maneuver or lane change.

2.6   ROLE OF 5G IN ACCIDENT PREVENTION SYSTEMS

Every year, 1.35 million lives are lost globally to road accidents. The majority of these crashes (approximately 94%) are due to human errors. Here CAVs have a huge potential to save human lives. 5G technology will make the vehicle-to-vehicle and vehicle-to-infrastructure processes stronger and help CAVs to better analyze a situation with data from various sources. CAVs have had their own types of crashes in testing facilities and in real-time use, but that is rarer than the crash probability of a human-driven vehicle. 5G will give vehicles a better view beyond the field of view visible to them, steering control, smoother acceleration, enhanced cooperation between driving vehicles, coordinated braking, and more optimized driving patterns. V2I interaction will make it easier for vehicles to identify signage, barriers, speed-calming infrastructures, and other obstacles, and will respond accordingly to the situation thereby enhancing the safety of vehicles.

Let us look at the safety features journey throughout the inception of motor vehicles. From 1950s until 2000, we had cruise control, seat belts, and antilock brakes as the available safety features. However, in the new millennium, the first decade saw massive additions to the safety features of vehicles, such as electronic stability control, forward collision warning, blind-spot detection, and lane departure warning. From 2010 until the end of 2016, several new features were added, such as rear-view video systems, pedestrian automatic emergency braking, automatic emergency braking, rear automatic emergency braking, lane cantering alerts, and rear cross-traffic alerts. In the last few years, lane-keeping assist, traffic jam assist, and adaptive cruise control have been added. In the future, we can look forward to more advanced driver assist system (ADAS) features eventually leading to fully automated safety features.

With a higher level of vehicle automation, it is automatically expected that the levels of safety would become enhanced. The more the entire autonomous driving ecosystem is advanced, the more efficient it will be to protect the driver, the pedestrian, the cyclist, and the passengers within the vehicle.

Accident prevention systems involve crash prediction alerts, collision avoidance frameworks, multi-agent collision avoidance frameworks, ADAS with automatic steering control, and braking mechanisms. Further, several AI and machine-learning-based additions in the AV landscape are proposed to train the vehicle to conduct itself with a set of inputs available from various data points and sensors from connected devices. Several previous accidents that have taken place in Uber and Google self-driving cars have made it evident that more calibration and simulation need to be done on the prototypes in order to decrease crash probability. It will take some more years to eventually reach a point where a completely crash-free level of safety is achieved.

2.7 ROLE OF 5G FOR TRANSIT OPERATIONS

The commuter experiences over the public transit systems are key to understanding where the scope lies for improvement for public transit agencies. Information and communications technologies (ICT) have traditionally always been a high-cost alternative for studying public transit metrics [7]. However, in the era of fast data and more especially big data processing, the process has become much less costly to track the metrics of public transit operations [5]. Cloud-based open data sets such as general transit feed specification (GTFS) help in managing the challenges related to on-road safety, transit unit management, and vehicle location tracking, etc. Temporal parameters, fare collection, and revenue management can also be closely monitored and further rectified, leading to enhanced attractiveness of public transport services. 5G speeds will not only detect transit issues but would be easier with the help of AI-based solutions and machine learning to figure out the solution to complex situations and resolve the matter in a matter of minutes, literally! Figure 2.6 depicts the features which impact real-time passenger information along with transit operations.

Once the issues are identified in public transit and passenger transport, the urban mobility sector shall gain impetus in terms of increasing passenger numbers, revenues, reduced tariffs and congestion, and re-design of urban corridors to embed more space for non-motorized transport (NMT) alternatives like walking and cycling. Further, the safety of NMT users will be enhanced with 5G-enabled vehicle-to-everything (V2X) communications. So, fitness gets a boost along with the digital economy.

V2X technology requires a radio module, and each vehicle has a transmitter and spectrum attached to the service. The deployment cost can be hugely reduced if existing cellular networks are used for this purpose.

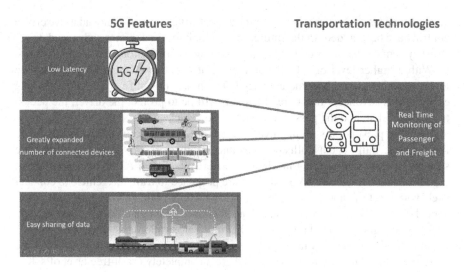

FIGURE 2.6   5G features affecting real-time passenger information and public transit operations

Several features applicable to V2X are: expanded bandwidth, low latency, significant numbers of connected devices, early sharing of data and network slicing, etc. Several subcategories of V2X are summarized in Figure 2.7.

V2X could include road work warnings for zones under construction, traffic congestion identification by giving traffic jam warnings, contextual information exchange with several infrastructure points, intersection collision warnings, overtaking vehicle

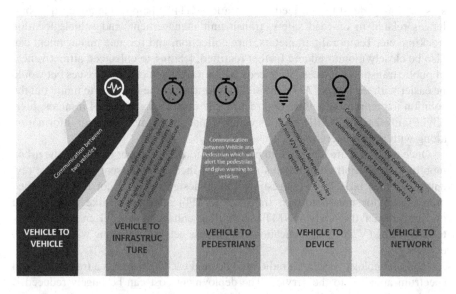

FIGURE 2.7   Subcategories of V2X communications

warnings, local hazard warnings, left-turn assist warnings, and green light optimal speed advisory (GLOSA), where a traffic light informs the upcoming vehicle of time and speed so they can decide whether they can pass the intersection without stopping and pre-plan their stops on intersections.

Integration of MaaS platforms would again give a multitude of options in terms of trip choice to the new smart commuter. MaaS is a platform where the commuter shifts from private transport vehicles to public transport. It provides a single window gateway where seamless travel is ensured and only a single payment account is required for all different modes used during the trip. It provides customized service to each commuter based on their specific travel and trip requirements and also gives them easy options to pay the fare. When the same concept is applied to the movement of goods, it is called transport as a service (TaaS).

Better management of smart mobility cards for seamless transport in a multimodal environment will also reduce fraud and further assist public transit organizations to help low-income communities have access to public transport systems. Further, as origin and destination matrices are processed more quickly, this would reduce the chances of empty vehicle dispatch or extremely overcrowded vehicles being operated, as it would adjust accordingly to the peak hour or off-peak hour demand and roll out the fleet as per the demand.

2.8   ROLE OF 5G IN ADVANCED DRIVER ASSISTANCE SYSTEMS (ADAS)

With 5G technologies embedded in AVs, the vehicle also assists the driver by letting it explore the environment with the help of radar and cameras, which helps the driver to take action based on the data received. ADAS is the first step towards fully autonomous driving. With 5G, fast cloud-sharing is possible, leading to real-time and reliable information being communicated between vehicles and service providers, which are using cloud-based technologies to assist. The faster gathering of information from nearby vehicles and infrastructure is possible with 5G. It may be particularly helpful in protecting vulnerable road users, such as pedestrians and cyclists, where the vehicle will get an alert if a VRU enters the same geographical area. Also, while road construction is going on in a particular area, this technology can share the details with road workers and emergency vehicles so they can change routes or plan ahead to leave the area. The technology used here is called geofencing. In geofencing, the geographical area pockets are marked, and further, which geographical area when the alert notifications are to be distributed is considered. Blind-spot warning mechanisms can also form a part of ADAS especially when reverse or rear movement is required. It can alert the driver whenever the driver drifts outside their own lane while driving, known as lane departure warning. ADAS, when coupled with an active safety system, will also help in actively controlling braking or steering. Due to these everyday big and small ways in which ADAS provides to the driver, it is also referred to as "assistance".

Ericsson technologies have tested ADAS in several cases with 5G, such as the 5G aquaplaning alert, where, wherever a situation of contact with water arises leading to

FIGURE 2.8   5G Aquaplaning alert (Ericsson)

aquaplaning, the connected cyber-tires alerts the vehicle, and the gravity of the water hazard is detected and further monitored, data is shared with other vehicles via the cloud, and the succeeding vehicle is allowed to pass safely with a timely alert. Figure 2.8 shows how the aquaplaning alert is given in the ADAS system.

Another ADAS case study is about alerting the vehicle against unseen pedestrians; in this case, both the pedestrian and the driver receives warnings about the presence of the pedestrian. It utilizes sensor data to share advanced safety information with drivers to enhance safety on the road. When the pedestrian is easily visible to the driver, then augmented reality (AR) technology is used to enhance visibility, and potential warnings or alerts about the pedestrian close to the vehicle are given. Figure 2.9 shows the unseen pedestrian scenario. However, in the case that the driver has not been able to see the pedestrian, then the vehicle, along with cloud-connect fast communication and sensors, is able to detect the proximity of the driver and pedestrian and further alert both.

Augmented road sign information helps the driver when they have seen a specific road sign but have not been able to comprehend or recognize it. This technology will help to automatically explain the meaning of such a road sign to the driver and assist by responding to his gaze.

According to the Insurance Institute of Highway Safety, the use of several of these technologies has helped reduce collisions massively. For example, a 27% reduction was found in front-to-rear crashes by installing forward collision warning systems. Further, if the system can automatically pull the brakes, then this percentage nearly doubles. Similarly, a 17% reduction in crashes is seen if rear-view cameras are deployed. Further, if rear-view cameras are coupled with automatic braking, then a 78% reduction in crashes is possible. ADAS also ensures that a safe gap is maintained between the vehicles, and for that, it may automatically regulate the speed of

FIGURE 2.9 Hidden pedestrian alert (Ericsson)

the vehicle. High-end ADAS features include control of steering and propulsion in the case of stop-and-go traffic in congested urban corridors.

2.9 ROLE OF 5G IN LOGISTICS OPERATIONS

The logistics industry will evolve around the newer possibilities after 5G, and gradually this will lead to innovative and more revenue-oriented optimized business models in the shipping, delivery, and logistics domains. The retail industry and e-commerce giants, such as Amazon and Domino's, have already started using drone delivery systems, which are able to access even non-reachable pockets of districts, rural areas, etc. This also saves on the fuel earlier spent on the conventional truck-based logistic system. This also saves the retailers a good percentage of inventory in their business models. With the advent of 5G technology, the tracing, tracking, truck platooning, and managing of drone vehicles along with streamlining last-mile delivery will not only get faster but will also make sure multiple service locations are covered in a shorter period of time at once.

In order to have optimized transport costs, freight logistics need to be robust and require accurate goods flow management so that costs are minimal and customer satisfaction is high. The three critical dimensions that enhance logistics efficiency with 5G are, firstly, simplification of communications and signal processes, eventually leading to the second dimension. The second dimension is when vehicles can operate themselves, i.e. autonomous vehicles. The third dimension is massive machine-type communications that expand IoT and wireless internet. When this capacity is put to use in logistics, each unit, whether parcel, packet, mail, or container, can be easily located and tracked in the distribution chain. Drones are also being used as autonomous delivery vehicles in various parts of the world for delivering various products.

FIGURE 2.10 Delivery logistic services through drone delivery and autonomous car delivery

Some of these can be seen in Figure 2.10. As you can see, Costa Coffee, Dominoes, Amazon, Pizza Hut, etc. have already started pilot runs in the automation of delivery logistics.

Logistics carriers can be through roadways, railways, airways, and ports. However, for the use of 5G technologies, only railways, trucks on roads, and port management is considered. If 5G networks are deployed in rail networks, the benefits could include onboard entertainment and multimedia services for commuters, an increased number of transit units in the rail network, safer train operations, and enhanced reliability of railway communications. Currently, the technology on which trains rely is GSM, which will soon (2030) be obsolete. Therefore, in order to make sure that train operations are operating safely, a 5G upgrade is needed. If the right transition from GSM to 5G is made by 2025, the new system will definitely expand services in all countries before GSM goes off air. The future railway mobile communications system (FRMCS) is aimed to integrate 5G spectrum-based technologies with higher potentials into train operations. This will aid the extensive use of IoT features in rail, which will also be able to monitor all the assets in the whole network along with energy consumption and savings. Additionally, information regarding rolling stock, wear of axles, peak electricity consumption, real-time ridership data for better distribution of passengers, ticketing queues, power grids, and other components of trains could be tracked faster. The number of connected devices will shoot up and so will the need for massive data storage and management. 5G deployment will make sure that railway operators can connect sensors and actuators with smart city applications, which would create a great data set for machine learning needs and help the system improve its collective intelligence.

2.10 SUMMARY

The major changes expected with 5G technologies in the transportation sector are, firstly, a huge revolution in connectivity between vehicles and infrastructure, leading to a massive rise in the use of CAVs. Secondly, an increase in the number of connected devices will lead to highly efficient logistic handling and smart e-commerce. Thirdly, enormous amounts of data would be available for all transport operations, which will enhance the quality of urban transportation with the inclusion of MaaS-based platforms.

In a report by the McKinsey Global Institute, around one-fourth of the globe will have 5G available by 2030 [9]. Countries like the USA, Japan, and the Republic of Korea are using 5G on a large-scale level across their countries. Countries like Canada, China, India, and within the European Union will soon deploy 5G networks but only in their major urban areas for now. This will widen the connectivity gap between urban and rural areas. This may also affect 5G reaching out to remote areas in developing countries. In addition, opportunities in the transport sector in these cities may not be realized due to limited deployment [4]. Further, affordability and accessibility equations need to be combined so that wider reach and more profitability can be realized. Systems like smart cards for seamless travel and single-point collection could be subsidized for vulnerable communities and people in order to keep the system affordable for all users. 5G-enabled cities may be able to prioritize more space for pedestrians and cyclists if stronger policies are developed. Further, these cities may have better operational public transport. In addition, the creation of new jobs and services will enhance everyday living experiences. Figure 2.11 shows a SWOT analysis of the application of 5G in the transportation sector.

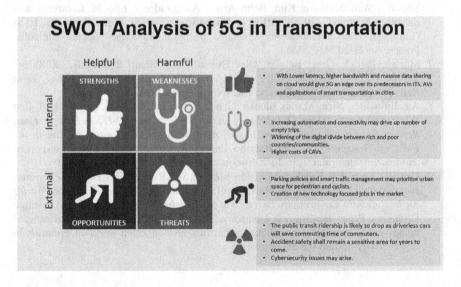

FIGURE 2.11 SWOT analysis of 5G application in the transportation sector

The strengths of 5G includes faster speed and ability to connect to multiple devices at one time. 5G may create opportunities for Non-motorized (NMT) and Vulnerable Road User (VRU) friendly urban spaces along with employment generation. 5G has certain weak points which includes need of expensive technology and the digital gap between communities due to higher costs.

The challenges consist of developing acceptable accident safety systems and dealing with a decrease in the use of public transportation. Passengers mostly favor public transportation as they do not have to drive. With driverless revolution, this reason would no longer work in favor of public transportation. Additionally, a huge exchange of data may spark privacy and cybersecurity debates.

REFERENCES

1. Pichai, Sundar (2021). AI for more efficient traffic lights. https://blog.google/outreach -initiatives/sustainability/sustainability-2021/
2. Toyota Research Institute (2021). Blog: Toyota Research Institute bets big in vegas on Toyota guardian autonomy. https://www.tri.global/our-work/automated-driving/
3. Tesla (2021). Autopilot and full self-driving capability. https://www.tesla.com/support/ autopilot
4. Limi, Atsushi and Diehl, Adam (2015). A new measure for Rural access to transport. Knowledge Note 23. World Bank Group. https://www.worldbank.org/en/topic/trans-port/brief/connections-note-23
5. Wang, Winnie et al. (2015). Advances and challenges in intelligent transportation. The evolution of ICT to address transport challenges in developing countries. Note 26. World Bank Group. https://www.worldbank.org/en/topic/transport/brief/connections -note-26
6. Kekki, Sami, Walter Featherstone, Yonggang Fang, Pekka Kuure, Alice Li, Anurag Ranjan, Debashish Purkayastha, Feng Jiangping, Danny Frydman, Gianluca Verin, Kuo-Wei Wen, Kwihoon Kim, Rohit Arora, Andy Odgers, Luis M. Contreras, and Salvatore Scarpina. (2018). "MEC in 5G networks." ETSI White Paper 28. ETSI (European Telecommunications Standards Institute), Valbonne– Sophia Antipolis, France. Accessed May 2020.
7. Marsch, Patrick, Ömer Bulakçı, Olav Queseth, and Mauro Boldi, eds. (2018). *5G System Design: Architectural and Functional Considerations and Long Term Research.*Chichester, West Sussex, UK: John Wiley & Sons.
8. Asselin-Miller, Nick, Marius Biedka, Gena Gibson, Felix Kirsch, Nikolas Hill, Ben White, and Kotub Uddin. (2016). *Study on the Deployment of C-ITS in Europe: Final Report: Framework Contract on Impact Assessment and Evaluation Studies in the Field of Transport.* London: Ricardo Energy & Environment. https://transport.ec .europa.eu/system/files/2016-10/2016-c-its-deployment-study-final-report.pdf
9. Grijpink, Ferry, Eric Kutcher, Alexandre Ménard, Sree Ramaswamy, Davide Schiavotto, James Manyika, Michael Chui, Rob Hamill, and Emir Okan. (2020). *Connected World: An Evolution in Connectivity Beyond the 5G Revolution.* McKinsey Global Institute Discussion Paper. McKinsey & Company. https://www.mckinsey.com/industries/tech-nology-media-and-telecommunications/our-insights/connected-world-an-evolution-in -connectivity-beyond-the-5G-revolution

3 Network Management in Smart Cities

M. Deepika and A. Angel Cerli

CONTENTS

DOI: 10.1201/9781003227861-3

3.1   INTRODUCTION

The internet of things (IoT), like any other system, needs a mechanism for evaluating events that take place within it. Forensics is the term used when such an examination is conducted for legal purposes. On the other hand, the IoT presents several challenges in forensics [1]. Data collection from devices with limited interfaces, storage, and processing capabilities is difficult. As an alternative, the gathering of little data bits from these devices can offer an unparalleled view of events from a variety of perspectives. There will be an excess of forensically relevant data in the future due to the development of linked electronics. Our digitally connected lives leave traces that might pave the way for a golden age of forensics. Untrustworthy human memory will be supplanted by concrete proof.

The benefits of IoT forensics are not without cost. The first issue that comes to mind is the issue of privacy. Fortunately, specialists in general IoT and, more particularly, IoT forensics are aware of the issue and working to resolve it. This chapter focuses on the challenges that a forensic investigator has while investigating IoT-related concerns. Currently, more than half of the world's population lives in or near cities [2]. By 2050, the proportion of people living in cities will have grown to 70%. Smart cities must provide a wide range of services in a timely and effective manner. The solution is to capitalize on the current growth of networked information technologies. Significant investments in smart cities will be undertaken during the next ten years. Most of these technologies will be in widespread use by 2020. Smart houses rely on information and communications technologies (ICT) to elevate the housing and living experience. The cost of creating supporting technologies for smart cities is expected to be approximately $100 billion.

The number of elderly individuals is rapidly increasing. Smart homes and communities may be used to cost-effectively fulfill the needs of this demographic. In recent years, the following factors have increased interest in smart homes and cities: China and India account for 40% of the world's population. Many countries, notably Japan, Europe, and even China, have experienced an increase in the number of people over the age of 65 who require smart homes and smart cities to improve their quality of life [3].

Municipal apps rely on human-centered controls that are reactive for most of their functionality today. Cyber-physical devices (CPDs) in cities employ real-time monitoring data from wireless sensor nodes (WSNs) as well as user feedback to address this challenge. User control and machine-centralized detection–failure prevention paradigms have been combined in a new approach to city administration. According to manufacturers, the control framework aims to forecast and prevent future system failures. In addition, it keeps an eye on its systems' performance and looks for abnormalities [4]. Failure detection and recovery needs in smart cities are becoming more precise and efficient. Because this self-contained framework includes components for the user, it improves user experience and allows for better action options.

There will be a wide range of devices in future smart cities, including WSNs, CPDs, IoT devices, and mobile users. In the area of control, communication between various devices and systems is monitored to ensure that it is both functional and successful.

The data from smart cities will be vulnerable to a variety of assaults in the future. A safe environment must be provided by service providers, and interoperability is another concern. Aspects of the data gathering procedure that are essential to this study's authors include security. Low energy efficiency can be blamed on a controller that can't keep up with the network's changing demands. In the absence of sufficient resources, power dissipation is excessively high. For example, a network controller must be capable of dynamic traffic monitoring and resource allocation.

In almost every aspect of municipal management, from surveillance systems to agricultural operations, smart communication devices (SCDs) are employed [5]. There are more and more people who own at least one smart electronic gadget that can communicate via the internet thanks to reductions in the cost of producing electronic equipment. Cellphones, smart buildings, and other electrical devices with a radio frequency (RF) receiver can all be affected by SCDs. Reactive and active SCD devices are the two types of SCD devices. Non-intelligent devices, reactive SCDs, just take in and respond to inputs. When it comes to power management, active SCDs have their own set of application-specific performance indicators.

When it comes to content delivery, cloud computing has become the de facto platform of choice. A single touch or blink of the eye may send data from set-up boxes to wristband watches to sporting equipment to glasses. Using internet infrastructure, computation, and storage, cloud computing is a service delivery paradigm. Performance, security, usability, and accessibility have attracted substantial worldwide investment. It has been more than a decade since the term "cloud computing" entered the business lexicon. Today, cloud computing is an integral part of every modern IT strategy. This chapter will cover the fundamentals of cloud computing and how they apply to smart homes, smart couples, and more.

3.2   FORENSICS

As the name implies, forensic science is the application of scientific methods to legal concerns that occur in court proceedings and criminal investigations [6]. Evidence collection and analysis are two of the most important aspects of forensics. There should be a chain of custody for all evidence from the time it is obtained until it is presented.

3.2.1   DIGITAL DEVICE FORENSICS

The study of digital evidence is called digital forensics. E-evidence, which is sometimes known as digital evidence, can be easily falsified. On digital devices (PC, smartphone, or IoT), the last access time of the file is updated. As a result, the file might be used as evidence [7]. Evidence tampering is an example of an unintentional yet substantial alteration. Even more concerning is the potential for hazardous alterations. To safeguard the integrity of digital evidence and its usefulness in court, electronic evidence and handling protocols have been put in place.

In the first phase, a forensically exact duplicate of the evidence must be created. An original digital record's forensic copy is matched bit-for-bit with the forensic copy. Tools that have been specifically designed for this purpose and have been evaluated and verified so they work according to a needed specification must be used to do this task. Prior to and after copying bits, the tools create a cryptographic hash of the original and copied data. As a bonus, these technologies also track all actions done in order to certify that the chain of evidence is present.

Any digital evidence, including personal data, poses an ethical dilemma in terms of data privacy. In today's world, digital gadgets have become an essential part of our lives. Users' daily actions are tracked by a wide range of personal devices, from smartphones and laptops to cloud and IoT devices. This information is mostly irrelevant to the case that required its collecting. However, a forensic investigator's job typically entails reviewing a range of documents to determine which ones are pertinent to an inquiry and which ones are not. Investigating the contents of digital devices is a violation of privacy on a grand scale. Specifying what type of data and evidence an investigator should look for is essential to protecting user privacy as much as feasible. Future research on the IoT will continue to examine this issue.

There are a number of devices and formats in which digital evidence may be found, which complicates issues [8]. Computers, cellphones, digital cameras, GPS systems, and any other device (item) that captures data in a digital format are all examples of such items (equipment) (and it seems that it will eventually include everything). Data can be stored on a separate media by each of these devices. Thanks to de facto uniformity, most situations are made easier. Various software uses different data formats to produce digital recordings on devices. Specialized expertise and equipment are required to read and understand a specific data format. A subject matter expert is generally responsible for collecting evidence utilizing specialized technologies.

3.2.2 OTHER DIGITAL FORENSICS

Other digital forensic data sources exist. When it comes to IoT forensics, the collection of data from these devices can lead to a number of problems. We can learn a lot from these devices about what makes IoT evidence-collecting unique [9]. There are several issues with digital evidence that are related to the previous section. When it comes to memory, this is usually non-volatile. A volatile working memory, such as RAM, may contain forensically significant data. Live forensics is the process of creating a memory evidence copy without shutting down the device. This therapy must be properly recorded because it has an influence on memory content. There are similar difficulties in network forensics as well. Network equipment such as routers and firewalls can provide some evidence, but the bulk is only available in flight. A gadget that processes the data is the only way to collect it. It is possible to store network data using devices and procedures. Network data sniffing may be problematic owing to the data's sheer magnitude, but other factors must be considered such as the quantity and placement of sniffer devices required. Moreover, network data may contain a huge amount of irrelevant information, making the privacy issue even more complex [10]. As a result, the investigation's breadth is questioned.

It's a relatively new trend in digital forensics to use cloud forensics. Device and network forensics shouldn't, in principle, be that different [10]. In the cloud, multiple clients of a single cloud service provider share the same virtual architecture. Data or virtual resources important to an inquiry are hard to discover or distinguish because of this. It is also difficult to gain access to the cloud infrastructure required to create forensic copies. There are no central data processing centers in place, making it impossible to acquire data without the help of cloud service providers. There is a possibility that data will be held in several countries, each with its own set of rules.

3.2.3 THE NEED FOR IoT FORENSICS

Forensics of the IoT includes devices, networks, and cloud forensics. One example is a persistent storage device that uses well-established file systems and formats [11]. As with any other digital gear, these "objects" can be handled as such. "Things" may use proprietary file systems and formats, which is unfortunate. In fact, they may lack persistent memory to save user data, as well as a power supply that drastically limits, if not precludes, the duration of live forensic analysis. Because of limited RAM, it may be necessary to convey all information at once. A proprietary closed format or an open standard can be used to convey the data. A network's data is encrypted via encryption. Processed IoT information may reside on the opposite side of the world. All of this makes IoT forensics more difficult than standard digital forensics.

IoT device forensics, network forensics, and cloud forensics are the three areas of an IoT ecosystem for forensics. The focus of this chapter is on (IoT) device forensics, even though the other two areas are very important; as the book focuses on ubiquitous computing systems, this is in line with the book's message. The other two areas have made more progress. In order to understand IoT system forensics, they are briefly discussed below.

In one of the earliest articles on IoT forensics, the distinctions between regular digital forensics and IoT forensics were described in a brief overview. In an issue of *IEEE Security & Privacy* on digital forensics, researchers added to this list. Forensic issues and possibilities stem from the identified discrepancies, which will be discussed in the next two sections.

3.3 CHALLENGES IN IOT FORENSICS

Issues connected to IoT forensics are systematized here based on current literature. The major issues are addressed initially, followed by others as they emerge during the various stages of a forensic investigation [12].

3.3.1 GENERAL ISSUES

In the field of IoT forensics, there is no standard approach or framework available. Digital forensics does not have a single generally acknowledged approach, but there are many that practitioners and researchers identify and use [13]. We are in the beginning stages of IoT forensics, which uses techniques and concepts from traditional digital forensics which may or may not apply to IoT forensics. IoT forensics tools are few. Demand for new software and hardware will increase. IoT forensics tools and their relevance for IoT are discussed in detail. According to the authors, existing traditional computer forensic methods are inadequate for cybercrime investigations using IoT devices after a thorough examination was conducted. In light of IoT's pervasive nature, it might be difficult to determine which country is responsible for a particular problem. Depending on the IoT system's device configuration, cloud location and provider locations may be spread across many nations. As a comparison, the internet has a similar global reach. IoT only shifts the problem from the digital to the physical world, and that's all it does.

3.3.2 EVIDENCE IDENTIFICATION, COLLECTION, AND PRESERVATION

The first step in IoT forensics is to identify evidence sources that can be accessed. Researchers must identify which gadgets record important data. How the IoT interacts with its environment is a topic that must be addressed. It will be left up to the investigator to decide which of the various sources he wants to employ. In addition, it is necessary to know where and how the data is kept. Consider the limitations of data gathering before acquiring evidence (physical, proprietary standards, and legal issues). Finding IoT systems and identifying IoT devices that might be used as evidence in an inquiry is tough. As a result of this, the device may have information on several users in addition to those under inquiry. A challenging task is identifying a certain user's data.

With so many diverse technologies, it's challenging to create a process for obtaining evidence that is consistent across all of them. The restricted capabilities of gadgets, their many interfaces, and their storage formats make data extraction challenging. There is a possibility that it will be impossible to extract data without altering the equipment or the data, which may be troublesome in forensics and may be deemed evidence tampering. There is no onboard data storage in traditional digital forensic software solutions. In order to create forensic pictures of an IoT device, there are only a handful of options available. Forensically sound collection of the device's leftover evidence may be difficult, if not impossible. In some circumstances, data encryption might make it difficult or impossible to collect evidence. Several formats are available for cumulative datasets.

IoT crime scenes contain both physical objects and the surrounding environment, as well as forensic evidence. Retaining evidence in its original form may be challenging. Components of IoT may interact on their own. A crime scene's borders might be difficult to define and identify from the surrounding area. Whether an IoT gadget should be retained as evidence is a practical problem. When it is taken from the IoT ecosystem, there is a clear loser.

3.3.3 EVIDENCE ANALYSIS AND CORRELATION

When confronted with an IoT system, a digital forensics investigator must first learn how to analyze physical evidence [14]. A combination of IT skills and experience in adjacent disciplines may be necessary. IoT devices may generate a lot of data, and that's the most serious issue at this point in the research. For an investigator and the tools he or she uses, that volume of data might be daunting. Traditional digital forensics has fewer possible evidence sources than IoT. For example, a sensor that monitors a physical characteristic in short time intervals might generate a large amount of data. Evidence from several sources is more difficult to link. In forensics, it is necessary to create a timeline. Many gadgets may have faulty clocks, making them difficult to work. Reenacting historical events is difficult because of this. Although more evidence should lead to a more accurate reconstruction, the time and effort required may not make this worthwhile.

During this time, the question of privacy is quite important. As a result of evidence gathering and analysis, it is possible to identify a person's identity and activities. However, it's not always easy to tell if the person being examined is the one under investigation or not. Some of the information received from an IoT device may be about people who aren't relevant to the inquiry. It would be ideal if such data could be removed at the point of capture; however, due to time and resource constraints, this is rare. Non-essential personal information can be found in even the most relevant data. There's a similar problem in traditional digital forensics, but in IoT, data is collected continually and indiscriminately from within the sensors' reach, and it's generally done without the participants' consent.

3.3.4 PRESENTATION

IoT situations might make delivering forensic results difficult [15]. In forensics and law, IoT is an emerging method. Virtual evidence is only just beginning to be accepted by courts, and the physical/virtual mix presented by IoT may be confusing to some. Concerns regarding whether a court will accept the use of a technique or equipment that is not yet standardized are also present in this phase, as well as in the preceding phases. Although forensic practitioners are also concerned with other aspects, the abovementioned concerns should nonetheless be addressed.

3.4 OPPORTUNITIES OF IOT FORENSICS

In general, the IoT provides new forms of evidence in forensics. Everyday events that were not previously recorded or stored are now being captured via the IoT. These days, they're even kept as digital data [16]. In turn, this makes it easier to conduct searches, filter out irrelevant information, and cross reference, aggregate, and conduct other data processing, which helps turn data into evidence. Contextual evidence collected without the criminal's knowledge can be preserved via IoT technologies. Everything happens automatically, without the need for human involvement, as a result of IoT operations. IoT evidence is more difficult to remove in physical and digital forensics. When it comes to proof, there's generally more than one piece, and it's kept in the cloud, out of the reach of anyone who would want to delete it. Most suspects are completely unaware of what evidence is being gathered against them, as mentioned in the previous paragraph. Since the data in cloud cannot be removed, other evidence collection is not needed.

There are more evidence sources available to digital forensics because of IoT. A wide range of forensically useful data is generated by devices that are connected to the internet. Evidence might come from any device that collects, analyzes, stores, or sends data. Any sensor, no matter how small, could have a significant influence. Data gathered by IoT systems may be used to create a composite image of events by combining all the data. This may be done by using data from many IoT devices at various locations visited by the suspect, for example. In addition, wearable activity trackers may be used to estimate movements.

3.5 CLOUD COMPUTING SECURITY

At the very least, the level of security is equivalent to the level that traditional IT departments give [17]. Failure to do so would result in higher costs and the potential loss of data, as well as the loss of the company. As a result, clients can thereby offset the benefits of cloud computing by avoiding other possible costs. Cloud service providers create rules and procedures to ensure that tasks are done consistently. Cloud providers and clients agree on SLA requirements so that each party can adequately evaluate, avoid, and control security threats. Consumers are responsible for safeguarding the operating system, data stored in the cloud, and network security due to the division of tasks with the service provider.

The legal protection of personally identifiable information (PII) in the cloud is known as cloud governance. Many nations have different rules about how to obtain PII data in the event of an inquiry or enforcement action; this is shown in Figure 3.1. This makes it difficult to determine where data is stored and how to comply with foreign regulations [18].

3.5.1 EFFECTIVELY MANAGE IDENTITIES

Customers should investigate if their cloud provider has policies in place to control who gets access to their data and apps. This access will be regulated and managed by established norms. Some well-known standards are as follows [19]:

- Federated identity management (FIM)
- Identity provisioning and delegation
- Single sign-on, single sign-off (SSO)
- Identity and access audit
- Robust authentication
- Role entitlement and policy management

Cloud providers must develop mechanisms for limiting access to cloud infrastructure by their employees. It should also be possible to show clients that this is done immediately as required by new laws.

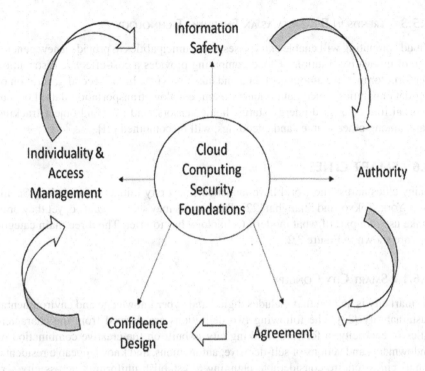

FIGURE 3.1 Cloud computing security fundamentals

3.5.2 KEY CONCERNS ABOUT CLOUD COMPUTING

Even though cloud computing is still in its early stages, there are various concerns about the technology [20].

- A new law has allowed internet firms to store data on servers that are not connected to their local networks. However, some businesses are concerned about having their data stored elsewhere other than on their local infrastructure servers.
- There are some serious security and data security issues in the digital era. Data security: when data is shared across the network, the risk of illegal data exposure increases. Security is also an issue when it comes to encryption, authentication, and authorization methods. It is also critical to be aware of these issues.
- Businesses are becoming increasingly concerned about losing service and, as a result, customers, necessitating high availability.
- Regulatory compliance and audits are necessary for various IT infrastructures. Companies can use cloud computing services to ensure that they are abiding by the laws of the land, water, and air.
- In the event of an emergency, the US Department of Homeland Security (DHS) issued guidance on how service providers should handle their Platform as a Service (PaaS) and Infrastructure as a Service (IaaS) services.

3.5.3 Trends in Big Data as an Enabling Technology

Cloud computing will enable enterprises and municipalities to provide a new genera-tion of innovative solutions. Cloud computing provides a cost-effective distribution platform for massive amounts of data and data analytics. In the second generation of big data analytics, voice data, video stream, car flow, transportation data, hospital data, airline data, grid energy status, home sensors, and user and object tracking data, among other sources and encodings, will be combined [21].

3.6 SMART CITIES

Many cities across the world have launched smart city initiatives, including Seoul, New York, Tokyo, and Shanghai [22]. These cities may seem advanced, yet they only make use of a part of what modern technology has to offer. The three main catego-ries are shown in Figure 3.2.

3.6.1 Smart City Concept

A smart city is an idea that includes digital and cyber knowledge and environmental sustainability [23]. The following two definitions are derived from the character-istics of each city: a forward-thinking city is built on the creative combination of endowments and actions of self-decisive, autonomous, and knowledgeable residents. Smart cities require considerable planning to establish uniformity across city ser-vices. This is something that a human-centric paradigm built on ICT infrastructure can accomplish.

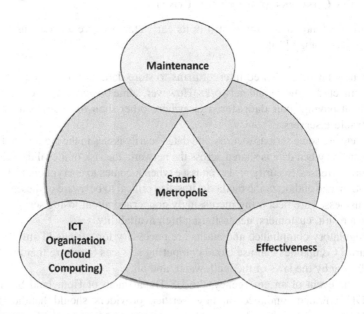

FIGURE 3.2 Smart city organization

3.6.2 CLOUD COMPUTING BENEFITS IN THE CONTEXT OF SMART CITY

New York has been named one of the world's best cities for internet connection. Smart cities propose a new idea of what habitually available services should be in the internet age. They include waste management as well as the efficient utilization of natural resources such as electricity, water, and air [24]. Smart cities include a diverse variety of economic and technological services. Berlin has made one of the most optimistic and bold moves in recognizing cloud computing as a natural resource. It will provide data analysis, analytics, and other services to smart cities across the world.

3.7 SMARTER GRID

Only a small portion of the energy is derived from renewable sources, such as hydroelectric electricity. According to the World Resources Institute, the energy consumption of major economic powers such as China will more than quadruple that of the United States by 2040. An outage, such as the one that happened in North America in 2003, disrupts businesses and the economy. Power grid outages might be avoided if diagnostic information was available [25].

Cloud computing can assist smart grids in dealing with a wide range of challenges and opportunities. New paradigms must be created to enable optimal power generation and consumption, as well as to forecast the grid's condition across a wide area. Cloud computing is a crucial component of today's technology, and this is described in Figure 3.3.

3.8 SMART HOME

Home automation is being migrated to the cloud by IBM. When a customer agrees to install home automation devices, the objective is to provide a simple installation procedure [26]. IBM has identified three key aspects of current smart home devices. These features include ease of use, vendor agnosticism, and interoperability. A smart house defines and provides many new capabilities. Just a few examples include entertainment and smart TVs, energy management, safety and security, and health and convenience; these capabilities are discussed in Figure 3.4.

In smart homes, sensors such as electricity meters and monitoring devices will be placed. These devices will communicate with one another and contact cloud-based services to provide essential functionality. Cloud computing offers a sensible foundation for integrating interoperable smart home services.

3.9 SMART CITY DATA PLAN CHALLENGES

The smart city network offers significant capacity and throughput improvements, as well as improved quality of service (QoS) in terms of latency, battery use, device cost, and reliability [27]. Preventative and control measures would eliminate possible

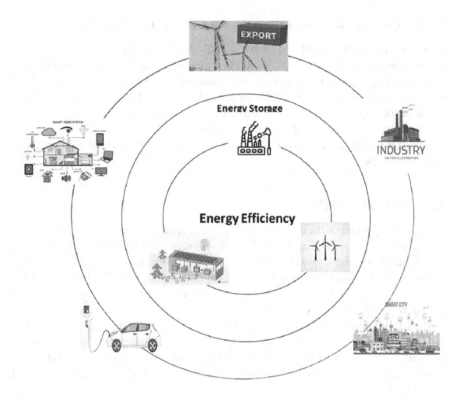

FIGURE 3.3   Smart grid environment

risks and failures before they happened. A smart city network can manage many devices. The SCD network's deployment is riddled with problems. According to a study conducted by the US Department of Defense, correlations between disparate data sets might be more accurately examined, and effective models could be employed. However, the application is still in its early phases.

3.9.1   Compatibility between Smart City Devices

Future smart cities will have several smart device networks, which will generate a large amount of raw data [28]. Communication between the network element (NE) and the SCD, as well as its consequences, is a crucial challenge for future smart city networks. The network topology may be expressed using a few subroutines. In the future, smart cities will have billions of sensor nodes, and making these devices more complicated than necessary would increase both capital and operational expenses. Using application-defined simple and less expensive SCD, on the other hand, may result in device swap compatibility problems. SCD networks may feature a variety of consumer devices. Most of these gadgets are simply plug-and-play. Furthermore, the network infrastructure is made up of NEs from many manufacturers, each with its own set of embedded rules and

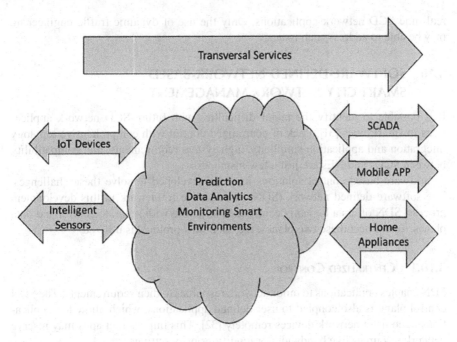

FIGURE 3.4   Cloud with big data analytics

applications. Because of hardware restrictions, determining the rules for a new device is challenging.

3.9.2 SIMPLICITY

To make it easier to run a switch's operating system (OS) from within the OS, software-based control is required [29]. Engineers are working on a network that will allow them to operate the SCD network using applications. It is inefficient for a big network since engineers must manually control the whole network.

SCD network management devices are more sophisticated than those used in typical SCD networks. Designing and implementing SCDs is also a difficult process. NEC has developed and will implement a new NE management plan in the future.

3.9.3 MOBILITY AND GEOGRAPHIC CONTROL

Smart cities will rely on SCDs to fulfill a variety of functions in the future. These dispersed devices generate a large volume of data that must be sent all at once. This huge packet load emphasizes the need for a large communication capacity [30]. In a normal network structure, each switch makes decisions based on its local information. Smart devices may connect to the network from anywhere and move quickly. Such QoS issues may result in a poor user experience and incorrect judgments in real-time SCD network applications. Only the use of dynamic traffic engineering may be able to address such issues.

3.10 SOFTWARE-DEFINED NETWORK-BASED SMART CITY NETWORK MANAGEMENT

It is possible to identify the major difficulties with future SCD network applications in smart cities [31]. Lack of centralized control with comprehensive topology integration and application simplicity, high system requirements, and compatibility between SCDs and NEs are just a few instances.

Software-based control solutions must be developed to solve these challenges. The software-defined network (SDN) is a feasible framework in this development process. SDN offers a logically centralized structure with separate control and data planes. To connect these two planes, the open flow protocol is utilized.

3.10.1 CENTRALIZED CONTROL

SDN enables applications to tailor network resources to their requirements. The SDN control plane is also coupled to user-defined applications, which allow the applications to connect network devices remotely [32]. This implies that apps may reserve network resources like bandwidth or modify priority settings.

Because of its high level of operation abstraction, SDN makes it easier to deploy new protocols and network services. The policy control for all network devices is consolidated by the logically centralized controller.

3.10.2 SIMPLICITY AND INERRABILITY

SCD networks are intended for specialized purposes [33]. In each situation, this design paradigm necessitates a range of activities. SCD packets may need to be pre-processed to deal with the scenario, or packets received from a specific SCD may need to be sent to many controllers. This type of application-specific activity is possible with the SDN paradigm. The SDN controller is a source of security and privacy concerns. Due to the simplicity of SDN, programmers may create generic apps and libraries and freely share them with other users.

The simplicity with which the new apps and libraries are deployed contributes to their user-friendliness [34]. The standard is presented by SDN. When the network is used, the newly added activities will be available. By providing a variety of device services and raw data streams, SDN enables scalable and effective programming.

3.10.3 VIRTUALIZATION

The smart city abstraction is divided into two components. To begin, to improve the user experience, the services must be abstracted. Second, the network controller should differentiate between user-specific data as a networking goal and user input as a generic network condition [35]. Virtualization should be used to separate network resources and network applications. The great majority of SDN applications are cloud-based, allowing for almost limitless calculation capacity and service rate. The virtualization of different, frequently geographically distributed resources gives better control over system resources while lowering capital expenditure (CapEx) and operating expense (OpEx).

3.10.4   COMPATIBILITY

Smart city networks based on SDN provide huge capacity and throughput gains. They offer better QoS in terms of latency, battery usage, device cost, and dependability [36]. The autonomous network management architecture and network densification are considered. Despite the guarantees, a slew of hurdles lies ahead. The SCD idea encompasses a wide range of devices as well as operating systems and protocols. The firm interoperability between SCD and NEs, as well as between users, is critical for smart city applications. Inter-device communication should also be autonomously controlled and protocol-updated. The distance between two connected devices has grown in proportion to the growth of cities. The number of network-connected devices is growing at a breakneck pace. To improve the network infrastructure, new network equipment will be necessary. Monitoring the compatibility of existing and newly deployed infrastructure is critical [37].

SDN offers a simple yet effective way of resolving compatibility concerns. The data plane is made up of SCDs and dumb switches, while the SDN controller handles the control plane. On network equipment, there will be no pre-programmed action sets or goals. Interoperability suffers as a result of the separation of control and data levels.

3.10.5   CHALLENGES OF SDN IN SMART CITY APPLICATIONS

Smart city networks can fulfill a lot of the requirements for the next generation [38]. Many concerns, however, such as resource management and user satisfaction, remain unresolved. The network controller must fulfill the criteria for self-analyzing and dynamic configuration. SCDs will be utilized for monitoring and analysis in future smart cities. When it comes to network power use, there are two major things to consider. The total energy efficiency of the network structure is another issue for network management. It should include auto-discovery capabilities as well as an adaptive power control mechanism.

3.11   SOFTWARE-DEFINED THINGS FRAMEWORK

The use of SDN in SCD management gives a practical answer to infrastructure-related issues [39]. These include avoiding a heavy traffic load and lowering reaction time by performing the optimization procedure at the control plane layer. This chapter presents a framework for self-adaptive reactive smart communication devices (R-SCD) network management.

3.11.1 REACTIVE SMART CITY DEVICE MANAGEMENT

R-SCDs are less competent electronics that can only do a few tasks or activities. When they detect a certain condition, they emit a continuous data packet [40]. This chapter discusses two types of events: continuous events and discrete occurrences. R-SCDs attempt to recognize events, whether continuous or discrete, and send an acknowledgment message if they do. The main purpose of these devices is to increase the number of occurrences over a long period. They might be placed at various times or in different locations.

By keeping all IoT devices active, the network's lifespan is shortened by 40% in a high event detection situation. Most R-IoT devices are in suburbs and cannot be switched off unless the batteries are changed [41]. The battery management of the SCD network must be regulated. Scheduling the R-SCD on/off times is a straightforward yet effective approach. According to the study, SDNs enable intelligent R-ScD network management. It concludes with an examination of the technologies underlying SDNs [42]. SDN offers a centralized control system for dummy switches that are designed to take a certain action when they meet a new device. The SDN controller will be able to determine the kind of device and add it to the relevant device list. During the optimization process, control packets are transmitted to the state-changing devices.

3.11.2 SMART MOBILITY AND SMART TRAFFIC MANAGEMENT

Every smart city initiative must include smart mobility. Mobility and transportation will be made easier for city dwellers and tourists [43]. Because of advances in computer power, smart traffic management can now process, assess, and make a range of optimum judgments in real time. In the United States, this may save over 5 billion hours of commuting time.

3.11.3 SMART ENVIRONMENT

A smart environment necessitates the rapid expansion of ubiquitous computing. Devices, networking, middleware, and applications all contribute to the development of a smart environment [44]. WSNs may be utilized for several applications in smart homes and cities. WSNs can conserve energy, decrease pollution, and monitor noise and the environment.

WSNs link our surroundings in ways we can't even conceive. While smart homes provide a comfortable and smart-economic living, it is increasingly difficult to avoid using home video messaging, and alarms for mobile phones, doors, windows, and light control applications.

3.11.4 SECURITY

The security of smart home and city apps is nearly comparable to that of the WSN application environment [45–47]. WSN security issues are thoroughly covered, including specific and physical assaults, security measures, and requirements. Security and privacy concerns are also comparable.

Technology for smart homes hackers, malware, and other threats can all render WSNPs vulnerable. An attacker can get access to the system if there is no consistent authentication. An attacker can make the network or equipment unavailable by injecting a huge volume of data and/or requests. It may also modify the database and stock information. Data manipulation, data injection, and denial-of-service assaults are all part of this.

Attackers can steal and alter data, create system failures, and even restrict system function [48, 49]. Active attacks against hospitals and healthcare facilities may endanger people's lives. Passive attacks acquire information without the user taking any action, whereas active attacks require the user to act. Smart home apps must be accessible, private, and secure. They must also prevent distributed denial-of-service (DoS) assaults that cause system failures. These requirements must be met to create robust applications.

3.11.5 ADVANCED OPTICAL NETWORK ARCHITECTURE FOR NEXT-GENERATION INTERNET ACCESS

Future smart cities will rely on digital technologies to decrease costs and reduce resource use. Communications efficiency has the potential to boost production while reducing the barrier of huge and diverse geographical distances that limit the maintenance of QoS, and extending current communication infrastructures is a long-term objective [49]. This chapter offers a new network design suitable for providing end users with internet access and intercommunication, resolving interoperability issues, and supplying highly accessible bandwidth to fulfill connection requests for many years to come.

3.12 CONCLUSION AND FUTURE WORK

In IoT forensics, there is now a desire for practical solutions to challenges that arise during IoT-related research. This criterion will help to enhance research through practice. Data from many IoT devices may be connected to create a very detailed event reconstruction. Suspects of crimes are usually unaware that recordings are being made and are unable to delete evidence. Cloud computing refers to the advent of common paradigms in IT infrastructure and delivery based on virtualization and containers.

A few examples of IoT use include new devices, interfaces, storage mediums, file systems, network protocols, dispersed cloud storage, and unclear authority and jurisdiction. The amount of data that must be maintained, stored, and evaluated is massive. Even presenting the findings might be problematic. So far, the three major pathways of IoT forensics research have been the development of novel models and interfaces, the building of systems with a pre-prepared repository for evidence, and the forensics of real-world IoT systems. Because it is in its early phase, there are numerous avenues for future research.

However, because of the huge data load from sensor and actuator devices, as well as cost restrictions, network devices and applications have to be separated into layers. The future of smart cities may be improved through increasing self-awareness and improving reasoning. Cities of the future will need to not just assess fluctuating data but also forecast future failures or requirements.

REFERENCES

1. Obaidat MS, Misra S. *Principles of Wireless Sensor Networks.* Cambridge, UK: Cambridge University Press; 2014.
2. Energy consumption by sector. *US Energy Information Administration (EIA),* March 2015 monthly energy review. March 2015.
3. Louis J-N, Caló A, Pongrácz E. Smart houses for energy efficiency and carbon dioxide emission reduction. In: The Fourth International Conference on Smart Grids, Green Communications, and IT Energy-aware Technologies (ENERGY 2014), Chamonix, France; April 2014.
4. Attia II, Ashour H. Energy saving through the smart home. *Online J Power Energy Eng.* 2011; 2:223–227.
5. Barley D, Deru M, Pless S, Torcellini P. Procedure for measuring and reporting commercial building energy performance. Technical report. National Renewable Energy Laboratory, NREL/TP-550-38601; October 2005.
6. Corucci F, Anastasi G, Marcelloni F. A WSN-based testbed for energy efficiency in buildings. In: IEEE Symposium on Computers and Communications (ISCC), Kerkyra, Greece; June 2011. p. 990–3.
7. The Edison Foundation. *Utility-scale Smart Meter Deployments.* Washington, DC: Institute for Electric Innovation (IEI); September 2014.
8. Cees Links. After the smart phone: The smart home. White paper. GreenPeak; October 2014.
9. Santini S, Ostermaier B, Vitaletti A. First experiences using wireless sensor networks for noise pollution monitoring. In: Workshop on Real-world Wireless Sensor Networks (REALWSN'08), Glasgow, Scotland; April 2008. p. 61–65.
10. Bhusari P, Asutkar GM. Design of noise pollution monitoring system using wireless sensor network. *Int J Software Web Sci.* 2013; 1:55–58.
11. Tan W, Jarvis S. On the design of an energy-harvesting noise-sensing WSN mote. *EURASIP J Wireless Commun Networking.* 2014; 167:1–18.
12. Roseline RA, Devapriya M, Sumathi P. Pollution monitoring using sensors and wireless sensor networks: A survey. *Int J Appl Innovation Eng Manage.* 2013; 2(7):119–124.
13. Odey AJ, Daoliang L. AquaMesh: design and implementation of smart wireless mesh sensor networks for aquaculture. *Am J Netw Commun.* 2013; 2:81–87.
14. Hassard J, et al. Innovative multi-species sensor development for mobile/portable sensor networks. In: *Security & Resilience for the Public & Private Sectors,* London, UK; 2010.
15. Williams M, Villalonga P. ITI-SENSE: Sensor technologies for air quality. In: Citizens' Observatory Coordination Workshop, Brussels, Belgium; January 2013.
16. Sirsikar S, Karemore P. Review paper on air pollution monitoring system. *Int J Adv Res Comput Commun Eng.* 2015; 4(1):218–220.
17. Yaacoub E, Kadri A, Mushtaha M, Abu-Dayya A. Air quality monitoring and analysis in Qatar using a wireless sensor network deployment. In: The 9th International Wireless Communications and Mobile Computing Conference (IWCMC), Sardinia, Italy; July 2013. p. 596–601.

18. Mishra SA, Tijare DS, Asutkar GM. Design of energy aware air pollution monitoring system using WSN. *Int J Adv Eng Technol.* 2011; 1(2):107–116.
19. Mansour S, Nasser N, Karim L, Ali A. Wireless sensor network-based air quality monitoring system. In: 2014 International Conference on Computing, Networking, and Communications (ICNC), Honolulu, HI, February 3–6, 2014. p. 545–550.
20. Virone G, et al. An advanced wireless sensor network for health monitoring. In: The Transdisciplinary Conference on Distributed Diagnosis and Home Healthcare, Arlington, VA; April 2006.
21. Hyojeong S, Talipov E, Hojung C. IPv6 lightweight stateless address autoconfiguration for 6LoWPAN using color coordinators. In: IEEE International Conference on Pervasive Computing and Communications. PerCom 2009, Galveston, TX; March 2009. p. 1–9.
22. Dhobley A, Ghodichor NA, Golait SS. An overview of wireless sensor networks for health monitoring in hospitals via mobile. *Int J Adv Res ComputCommun Eng.* 2015; 4(1):169–171.
23. Oliver N, Flores-Mangas F. HealthGear: A real-time wearable system for monitoring and analyzing physiological signals. In: International Workshop on Wearable and Implantable Body Sensor Networks, Cambridge; April 2006. p. 64–7.
24. Gautam KK, Gautam SK, Agrawal PC. Impact and utilization of wireless sensor network in rural area for health care. *Int J Adv Res Comput Sci Software Eng.* 2012; 2(6):93–98.
25. Malan D, Thaddeus FJ, Welsh M, Moulton S. CodeBlue: An ad hoc sensor network infrastructure for emergency medical care. In: Workshop on Applications of Mobile Embedded Systems (WAMES 2004), Boston, MA; June 2004.
26. Tennina S, et al. WSN4QoL: A WSN-oriented healthcare system architecture. *Int J Distributed Sensor Netw.* 2014; 2014:1–16.
27. Kouroubali A, Chiarugi F. Developing advanced technology services for diabetes management: User preferences in Europe. In: Wireless Mobile Communication and Healthcare, Mobihealth, Kos Island, Greece; October 2011. p. 69–74.
28. MobiHealth in Zambia: Focus on Telemonitoring High Risk Pregnant Women. Technical report. MobiHealth; August 2014.
29. Milenković A, Otto C, Jovanov E. Wireless sensor networks for personal health monitoring: Issues and an implementation. *Comput Commun.* 2006; 29:2521–2533.
30. Institute of Electrical and Electronics Engineers. IEEE Std 802.15.1-2005, wireless medium access control (MAC) and physical layer (PHY) specifications for wireless personal area networks (WPANs); June 2005.
31. Institute of Electrical and Electronics Engineers. Part 15.3: wireless medium access control (MAC) and physical layer (PHY) specifications for high-rate wireless personal area networks (WPAN); September 2003.
32. Institute of Electrical and Electronics Engineers. IEEE Std 802.15.4-2006, wireless medium access control (MAC) and physical layer (PHY) specifications for low-rate wireless personal area networks (WPANs); September 8, 2006.
33. Fredman A. Mechanisms of interference reduction for Bluetooth. pdf ebooks; February 2015.
34. Khair MAI, Misic J, Misic VB. Piconet interconnection strategies in IEEE 802.15.3 networks. In: Zhang Y, Yang LT, Ma J, eds. *Unlicensed Mobile Access Technology: Protocols, Architectures, Security, Standards, and Applications.* Boca Raton: Auerbach Publications; 2009:147–162: [chapter 8].
35. Goratti L, Haapola J, Oppermann I. Energy consumption of the IEEE 802.15.3 MAC protocol in communication link set-up over UWB radio technology. *Wireless Personal Commun.* 2007; 40:371–386.

36. Stabellini L, Parhizkar MM. Experimental comparison of frequency hopping techniques for 802.15.4-based sensor networks. In: The Fourth International Conference on Mobile Ubiquitous Computing, Systems, Services, and Technologies (UBICOMM); 2010. p. 110–6.
37. Popovski P, Yomo H, Prasad R. Strategies for adaptive frequency hopping in the unlicensed bands. *IEEE Wireless Commun.* 2006; 13(6):60–67.
38. Hsu AC-C, et al. Enhanced adaptive frequency hopping for wireless personal area networks in a coexistence environment. In: Global Telecommunications Conference (GLOBECOM), Washington, DC; November 2007. p. 668–72.
39. Stabellini L, Shi L, Rifai AA, Espino J, Magoula V. A new probabilistic approach for adaptive frequency hopping. In: The 20th IEEE International Symposium on Personal Indoor and Mobile Radio Communications (PIMRC), Tokyo, Japan; September 2009. p. 2147–51.
40. Institute of Electrical and Electronics Engineers. 802.11a-1999 high-speed physical layer in the 5 GHz band; October 1999.
41. 802.11a. White paper. VOCAL Technologies; May 2012.
42. Institute of Electrical and Electronics Engineers. 802.11b-1999 higher speed physical layer extension in the 2.4 GHz band; October 1999.
43. Institute of Electrical and Electronics Engineers. IEEE 802.11g-2003: Further higher data rate extension in the 2.4 GHz band; October 2003.
44. Institute of Electrical and Electronics Engineers. IEEE 802.11n-2009 – Amendment 5 enhancements for higher throughput; October 2009.
45. Jun J, Peddabachagari P, Sichitiu M. Theoretical maximum throughput of IEEE 802.11 and its applications. In: Second IEEE International Symposium on Network Computing and Applications (NCA 2003), Cambridge, MA; April 2003. p. 249–56.
46. Wang X, Kar K. Throughput modelling and fairness issues in CSMA/CA based ad-hoc networks. In: The 24th Annual Joint Conference of the IEEE Computer and Communications Societies (INFOCOM 2005), Miami; March 2005.
47. Khanduri R, Rattan SS, Uniyal A. Understanding the features of IEEE 802.11g in high data rate wireless LANs. *Int J Comput Appl.* 2013; 64:1–5.
48. Understanding and optimizing 802.11n. Technical report. Buffalo Technology; July 2011.
49. Khanduri R, Rattan SS. Performance comparison analysis between IEEE 802.11a/b/g/n standards. *Int J Comput Appl.* 2013; 7:13–20.

4 Energy-Efficient Reinforcement Learning in Wireless Sensor Networks Using 5G for Smart Cities

M. S. Pramod, Arun Balodi, Aditya Pratik,
G. Satya Sankalp, B. Varshita, and R. Amrit

CONTENTS

DOI: 10.1201/9781003227861-4

4.1 INTRODUCTION

"A wA wireless sensor network (WSN) consists of a large number of sensors which monitor elements in the environment, such as temperature and humidity. These sensors are collectively connected to a node known as the base station. Artificial intelligence (AI) methods can be applied at the node level and network level. In order to increase network performance, an AI approach [1] known as reinforcement learning is used. Energy consumption [2] involves three states: transmission, reception, and being idle. Through the trial-and-error interactions with the present environment, reinforcement learning (RL) estimates the long-term reward of each state–action pair. To increase the network lifespan and decrease energy utilization, clustering is used as an efficient method, which provides necessary scalability. Clustering is the combination of the sensor nodes in a WSN environment. A cluster head is a node that accumulates data from cluster sensors and transmits this data to the sink (base station). In WSNs, data aggregation is a widely used technique to increase energy efficiency. The node density in sensor networks is very high. Here the same data can be sensed by different nodes and hence redundancy of data is present. This crisis can be reduced by using data aggregation. Clustering data aggregation is used, where the collected data is aggregated by each cluster head and communicates the combined data to the base station. RL [3], an AI-based approach, is used where the decision-maker observes, learns, and takes actions in the operating environment in order to increase the accumulated reward. One of the most widely used RL algorithms is Q-learning. The actions of this algorithm depend on the Q-function. The Q-function depends on the actions being performed at each and every state of the agent. This protocol is used to reduce energy consumption based on the network load. Using the Q-learning algorithm, we can create an effective and independent wake-up schedule for each node.

Smart cities are the future of sustainable development [4] where mankind is developing new strategies continuously. These cities can be simply defined as urban areas. By using different types of electronic methods and sensors, we can collect, manage, and assess data, which helps to improve the performance of various tasks being performed in the city. This data is processed and analyzed to perform different tasks, such as monitoring transportation systems, different kinds of plants (power, waste management, etc.), educational and health infrastructures, and other community services. Monitoring everything efficiently will help in the fast evolution of cities. The concept behind this is to integrate sensors that are connected to an internet of things (IoT) network [5] to optimize the efficiency of operations. This integration will help enhance quality and performance, and reduce costs and the consumption of resources. All this development in the field of smart cities is ongoing to ensure that these cities properly function. This in turn will help citizens to respond to challenges considerably better than the present-day cities. According to descriptions of smart cities, it is suggested that a wireless sensor network could be optimally implemented in these cities, and as we progress to implement energy efficiency in WSNs, we can surely expect breakthroughs in the vast range of possible applications of WSNs in these future smart cities.

Broadband cellular networks are expanding at a fast rate as described by Moore's law. The 5th generation of telecommunication [6] technology, also known commonly as 5G, began to be deployed worldwide in 2019, succeeding 4th generation (4G) networks which ran successfully for 13 years after being deployed in South Korea in 2006. However, the widely used standard long-term evolution (LTE) was not developed until 2009, and now the world is progressively advancing towards an even wider and more efficient networking standard in the form of 5G networks. The 5G network also finds use in fields like IoT and AI. Specifically, a reinforcement learning-based energy-efficient protocol is proposed for applications using IoT in 5G. In several countries, cellular network technology of 5G has been recently promoted. 5G has a wide range of data transfer capacity i.e. larger bandwidths and smaller wavelengths. 5G is the most important means of developing the global internet of IoT [7]. Energy efficiency in 5G would decrease costs, enhance decision-making, and provide the ability to communicate virtually with any device across distances. In the future, 5G will be used in different types of devices in wireless networks with higher data rates and lower power consumption (Figure 4.1).

4.1.1 Problem Statement

WSNs are limited by computational resources and energy thus limiting their use. Energy is consumed in different stages of operation in a node in a WSN. The consumption of energy depends on the size of the data and the distance of transmission for which the energy increases exponentially.

The distance between a base station and a sensor node can be quite large. Due to this, the consumption of energy of the node is very high, leading to a lot of losses. Hence the overall process of collecting and sending data becomes expensive.

To solve these issues, we use many AI techniques like RL to optimize at the node and network levels in order to make them adaptive in terms of energy consumption.

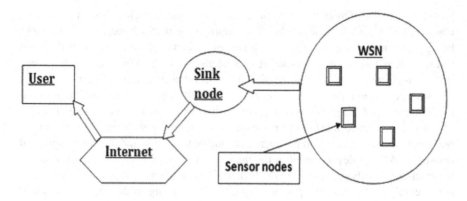

Wireless sensor network

FIGURE 4.1　An illustrative diagram of a simple WSN

4.1.2 OBJECTIVES

- To optimize the WSN at both the network and node level by using RL techniques
- To optimize the topology of networks for energy efficiency we use the Q-learning algorithm
- To use RL at the node level to make non-fixed and adaptive node duty cycles
- To decrease the overall consumption of energy over time
- To accomplish high scalability and to increase the network lifetime and energy efficiency using clustering (combining the group of sensor nodes in a WSN environment).

4.2 LITERATURE REVIEW

4.2.1 WIRELESS SENSOR NETWORK

The work of BenSaleh et al. [8] suggests that a wireless sensor network (WSN) is a set of connections consisting of several sensor nodes for observing physical or environmental conditions such as light, pressure, and temperature. Wireless sensors send and receive environmental information. WSNs have two design approaches, i.e. a low-level approach and a high-level approach.

In a study by Manikanda Kumaran and Chinnadurai [9], competent ad-hoc sensor routing (CASeR) protocol is used to reduce delay and increase the efficiency of energy usage in mobile WSN. The nodes work by sending information to the sink. The energy consumption depends on the time taken by the node to send the data to the sink; hence, the network lifetime can be assessed and increased accordingly.

The study of Wan-Kyu and Sang-Jo [10] proposes a Q-learning-based, data-aggregating, and energy-efficient routing algorithm. Many types of sensors are used in this study, and their work is to send the collected data to the sink. Three different data aggregation models, the representative aggregation model, lossy compression aggregation model, and lossless aggregation model, were used.

4.2.2 ARTIFICIAL INTELLIGENCE

Stephan et al. [11] use cognitive radio sensor networks, which have a network of sensor nodes. ESUCR has two transition states, idle state and busy state. If the channel is in an idle state, this is denoted as P_{idle}, and if the channel is in a busy state, this is denoted as P_{busy}.

Menaria et al. [12] present the NLFFT model (node-link failure fault tolerance model) in WSNs using AI. It has two levels, link level and node level, that can be used for the implementation.

Sreedharan and Dnyandeo Jageshwar [13] show that in a WSN area, a total of 1,000 nodes are initially used across the network. The node present in the center of all the nodes is the sink node. When the information from nodes is sent to the sink, the clustering algorithm is implemented.

4.2.3 DEEP REINFORCEMENT LEARNING

In a study by Sinde et al. [14], the deep reinforcement learning (DRL) algorithm in a WSN is used to extend the lifetime of the network through energy-efficient scheduling. This has three phases to extend the network lifetime: the cluster phase, duty-cycle phase, and route phase. A zone-based clustering is also used in the study. In DRL-based scheduling there are three modes, sleep mode, listen mode, and transmit mode. These modes are represented using a DRL model.

Sheng et al. [15] use an RL approach to solve scheduling and resource allocation. A DRL algorithm is applied and the agent learns based on reward. This is done by two things: one is based on the received reward and the other is assigning the task.

4.2.4 ENERGY EFFICIENCY IN WSN

The study by Warrier and Kumar [16] introduces the concept of energy harvesting based on energy-efficient routing. The increasing popularity of WSNs with the concept of "three any," that is, any person, anytime, and anywhere, led the authors to design routing protocols that consume small chunks of energy during communication, thus increasing the lifetime of these networks. An important factor here was power, as the radio transmission consumes large amounts of energy including the radio reception. Thus, the authors came to the conclusion that a key issue in WSNs is energy conservation. In WSNs, nodes are used to harvest energy from the environment. A replacement of energy becomes too costly for most of its applications, so a suitable solution needs to be found for this issue.

Energy consumption is one of the primary concerns in WSNs. In the research presented by Zaman et al. [17], a "position-responsive routing protocol" (PRRP) was adopted for designing an energy-efficient routing protocol. Here, PRRP helps in minimizing the consumption of excess energy in each node. This is done by decreasing the amount of time when a sensor node is idle and in a listening state. Reduction in the average communication distance further helps in minimizing energy consumption. The evaluation was done for the proposed PRRP keeping in mind the context of the lifetime of a network, consumption of energy, and throughput of the network per data packet and per individual. A significant improvement in terms of overall performance as well as energy efficiency is successfully shown in the outcomes of the paper.

Athanassoulis et al. [18] discuss how WSNs have the potential for a large spectrum of applications, comprising a research area that is developing quickly. The design aspect is affected by many factors including power consumption, network topologies, and transmission errors. Developing a WSN can introduce many challenges. One of the challenges to be concerned about is regarding implementation. This research describes a multi-criteria architecture for achieving a consistent form of message forwarding over a WSN. Furthermore, this is an energy-aware architecture. Using this structure, a directed acyclic graph (DAG) is established all over the network. Multi-source data aggregation is done using the given DAG which is directed to a single sink. The requirement of message transmission is decided by an evaluation of energy reserves and induced error by the intermediate nodes themselves. The requirement of a sink is compulsory to accumulate, process, and send the data for further processing to a more sophisticated system.

4.2.5 REINFORCEMENT LEARNING

Mavrin et al. [19] investigate how to improve the efficiency of exploration of the distributions learned by the distributional RL method. Here the authors propose a method of energy efficiency to be implemented in DRL. This method has two components, a decaying schedule that suppresses the intrinsic uncertainty and a calculated exploration bonus obtained from the upper quantiles of the learned distribution. The distribution of the value function is learned using the quantile regression deep-Q-network (QR-DQN) algorithm. Then, the intrinsic uncertainty is suppressed using the decaying schedule. Using the upper quantiles in the learned distribution, an optimistic exploration bonus for QR-DQN is estimated.

Klink et al. [20] highlight the drawbacks of curriculum reinforcement learning (CRL). CRL is used to improve the stability and learning speed of an agent. This is done by exposing the agent to a tailored series of tasks throughout the process of learning. One of the major questions arising from CRL is how a curriculum can be automatically generated for any given RL agent, avoiding manual design. This study proposes an answer to this by considering the generation of a curriculum as a problem of inference, where target tasks are approached by progressive learning of distribution over tasks. An automatic curriculum is generated through this approach, whose pace is easily integrated with deep RL algorithms and is controlled by the agent. The generated curricula with the proposed algorithm are conducted in experiments and are concluded to improve learning across deep RL algorithms and several learning environments, outperforming or matching the levels of existing CRL algorithms.

In Rakelly et al. [21], the authors point out the problems in efficient off-policy meta-reinforcement learning (meta-RL). Integrating existing off-policy RL algorithms with probabilistic context variables having an online inference during meta-training can help in achieving sample efficiency. This can also help in the fast adaptation of the algorithms. The introduced off-policy meta-RL algorithm, known as PEARL (probabilistic embeddings for actor-critic reinforcement learning), combines existing algorithms with new context variables with an online interference.

Meta-training: the necessary statistics are accumulated using a probabilistic encoder and encoded in context variables using past experience.

Meta-test time: sampling context variables helps in enabling exploration that is temporarily extended for the duration of the episode; this also helps to keep the variables constant.

Using the collected trajectories, a fast trajectory level is adapted by the author which helps to update the posterior over context variables. The experiments in the study successfully demonstrate that PEARL not only matches but also outperforms existing approaches in the field by 20–100 times. A significant improvement in asymptotic performance is also observed.

4.2.6 5G (5TH GENERATION)

Ahmad et al. [22] focus on a detailed review of the latest spectrum-sharing technologies in the direction of the development of 5G and recent 5G-enabling technologies. The network traffic loads have significantly increased over time due to the increased popularity of small-cell and IoT devices resulting in the advancement of the current network into 5G technology, thus demand for high capacity, ultra-low latency, and high data rate has increased. The main research area here is focused on the exploration of spectrum resources and the maximization of the utility of the bands of these spectrums. However, achieving a management scheme for this technology that is efficient as well as stable is a severe challenge, in the form of the scarcity of spectrum resources, faced by developers. Additionally, an in-depth look at cognitive radio (CR) technology in spectrum sharing related to the implementation of 5G has also been conducted. For completing the survey, issues and problems in current spectrum sharing and CR networks are discussed in detail, and a mechanism is provided to support the advancements of efficient 5G technologies.

Pisarov and Mester [7] present the concept of 5G technology and how it will affect our lives in the future. This paper discusses the impacts of 5G networks on recent technologies, such as IoT, AI, and smart driving cars, and also how 5G networks can become a keystone in the development of smart cities if current problems with 5G are resolved. The 5G system is termed a non-stand-alone network due to the requirement of having active 4G support for its initial connection. With growing urbanism, the need for relaxation has increased exponentially; this relaxation is required as an antidote to an exhausted society. With smart devices like Alexa and Google in people's homes, the approach to everyday activities has changed. With the intention of comfortable living, smart cities are under development. This paper also discusses the three main problems that AI can address – detection, estimation, and optimization. Further research, development, and time are required for 5G networks to become stand-alone systems.

4.2.7 SMART CITIES

Urban IoT is designed in such a way as to exploit advanced communication technologies that can support the services of the city and those required by citizens. Zanella et al. [5] review the technologies and protocols required for an urban IoT. The paper emphasizes the importance of proper city planning using IoT by monitoring different services.

Khorov et al. [23] review Wi-Fi technology and assess the connections between multiple devices used in many areas, such as grids and houses. These connections reduce the need for human intervention by allowing people to establish communication very easily.

Shah and Mishra [24] present an IoT-enabled monitoring system that monitors environmental conditions such as temperature. The data received can be viewed using an android application that has been specifically developed.

4.3 METHODOLOGY

We use the following algorithms to implement the proposed model:

4.3.1 CLUSTERING

WSNs use clustering to increase the scalability of the network. The simulation employs a node-to-sink prototype. The nodes collect the data from the sensors, and the data is sent to the node situated in the center of all the nodes. This receiving node is the sink node.

First, the sink node transmits a packet with a token set to 0. When the node receives the packet, the token is incremented and the packet is retransmitted.

4.3.2 GROUPING OF NODES

For the ease of transmission of data between the sensor node and the base station, we divide the nodes into multiple clusters. Each cluster has three different types of nodes:

Primary node (P-node): These are the nodes that collect the data at the ground level.

Base node: The base nodes are the nodes present at the intermediate level. They are responsible for the reception of data from the primary node and the transfer of data to the cluster head.

Cluster head: These nodes are the head of each cluster, i.e. these nodes make contact with the base station, and they contain the total data of the cluster. They are responsible for data transfer to the base station.

The primary nodes collect the data and send it to the base node. The base nodes collect data from different primary nodes, and they forward the data to the cluster head. The data in the cluster heads are stored and finally sent to the base station. The

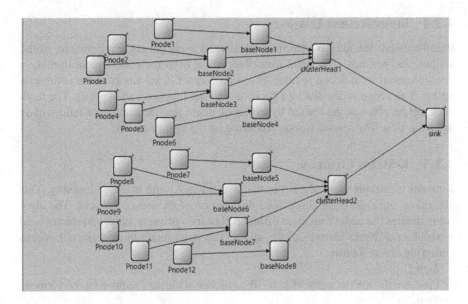

FIGURE 4.2 Sample cluster diagram consisting of two clusters

base station (sink) stores the data of multiple clusters, and finally, this is sent to the user (Figure 4.2).

4.3.3 Q-LEARNING

One of the most extensively used RL algorithms is Q-learning, where the environment is not required for modeling, and actions depend on the Q-function. We use Q-learning where the agent learns from the Q-function. The Q-function updates the values based on the actions performed at each state of the agent. Using the Q-learning algorithm, we can create an effective and independent wake-up schedule for each node.

The utility values are U(s) = maxQ (s, a).

Q (s, a) is given by the equation [25]:

$$Q(s,a) = R(s) + \sum P(s,a) maxQ(s',a') \tag{1}$$

where

s   = the current state of the agent
a   = the current action to some policy
s' = the next state where the agent ends
a' = the next best action picked using the current Q-value.
R   = the current reward observed from the environment
γ   = discounting factor for rewards

maxQ (s', a') = the maximum expected future reward given by the new state (s').

4.3.4 Reinforcement Learning

Reinforcement learning is effectively described using agents, environment states, actions, and rewards. The agent uses observation from the environment to make a decision about what action to take. The main contact in the environment is done by agents. The action is decided by a decision-making function called policy. The feedback can be given as the reward by which we determine the success or failure of an agent's action. The reward is received based on the agent's action.

4.3.5 K-Means Clustering

K-means clustering is an algorithm that is used in AI and machine learning. This algorithm implements the three-layer distribution of the sensor network. The algorithm divides the nodes into three different clusters – primary, base, and cluster head – based on different features of the nodes. The steps required to perform k-means clustering are as follows:

Step 1:
First, we decide the value of k, i.e. the number of clusters required to be formed.

Step 2:
For the available k clusters, we choose random points for each cluster and also select one point out of the set of random points as the centroid.

Step 3:
Once we select the centroid, we assign the points closest to the centroid and form another cluster.

Step 4:
After forming the cluster, we recompute the centroid to the newly formed cluster. This process is repeated until the entire set of nodes is classified into clusters based on the properties and features of the nodes.

4.4 DESIGN ASPECTS

4.4.1 Design Considerations

WSNs consist of a variety of sensor nodes which can be large in number and very small in size. The processing capability of each tiny node can be very small, and the power either consumed or radiated can be very low. While designing a WSN, certain factors should be kept in mind. The factors are listed below.

4.4.1.1 Fault Tolerance

In a WSN, the failure of a node or change in the topology of the network is quite possible. Hence, the designed network should be reliable and robust to adapt to the mentioned issues. The working of the network should be smooth and normal in every condition.

4.4.1.2 Lifetime

WSNs are expected to work for a long time (at least for six months to a year) with low power consumption. Using a 3V supply to power each node for a lifetime is considered sufficient in a WSN. The protocols designed in a WSN should be such that the consumption of energy by each node should be minimal and as low as possible to run for a lifetime.

4.4.1.3   Scalability

The design of a WSN should be such that it supports the addition of new components at any time during its lifespan. It should support the addition of new nodes at any time to enhance its working, and it should support large amounts of nodes in the network, as a WSN may require a new application of nodes at any time, and it should work with a large number of nodes such that its application can be vast.

4.4.1.4   Data Aggregation

The location of sensor nodes in a WSN raises the problem of the generation of similar data in neighboring nodes, as the nodes are located close to each other. Therefore, it is required to pile up the data and eliminate duplicate data generated in the network before transmission, as transmission and reception are costly in every WSN, so the duplication of data should be minimized. The data should be aggregated at each level in a WSN before transmitting it, and the redundant data should be eliminated and ensured that only the required data is transmitted.

4.4.1.5   Cost

As mentioned earlier, a WSN can have large amounts of sensor nodes, and each sensor node costs approximately 70 INR ($0.86), so the total cost of a network can be expensive. Therefore, the number of nodes in a WSN should be decided optimally and according to its necessity so that the cost of designing the WSN is limited.

4.4.1.6   Environment

WSNs should be designed as such to survive in any environment, even harsh and challenging, where deployed. It is already known that WSNs can be deployed in any challenging condition, thereby gathering information that a normal network could not do.

4.4.1.7   Heterogeneity Support

The WSN should support a variety of applications, and the protocols used to design a WSN should support different kinds of nodes to maintain heterogeneity.

4.4.1.8   Autonomous Operations

The operations in a WSN should be designed such that it can work autonomously in any condition where it is deployed. A WSN can be deployed in many harsh conditions that humans inhabit and where the deployment of another network is not possible. Therefore, the WSN should be able to organize, reorganize, and operate autonomously.

4.4.1.9   Limited Memory and Processing Capability

The sensor nodes are very structured simply and are primitive. They have very limited power, processing capabilities, and memory. The designs of WSNs should be very simple, considering the primitive nodes, and should not be too complex or demanding in terms of memory requirements and processing capabilities.

4.4.2 NODE CREATION

```
number_of_points = 20
Node={'id':0,'energy':0,'location':{'x':0,'y':0,},'isClusterHead':False,'isDead':False,
'threshold':0.1,'lastTimeCH':-1,'wantToSendData':False}
Node['id'] = i+1
Node['energy'] = 5000 # Energy of Each node is 5 miliJoules
Node['location']['x'] = X[i]
Node['location']['y'] = Y[i]
Node['isClusterHead']=False
```

Sample output of a node:

{'id': 1,	{'id': 2,
'energy': 5000,	'energy': 5000,
'location': {'x': 35.70129734495674,	'location': {'x': 39.045650567235214,
'y': -35.555472662442696},	'y': -146.95088393024912},
'isClusterHead': False,	'isClusterHead': False,
'isDead': False,	'isDead': False,
'threshold': 0.1,	'threshold': 0.1,
'lastTimeCH': -1,	'lastTimeCH': -1,
'wantToSendData': False}	'wantToSendData': False}

4.4.3 DISTANCE COMPUTATION

We consider the Euclidean distance between the nodes as

$$\sqrt{(x_2 - x_1)^2 + (y_2 - y_1)^2} \tag{2}$$

where (x_1, y_1) are the node 1 coordinates and (x_2, y_2) are the node 2 coordinates.

4.4.4 ENERGY PARAMETERS

Transmission energy is represented as

$$tran\_energy = 50 * pow(10, -6) * k + 10 * pow(10, -9) * (dist ** 2) * k$$

Receiving energy is represented as

$$recv\_energy = 50 * pow(10, -6) * k$$

Idle energy is represented as

$$idle\_energy = 40 * pow(10, -6) * k$$

where k = size of data being transmitted or being received,
   and dist = distance between base station and node.

4.4.5 WSN ENVIRONMENT

The node distribution considered for the training environment is as follows (Figure 4.3):
   Base station location

4.4.6 Q-LEARNING AGENT

For the environment created, we now use the Q-learning agent to train the environment for different actions. Here we have three different states of action – sleep, transmit, and dead. The agent first initializes all three states in the Q-table to zero (Table 4.1).

Once the values are initialized, we run the agent for the environment. First, the agent takes the initial values and the actions from the Q-table. The agent repeatedly keeps on checking the state and the value associated with that state. The agent also keeps learning about the environment and improves its response or action towards the environment. After many iterations, the agent develops the best action with respect to the environment.

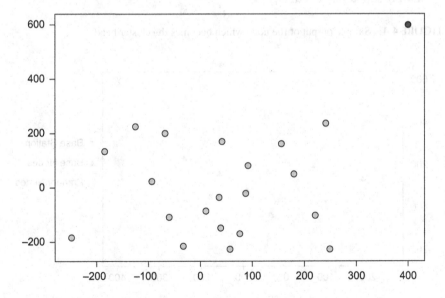

FIGURE 4.3 The environment where the agent will explore all the options

TABLE 4.1
Initial Q-Table

Action/State	Sleep	Transmit	Dead
Sleep	0	0	0
Transmit	0	0	0
Dead	0	0	0

4.4.7 CLASSIFICATION OF DIFFERENT NODES

The agent now classifies the different nodes present in the environment into clusters. For this, the agent uses the k-means clustering algorithm. Here the agent divides the set of nodes into primary nodes and base nodes. Once the nodes are classified into two different sets, the agent now selects the cluster head from the set of base nodes. This set is finally updated into the environment, and the agent again starts learning about the new environment (Figures 4.4, 4.5, and 4.6).

```
{'energy': -8.600000000000003,
 'id': 20,
 'isClusterHead': True,
 'isDead': True,
 'lastTimeCH': 42,
 'location': {'x': 42.273112850965106, 'y': 172.0339488309511},
 'threshold': 0.1,
 'wantToSendData': False}]
```

FIGURE 4.4　Sample output of the node which becomes the cluster head

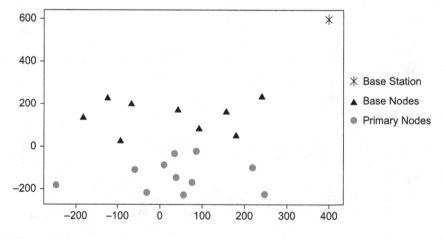

FIGURE 4.5　The classified environment with base nodes

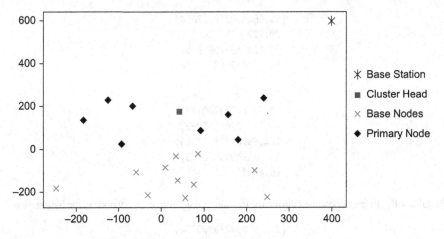

FIGURE 4.6   The classified environment with the cluster head

4.4.8   DATA TRANSFER DIRECTLY FROM PRIMARY NODE TO BASE STATION

The distance and energy required to transfer data directly from the primary node to the base station are calculated using the distance and energy formula given above (Figures 4.7 and 4.8).

4.4.9   SELECTION OF BASE NODES

The primary nodes select the base nodes on a random basis to transfer data. The base nodes are selected in such a way that the distance between them is not very long. On selecting the base nodes, the distance between the primary node and the selected base node is calculated, and using that distance, the energy consumed is also calculated (Figures 4.9 and 4.10).

After this, we calculate the distance and energy consumed in transferring the data from the base nodes to the cluster head (Figures 4.11 and 4.12).

We then calculate the distance between the cluster head and the base station and using the distance also calculate the energy required for data transfer from cluster head to base station (Figure 4.13).

$$[732.5601023720366,\\
829.5924694563054,\\
834.9986202141889,\\
789.0443117353392,\\
841.5122146561952,\\
844.0356801915049,\\
695.7258312898921,\\
896.2411655439563,\\
1016.3556360127052,\\
721.2624311366616,\\
924.6197259256109]$$

FIGURE 4.7   Distance between primary node and base station

[55.064430358732864,
 70.2223665378611,
 71.12226957595995,
 63.659092588189516,
 72.21428074155743,
 72.63962294363364,
 49.80344323240114,
 81.72482268155893,
 104.69787788547906,
 53.42194945691675,
 86.89216375707518]

FIGURE 4.8   Energy consumed during the transfer of data from primary node to the base station

[141.85494275990754,
 358.35634492292274,
 340.56710981340507,
 272.16007266391415,
 323.4216837203775,
 418.0638856038543,
 436.7320804280323,
 287.52219822174044,
 195.99344431063153,
 305.50362149093,
 155.51000243402657]

FIGURE 4.9   Distance between primary node and base node

[3.4122824785416648,
 14.24192699465168,
 12.998595628665592,
 8.807110515242703,
 11.86015855005239,
 18.87774124461926,
 20.473491007499728,
 9.66690144702618,
 5.241343021274463,
 10.733246274407344,
 3.8183360857030952]

FIGURE 4.10   Energy consumed during the transfer of data from primary node to base node

$$[114.8448984868682,$$
$$175.89041207897293,$$
$$183.02007513494928,$$
$$104.2466848505459,$$
$$228.97857838255075,$$
$$208.56853579276435,$$
$$112.50412272155417,$$
$$200.0463189363404]$$

FIGURE 4.11 Distance between base node and cluster head

$$[2.718935070845906,$$
$$4.493743706131091,$$
$$4.749634790240248,$$
$$2.4867371302329033,$$
$$6.643118935809394,$$
$$5.750083412273763,$$
$$2.665717762934652,$$
$$5.401852971998003]$$

FIGURE 4.12 Energy consumed during data transfer from base node to cluster head

$$[557.7844267659033]$$ $$32.51234667425673$$

FIGURE 4.13 Distance and energy values for the transfer of data from cluster head to the base station

To find the total energy consumed, we add all the energies calculated, i.e.

Total energy = Energy consumed during data transfer from primary node to base node + energy consumed during data transfer from base node to cluster head + energy consumed during data transfer from cluster head to base station (Figure 4.14).

4.5 RESULTS

Table 4.2 shows the final Q-Values the agent can obtain after being exposed to the environment. The agent learns from the custom environment by exploring and exploiting the environment to get the maximum possible results.

Figure 4.15 shows the energy consumption of each of the sample nodes transferring data directly to the base station. This model is flawed for the reason that the nodes spend a lot of energy transferring loads of data over huge distances simultaneously.

```
[41.32648212525673,
 53.39739260425674,
 50.00468600425673,
 47.962576124256735,
 51.015624164256735,
 54.05580568425673,
 58.73592109425673,
 46.92888291425673,
 40.472624766256736,
 47.99522773425673,
 41.08031755025674]
```

FIGURE 4.14 Total energy consumed during the entire data transfer process

---

TABLE 4.2
Final Q-Table (Showing the Best Action Generated by the Agent)

Action/State	Sleep	Transmit	Dead
Sleep	7.452424244535	69.36773284471019	13.5655655746335
Transmit	1.7744795807334843	55.663323234424	4.2345543156784
Dead	27.61242180234653	94.80461615040946	45.93663750088437

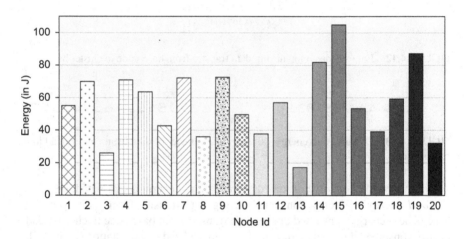

FIGURE 4.15 This plot shows the energy consumed during the transfer of data from all the 20 nodes to the base station

There is also a possibility of a bottleneck at the base station when receiving data from multiple sources simultaneously.

Bottlenecking occurs when multiple transmitters send data to a single receiver. From Table 4.2, we can see that there are three states of the node – transmit, receive, and idle. The idle state has the least energy consumption, and the transmit state has the highest energy consumption. When a bottleneck occurs, the node is in the

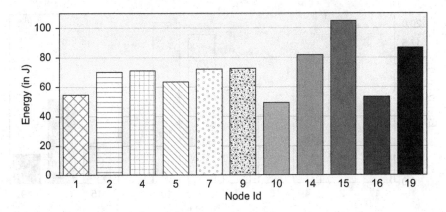

FIGURE 4.16   The plot shows the energy consumed by each primary node in transmitting the data from itself to the base station directly

transmit and receive states for the longest period of time, hence causing the node to become dead.

Figure 4.16 shows the energy levels after implementing the clustering algorithm. This figure shows the energy consumed by each primary node in sending data directly to the base station. This model also has the same flaw shown in Figure 4.15 in the sense that the primary nodes spend a lot of energy transferring loads of data over huge distances simultaneously, thereby creating the possibility of a bottleneck at the base station while receiving data from multiple primary nodes.

In the model used in Figure 4.17, there is a possibility of a bottleneck at the cluster head as the cluster head receives data from multiple primary nodes.

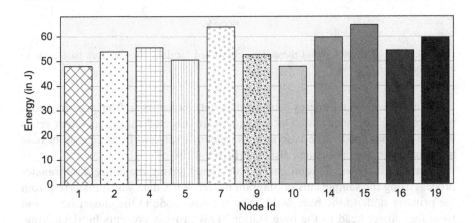

FIGURE 4.17   The plot shows the energy consumed by each primary node in transmitting the data from itself to the cluster head and from the cluster head to base station

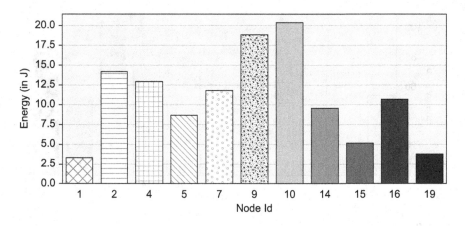

FIGURE 4.18   This plot shows the energy consumed during the transfer of data from primary node to base node

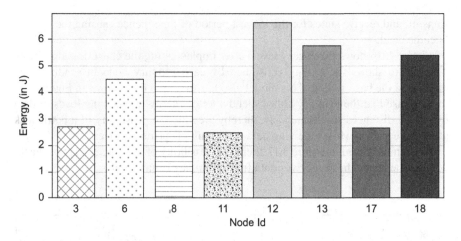

FIGURE 4.19   This plot shows the energy consumed for data transfer from base node to cluster head

Figure 4.18 shows the energy consumed for data transmission from primary nodes to a secondary base node layer. Once the nodes are clustered, the primary node sends its data to a base node. The base node is randomly selected from a group of base nodes based on availability and distance (Figure 4.19).

Figure 4.20 shows the total energy consumed during the entire data transfer process using the sample cluster diagram model. Here, data was transferred from the primary node to the base node, from the base node to the cluster head, and from the cluster head to the base station. This process prevents bottlenecking, and the overall energy levels are reduced as the primary nodes don't have to send data to a far-off node.

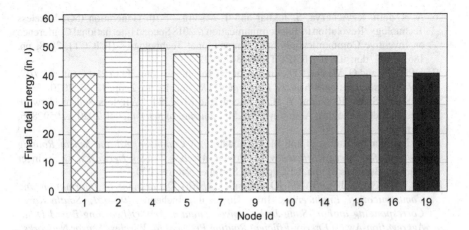

FIGURE 4.20 This plot shows the total energy consumed during the entire data transfer process using the sample cluster diagram model

4.6 CONCLUSION

The results obtained by the proposed model show an observable reduction in energy. This solution can really come into play in a real-world scenario where the nodes have wider distribution and would take a considerable amount of energy to directly transfer to the base station. By comparing Figures 4.16, 4.17, and 4.20, we can see the energy consumed during data transmission using different methods. The proposed model (Figure 4.20) is where the least energy is consumed overall. This is due to the fact that even though it increases the number of steps, the energy efficiency of the network will be conserved because of the multiple short-distance steps to transfer data. The nodes are also self-scheduling because of Q-learning, which will give optimal selection based on the final Q-table that the agent decides.

REFERENCES

1. C. Savaglio, P. Pace, G. Aloi, A. Liotta and G. Fortino, "Lightweight Reinforcement Learning for Energy Efficient Communications in Wireless Sensor Networks," in *IEEE Access*, vol. 7, pp. 29355–29364, 2019, doi: 10.1109/ACCESS.2019.2902371
2. M. Kozlowski, R. McConville, R. Santos-Rodriguez and R. Piechocki, "Energy Efficiency in Reinforcement Learning for Wireless Sensor Networks," 2018.
3. X. Meng, H. Inaltekin and B. Krongold, "Deep Reinforcement Learning-Based Topology Optimization for Self-Organized Wireless Sensor Networks," 2019 IEEE Global Communications Conference (GLOBECOM), Waikoloa, HI, 2019, pp. 1–6, doi: 10.1109/GLOBECOM38437.2019.9014179
4. H. Samih, "Smart Cities and Internet of Things," in *Journal of Information Technology Case and Application Research*, vol. 21, no. 1, pp. 3–12, 2019, doi: 10.1080/15228053.2019.1587572
5. A. Zanella, N. Bui, A. Castellani, L. Vangelista and M. Zorzi, "Internet of Things for Smart Cities," in *IEEE Internet of Things Journal*, vol. 1, no. 1, pp. 22–32, Feb. 2014, doi: 10.1109/JIOT.2014.2306328.

6. A. K. Jain, R. Acharya, S. Jakhar and T. Mishra, "Fifth Generation (5G) Wireless Technology 'Revolution in Telecommunication'," 2018 Second International Conference on Inventive Communication and Computational Technologies (ICICCT), 2018, pp. 1867–1872, doi: 10.1109/ICICCT.2018.8473011.

7. J. Pisarov and G. Mester, "The Impact of 5G Technology on Life in 21st Century," *IPSI BgD Transactions on Advanced Research (TAR)*, vol. 16, no. 2, pp. 11–14, 2020.

8. M.S. BenSaleh, R. Saida, Y. Hadj Kacem and M. Abid, "Wireless Sensor Network Design Methodologies: A Survey," *Hindawi Journal of Sensors*, vol. 2020, p. 9592836, 13 pages.

9. K. Manikanda Kumaran and M. Chinnadurai, *A Competent Ad-hoc Sensor Routing Protocol for Energy Efficiency in Mobile Wireless Sensor Networks*, © Springer Science+Business Media, LLC, part of Springer Nature 2020.

10. Y. Wan-Kyu and Y. SANG-JO, *(Member, IEEE) Department of Information and Communication Engineering*, Inha University, Incheon. *402–751, South Korea Corresponding author: Sang-Jo Yoo (sjyoo@inha.ac.kr) "Q-Learning-Based Data-Aggregation-Aware Energy-Efficient Routing Protocol for Wireless Sensor Networks" Received December 27, 2020, accepted January 10, 2021, date of publication January 13, 2021, date of current version January 20, 2021.*

11. T. Stephan, F. Al-Turjman, K. Suresh Joseph, B. Balusamy and S. Srivastava, "Artificial Intelligence Inspired Energy and Spectrum Aware Cluster Based Routing Protocol for Cognitive Radio Sensor Networks," *Journal of Parallel and Distributed Computing*, vol. 142, pp. 90–105, 2020.

12. V. K. Menaria, S. C. Jain, N. Raju, R. Kumari, A. Nayyar, (Senior Member, IEEE) and E. Hosain, (Senior Member, IEEE), "NLFFT:A Novel Fault Tolerance Model Using Artificial Intelligence to Improve Performance in Wireless Sensor Networks," Publication August 12, 2020, Current version August 24, 2020.

13. P. S. Sreedharan and P. Dnyandeo Jageshwar, "Spatial Correlation Based Clustering with Node Energy Based Multi-Hop Routing Scheme for Wireless Sensor Networks," ISSN 1846-6168 (Print), ISSN 1848-5588 (Online). https://doi.org/10.31803/tg -20210204153751

14. R. Sinde, F. Begum, K. Njau and S. Kaijage, "Refining Network Lifetime of Wireless Sensor Network Using Energy-Efficient Clustering and DRL-Based Sleep Scheduling," Received: 11 December 2019; Accepted: 25 February 2020; Published: 10 March 2020.

15. S. Sheng, P. Chen, Z. Chen, L. Wu and Y. Yao, "Deep Reinforcement Learning-Based Task Scheduling in IoT Edge Computing," *Sensors*, vol. 21, p. 1666, 2021. https://doi .org/10.3390/s21051666. Academic Editor: Taehong Kim Received: 31 January 2021 Accepted: 24 February 2021 Published: 28 February 20.

16. M. M. Warrier and A. Kumar, "An Energy Efficient Approach for Routing in Wireless Sensor Networks, Procedia Technology," vol. 25, pp. 520–527, 2016, ISSN 2212-0173.

17. N. Zaman, L. T. Jung and M. M. Yasin, "Enhancing Energy Efficiency of Wireless Sensor Network through the Design of Energy Efficient Routing Protocol", *Journal of Sensors*, vol. 2016, Article ID 9278701, 16 pages, 2016.

18. M. Athanassoulis, I. Alagiannis and S. Hadjiefthymiades, *Energy Efficiency in Wireless Sensor Networks: A Utility-Based Architecture* (2007).

19. B. Mavrin, S. Zhang, H. Yao, L. Kong, K. Wu and Y. Yaoliang, *Distributional Reinforcement Learning for Efficient Exploration* (2019).

20. P. Klink (Technische Universität Darmstadt), *Carlo D'Eramo (Technische Universität Darmstadt), Jan Peters (Technische Universität Darmstadt), Joni Pajarinen (Technische Universität Darmstadt, Aalto University) Self-Paced Deep Reinforcement Learning* (2020).

21. K. Rakelly, A. Zhou, D. Quillen, C. Finn and S. Levine, *Efficient Off-Policy Meta-Reinforcement Learning via Probabilistic Context Variables* (2019).
22. W. S. H. M. W. Ahmad et al., "5G Technology: Towards Dynamic Spectrum Sharing Using Cognitive Radio Networks," in *IEEE Access*, vol. 8, pp. 14460–14488, 2020, doi: 10.1109/ACCESS.2020.2966271.
23. E. Khorov, A. Lyakhov, A. Krotov and A. Guschin, "A Survey on IEEE 802.11ah: An Enabling Networking Technology for Smart Cities," *Computer Communications*, vol. 58, pp. 53–69, 2015, ISSN 0140-3664.
24. J. Shah and B. Mishra, "IoT Enabled Environmental Monitoring System for Smart Cities," 2016 International Conference on Internet of Things and Applications (IOTA), 2016, pp. 383–388, doi: 10.1109/IOTA.2016.7562757.
25. J. Wu, C. Zhang and G. Pu, "Reinforcement Learning Guided Symbolic Execution," 2020 IEEE 27th International Conference on Software Analysis, Evolution and Reengineering (SANER), 2020, pp. 662–663, doi: 10.1109/SANER48275.2020.9054815.

5 The Role of 5G Networks in Healthcare Applications

Narasimha Rao Vajjhala and Philip Eappen

CONTENTS

5.1 INTRODUCTION

The purpose of smart cities is to improve the quality of life of their residents by providing Information and Communication Technologies (ICT)-based solutions in key areas – smart economy, governance, mobility, environment, people, and living [23]. Smart cities employ a wide range of technologies, including cloud computing, network function virtualization, big data, internet of things (IoT), vehicle communication, proximity services, device-to-device (D2D) communication, and 5G networks [23]. The current healthcare system has several deficiencies, including an imbalance of medical resources and a non-individualized diagnosis and treatment model [13]. The healthcare systems in developing countries in Asia and Africa have additional problems: lack of infrastructure, overcrowded hospitals, overloaded medical staff, and lack of properly trained staff [13].

The increasing proliferation and availability of IoT devices and applications have created a growing demand for the adoption of 5G networks in developing countries [6]. Several vertical industries are primed to gain from the multi-Gbps speed and sub-10 ms low latency offered by the 5G networks [24]. The use of 5G networks

DOI: 10.1201/9781003227861-5

with IoT devices can potentially benefit developers of healthcare applications. For instance, several people require continuous monitoring for health problems and chronic diseases, including diabetes, heart disease, and cancer [17]. The patients in these cases would require continual surveillance by sending data to doctors and receiving diagnoses and treatment. Artificial intelligence and big data have already made significant advancements in healthcare applications [14]. 5G networks along with IoT devices can provide added value to existing technologies.

Applications such as Google's DeepMind Health and Bouy Health use cutting-edge technologies, including artificial intelligence and neuroscience, to provide high-quality medical care [14]. These applications rely on large datasets, and the use of 5G technologies and IoT devices can offer significant real-time datasets to these applications. However, data privacy and ethical issues need to be discussed and considered before deploying these technologies with healthcare applications [9]. This chapter explores the current healthcare applications using the 5G networks in conjunction with IoT devices. This chapter aims to develop a summary of the state-of-the-art technologies used in healthcare applications using 5G networks. This chapter also explores the possible advancements in healthcare applications as the deployment of 5G networks continues in several developed and developing countries.

The chapter begins with an explanation of the technologies constituting 5G. The differences between 4G and 5G technologies are explained in this section. The next section explains the various applications of 5G technologies. Smart healthcare applications, especially in the context of 5G and IoT, are discussed in the following section, followed by the challenges impeding the use of 5G in smart healthcare applications. The chapter ends with a set of recommendations for leadership, followed by a conclusion.

5.2   5G NETWORKS

5G is not a single technology but a combination of several technologies, including IoT, big data, cloud computing, and artificial intelligence [13]. 5G mobile communications standards are developed by a third-generation partnership project (3GPP) – a consortium of telecommunication standards organizations from the USA, Europe, and Asia [7]. 3GPP has different standardized technologies for smart cities scenarios integrating smart city applications in 5G networks [23]. The deployment of 5G devices is also expected to provide extensive connectivity, including both long-range – spanning metropolitan and municipal areas, and short-range – campuses and buildings [6]. The wide span of connectivity can help achieve seamless service mobility and availability. Major telecommunication corporations in the USA, including AT&T and Verizon, deployed 5G networks in 2019 [24]. Chinese mobile service providers also deployed a significant amount of 5G base stations in 2019 and have been ahead of other countries as of the end of 2020 [24].

5G networks are considered a significant development following the existing 4G networks, not only because of the multi-Gbps wireless bit rate but also for the ability to support reliable low-latency communications that are essential for applications like telesurgery [2, 24]. The wave frequencies used in 5G are between 30 and 300 GHz, having wideband advantage [3]. 5G networks promise several benefits over 4G, including a higher number of active nodes per unit area, higher operational frequency range (24–100 GHz), and spectrum sharing [7].

5G technology offers a transmission speed of up to 10 Gbps data transfer rate, which is around 10 to 100 times more than what 4G and 4G long-term evolution (LTE) can offer. The latency of 5G networks is < 1 ms, equal to a nearly zero data response time [1]. 5G networks operate at microwave frequencies, allowing a broad bandwidth accommodating many devices to connect simultaneously, for instance, up to one million devices per square kilometer [4]. This is nearly 100 times the connectivity offered by 4G networks. The energy consumption of 5G is less than that of 4G, enhancing a connected device's battery life [4].

Some of the key features of 5G networks include the multi-Gbps speed, sub-10 ms low latency, and significant coverage and connectivity. One of the critical issues involving 5G networks is network coverage. 5G networks use a higher frequency than 4G networks, so there is a potential for significant attenuation and penetration loss resulting in coverage issues. The performance of applications using 5G networks is also likely to affect the quality of experience [24]. Another drawback of 5G networks is the issues related to energy consumption, as the signal processors and the radio frequency hardware consume a significant amount of power [24].

5G networks can be deployed in standalone and non-standalone modes [3]. In standalone 5G architecture, 5G-compliant devices will directly connect to a 5G core network through 5G base stations [7]. In the non-standalone 5G architecture, the 5G-compliant devices will connect to a base station through 4G LTE base stations to get into the 5G core network [7]. This allows spectrum sharing between 4G LTE and 5G using the same infrastructure.

D2D communications improve channel reliability, system throughput, operational cost reduction, and energy efficiency [1]. D2D communication can happen when one terminal collaborates with other terminals to improve the communication features between the base station and terminals or could also happen directly between two terminals without including the base station [1]. Authentication management in 5G is complex considering the significant number of connected devices because of which different authentication models can be implemented for different applications [3]. Two types of authentication – entity authentication and message authentication – are used to manage authentication in 5G networks [3].

5.3 APPLICATIONS OF 5G NETWORKS

Smart healthcare is one of the main applications leveraging 5G networks by improving asset management in hospitals, and assisting in remote monitoring, assisted living, and telemedicine [1]. Smart antennas used in 5G network communication have utilized several innovations, including beamforming, where the radiofrequency energy is focused on a contract beam where required [1]. According to [1], machine-to-machine communication (M2M) and IoT are the two main pillars of smart healthcare using 5G networks. Some of the domains that can benefit from the deployment of 5G networks include smart mobility, smart health, smart energy, and industrial and consumer applications [6].

According to [7], three main 5G usage scenarios are possible, including enhanced mobile broadband (eMBB), massive machine-type communications (mMTC), and ultra-reliable and low-latency communications (URLLC). Smart mobility applications could range from autonomous driving and connected vehicles, while smart energy applications include grid networking and power-consumption-saving devices. Industrial applications using 5G networks include 3D printing, AI-supported factories, and cyber-physical systems. Consumer applications include smartphones with 4K/8K streaming, blockchain-based fintech applications, and holographic technology applications [6].

5.3.1 SMART HEALTHCARE APPLICATIONS

Smart health involves using traditional healthcare processes integrated with modern communication technologies to provide a high-quality healthcare system. A wide range of technologies, including communication networks, data analytics, sensors, and IoT devices, can be used to monitor health conditions and transmit metrics to remote servers that can be accessible by healthcare professionals for diagnosis and treatment [21], [23]. The technologies used by smart healthcare devices can be classified into short-range and long-range based on the communication range between the devices and the servers. Some of the key short-range wireless technologies in smart healthcare include Wi-Fi and Bluetooth, while long-range wireless technologies include WiMAX and body area networks (BAN) [1].

[1] have categorized the major requirements of smart healthcare systems into three categories, namely, things-oriented, app-oriented, and semantics-oriented. Things-oriented smart healthcare systems are focused on responsiveness, low power consumption, higher efficiency, and flexible application. App-oriented smart healthcare architectures focus on the authenticity of the data transmissions between smartphone applications and various sensors. Semantic-oriented systems focus on user experience and computing abilities by handling natural language execution methods.

Telehealth provides healthcare using telecommunication technologies remotely [8]. Telehealth includes the remote provision of clinical healthcare, health education, and public health services. Telemedicine [10] is a remote clinical service including consultation, diagnosis, and treatment. Telemedicine includes utilizing communication infrastructure such as 4G and 5G internet by a healthcare professional to remotely deliver healthcare to a patient. Patients can remotely access telenursing and telepharmacy services without direct physical contact with a nurse or a pharmacist using telehealth.

For instance, Canada has remote delivery of prescription drugs and telemedicine for consulting patients from remote locations [19]. In particular, the province of Nova Scotia successfully implemented telemedicine during the pandemic to avoid crowded hospitals and clinics and manage physician and nurse shortages [15]. Most telehealth providers face poor network speed and connectivity; thus, 5G can do miracles in telemedicine. As per [5, telesurgery allows surgeons to perform surgical procedures remotely. For multiple reasons, healthcare teleservices using 5G are highly encouraged due to a lack of hospital capacity and human resources.

Telehealth-based health education programs are possible only through a high bandwidth 5G network. High-quality teleservices require unique and sophisticated technologies for proper functionality; thus, 5G can transform future telemedicine platforms. For instance, high-quality, low-latency, and jitter video streaming is required for a telemedicine consultation or follow-up between a doctor and a patient. Uninterrupted 4K video streaming is ideal for monitoring patients via telenursing. It is also possible to remotely deliver drugs using unmanned aerial vehicles (UAV), with the help of secure connectivity by sending and receiving control instructions without delays [15]. Low-latency communication between the patient and the surgeon and connectivity between many devices such as sensors, robots, cameras, and augmented reality (AR) devices are ideal for telesurgery [16].

5.3.2 INTERNET OF THINGS (IoT) DEVICES IN HEALTHCARE APPLICATIONS

The increase in IoT devices over the last five years has also increased the need and demand for 5G networks. Connected IoT devices form a key component of smart cities, providing a range of solutions to different problem areas, including transport management, environmental pollution, healthcare, and public safety [23]. Some requirements of IoT applications include low latency, and higher bandwidth and security [6]. IoT devices mainly exchange small data packets with high energy efficiency and low data rates.

Various accessories, such as wearable devices, are connected through the internet and mobile devices to do continuous health monitoring [12]. A cloud database is used to collect and store ongoing information from mobile devices. Data collection with sensor devices has encouraged many people to be active and perform more physical activities and collect various data. The wearable sensors collect the number of steps, heart rate, and details of jogging, climbing, walking, and other exercises [16]. Wearable device information must be refined by various machine learning programs to be able to analyze a person's health status [11].

Insulin pumps deliver pre-programmed and user-adjusted insulin doses, and 5G could improve the insulin pump data exchange efficiency between patients and healthcare professionals. Insulin pumps help type 2 diabetes patients improve blood glucose control and better management of blood glucose. They can also help to delay or prevent the development of diabetic retinopathy, nephropathy, and neuropathy [25]. A pacemaker is an implanted device to assess and regulate abnormal heart rhythms. A pacemaker records heart rate and rhythm when an irregular heart arrhythmia is seen; the data is usually transmitted to an external device [25]. 5G technologies can help share patient information with medical professionals more easily, thus managing proper monitoring of patients in remote locations [16]. Doctors and nurses are always required to check different reports or x-rays in the operation theater, and 5G is expected to make it possible to see reports and x-rays from remote locations using technologies such as Google Glass. Blood pressure monitors can be transformed with 5G technology, and doctors can check patients' blood pressure remotely [25].

Studies point out that the ramifications of patients not taking drugs on time and as per medical practitioners' prescriptions could be severe. An automated pill dispenser could bring IoT, wireless M2M, and mobile phones together [16]. Sensor-based drug dispensers monitor medication usage and send reports to a central server through the wireless network [25]. These can be equipped with a 24/7 connection to the client, family members, doctors, nurses, and a medical alert central station or a monitoring center.

Some of the application areas expected to benefit from the deployment of 5G networks include autonomous driving, virtual reality, augmented reality, IoT, and healthcare applications. The number of connected devices is expected to reach more than 75 billion by 2025 [6]. Smart cities involve the interconnection of devices that produce and share large amounts of information within a transparent, decentralized, autonomous, and immutable system [18]. The use of IoT devices is a key aspect of smart cities. However, IoT devices still suffer from privacy and security issues [18]. 5G networks in conjunction with IoT devices can be used in a diverse set of health applications, including in cases where patients need to be monitored continually for treatment that requires a long duration of treatment, for instance, in cases of diabetes, heart disease, and cancer [17]. These patients might need continuous observation using IoT devices. However, there are issues with privacy and security in 5G networks that need to be addressed in this case.

5.3.3   5G NETWORKS IN HEALTHCARE APPLICATIONS

Healthcare systems will benefit from 5G networks, as internet connectivity would be reliable for medical devices with greater bandwidth and coverage. Technologies like telemedicine, augmented reality, and virtual reality, which play an important role in rehabilitation, would benefit from using 5G technologies [13]. Smart health applications are likely to be one of the key application areas utilizing 5G networks [6]. As the use of smart wearables has increased significantly over the last decade resulting in a large user base, a significant number of applications covering mobile-based condition monitoring and diagnosis are now available. This has resulted in a huge amount of data generated continually, so smart health is likely to be a major sector using 5G networks.

Wearables with versatile sensors can monitor physical activity helping in the rehabilitation of patients with chronic ailments, including spinal cord injuries and chronic pulmonary diseases. Some researchers have grouped the IoT devices used in smart healthcare as the internet of medical things (IoMT) [4]. IoMT device applications include non-interventional blood sample analysis, monitoring drug intake, and seizure prediction [4]. Precision medicine using 5G networks, big data, artificial data, and machine learning can help provide individualized and personalized medicine [13]. As 5G networks support low latency and high bandwidth, massive medical devices can connect to a central cloud computing server without any network congestion and support a truly immersive virtual reality, creating an interactive experience in telemedicine [13].

Innovations are also increasing interest in augmented and virtual reality-enabled surgery, which needs the low latency and high bandwidth offered by 5G networks [6]. 5G-powered sensors in ambulances can relay the patients' vitals in the case of emergencies and help the emergency room staff prepare and make life-saving decisions in time [4]. 5G networks will also reduce the overcrowding in hospitals, mainly as observed during the Covid-19 pandemic, by allowing a seamless delivery of teleconsultation and tele-expertise [4].

The healthcare system will benefit significantly from reliable 5G connectivity for huge medical devices, with higher bandwidth and better coverage than 4G. AR and virtual reality (VR) will undoubtedly benefit from 5G and contribute to intelligence medicine when 5G evolves. Integrating AR and VR is crucial for telemedicine due to its technical characteristics [13]. VR and AR can be used to do extremity rehabilitation exercises. VR and AR in the healthcare industry are not novel; however, they have not been fully developed due to latency issues. Latency is described as the response time between sending and receiving data from terminal devices [20]. Technically, 5G is expected to offer a ten-fold decrease in latency compared to 4G LTE. This reduction in latency would significantly help VR technology and telemedicine. VR is expected to streamline telemedicine, teleconsultation, and remote surgery with high bandwidth and low latency of 5G [22].

Vital signs such as blood pressure, temperature, and pulse could be streamed to cardiac monitors in a hospital with minimal latency during remote surgery using 5G [25]. 5G is super potent and robust to support multiple medical gadgets simultaneously, such as sensors, medical equipment, and cameras; however, current LTE allocations of the 4G spectrum cannot meet such massive requirements [13]. 4 k and 8 k ultra-high-definition monitor systems or televisions can provide clear and sharp videos with detailed content and high-resolution information [22].

Considering the nature of these innovations, 5G networks also need to address data privacy, security, and low power requirements to enable practical deployment and wide use of these technologies [6]. Healthcare applications can benefit from using 5G networks, provided some of the key requirements and expectations are addressed. These requirements include communication range, bandwidth, latency, reliability, power consumption, security, and privacy [6].

5.4 CHALLENGES IN THE DEPLOYMENT OF 5G NETWORKS IN HEALTHCARE APPLICATIONS

The full deployment of 5G networks will take close to another decade as the policy-makers, governments, medical research institutes, and hospitals in several countries are still preparing plans for the data center architecture, medical equipment procurement, and the necessary telecommunication infrastructure [13]. Smart healthcare systems will keep evolving as 5G networks help improve the quality of medical resources and reduce healthcare costs. However, major security, data privacy, and ethical issues related to the use of 5G networks must be addressed before widespread deployment and use.

Speed of data transfer is a critical challenge that has affected the execution of telemedicine using 4G LTE. The essential requirement is low latency and bandwidth, which can help gigantic medical devices connect with servers, central on-demand computing platforms, or connectivity between devices without network congestion. 5G truly supports AR applications, immersive VR, and zero-delay response by creating an interactive experience for telemedicine. Telemedicine services added with a high-resolution 4 k or 8 k monitor and 360 degrees VR can provide doctors a live view and help them make immediate decisions and diagnoses. It also helps in treatment strategy, helps medical staff with the operation, and acts as a powerful training tool. 5G can help revolutionize low-latency video streaming, significant interventions, and 3D high-resolution imaging [22].

5.4.1 SECURITY AND DATA PRIVACY ISSUES

Security is a key concern for IoT devices, especially in smart health applications, as it could put people's lives at risk. One of the major challenges with 5G networks is maintaining availability and withstanding attacks against availability. Attacks, such as denial of service (DoS) attacks, are possible considering the massive number of unsecured nodes in 5G networks [3]. Maintaining privacy and confidentiality has been one of the major concerns since the inception of 5G networks. Considering the massive number of connected nodes in a 5G network, there is more attention being given to privacy than traditional cellular networks. The anonymity of service is one of the basic security requirements in 5G networks [3]. Healthcare information generated by smart wearable devices is necessary to provide quality solutions through smart health applications. However, privacy is a critical issue when it comes to dealing with such sensitive personal data. Privacy protection is essential through all the phases involved in smart health applications, including collecting, transmitting, processing, and sharing such sensitive data [23]. Unless users' privacy concerns are addressed, smart health applications' usage and acceptance rates will be lower than expected.

Especially in personal health monitoring and vehicle routing, security, confidentiality, and data privacy are vital to prevent any leaks. An example of the security threats to smart city applications is the recent case of the hacking of a Tesla car where the hackers were able to open the door of the car while it was on the move

[23]. While this was a demo case and in a different scenario, this highlights the risks involved with IoT devices and nodes that are not secured. There is a need for end-to-end security solutions to be embedded in the 5G core architecture across all the domains and layers [23].

5.4.2 ETHICAL ISSUES

[26] state that users often suffer from consent fatigue due to numerous smart devices that are connected and may give their consent without proper knowledge of its consequences. Also, using technologies such as biometrics can help protect privacy, but these technologies are also susceptible to exploitation by hackers. Nabbosa and Kaar (2020) give the example of biometric data about a patient's health that insurance companies can use against the person. Also, technologies that detect facial expressions and emotions can place the mental privacy of the affected people in danger. Augmented reality technologies, such as smart glasses, have faced many protests about privacy, as they violated the privacy of people who did not want to be analyzed or photographed without their consent [26].

5.5 RECOMMENDATIONS FOR LEADERSHIP

As 5G is not one single technology, rather it is a group of technologies, there is a need for the base infrastructure to be set up before countries can leverage 5G for applications, such as smart healthcare. Several countries are struggling to implement and deploy 5G, as the base infrastructure is not yet properly set up, and, as mentioned in the previous section, it might take up to a decade for several countries to be ready to completely deploy and leverage the 5G technology. In addition to the challenges involved in smart healthcare applications using 5G technology as mentioned above, there are key ethical, security, and data privacy issues that need to be addressed. Hence, it is important for policymakers and leaders to focus on addressing these challenges before any major strategies and policies are designed. Several countries, especially in Asia and Africa, may set up 5G networks in urban centers but are likely to struggle to roll out and expand their networks to rural areas where the infrastructure is lacking and where significant investment is needed to upgrade existing systems. 5G networks in most of these countries are likely to operate along with existing 4G networks before they can evolve into completely standalone systems.

5.6 CONCLUSION

The emphasis on smart cities is increasing, with several developing and developed countries leveraging ICT-based solutions to improve quality of life. Smart healthcare is a core part of smart cities. While several countries have the infrastructure to deploy smart healthcare applications and leverage 5G technologies, other countries are only gradually catching up. The benefits of smart healthcare applications are significant and more relevant than ever in the post-pandemic world. However, policymakers have to frame policies and strategies in conjunction with businesses and telecommunication companies to set up a framework to facilitate seamless integration and deployment of these technologies. Policymakers would also have to consider various challenges, especially the ethical and privacy issues related to the deployment of these technologies, as this could influence the acceptance and adoption of these applications.

REFERENCES

1. Ahad, A., Tahir, M., Aman Sheikh, M., Ahmed, K. I., Mughees, A., & Numani, A. (2020). Technologies Trend towards 5G Network for Smart Health-Care Using IoT: A Review. *Sensors*, *20*(14), 4047. Retrieved from https://www.mdpi.com/1424-8220/20 /14/4047
2. Al-Turjman, F., Kamal, A., Husain Rehmani, M., Radwan, A., & Khan Pathan, A.-S. (2019). The Green Internet of Things (G-IoT). *Wireless Communications and Mobile Computing*, *2019*, 6059343. https://doi.org/10.1155/2019/6059343
3. Amgoune, H., & Mazri, T. (2018). 5G: Interconnection of Services and Security Approaches. Paper presented at the Proceedings of the 3rd International Conference on Smart City Applications, Tetouan, Morocco. https://doi.org/10.1145/3286606.3286795
4. Dananjayan, S., & Raj, G. M. (2021). 5G in Healthcare: How Fast Will be the Transformation? *Ir J Med Sci*, *190*(2), 497–501. https://doi.org/10.1007/ s11845-020-02329-w
5. De Mattos, W. D., & Gondim, P. R. L. (2016). M-health Solutions Using 5G Networks and M2M Communications. *IT Professional*, *18*(3), 24–29. https://doi.org/10.1109/mitp .2016.52
6. Ding, A. Y., & Janssen, M. (2018). Opportunities for Applications Using 5G Networks: Requirements, Challenges, and Outlook. Paper presented at the Proceedings of the Seventh International Conference on Telecommunications and Remote Sensing, Barcelona, Spain. https://doi.org/10.1145/3278161.3278166
7. Dogo, E. M., Salami, A. F., & Nwulu, N. I. (2019). Evaluative Analysis of Next Generation Mobile Networks in Future Smart Grid in Developing Countries. Paper presented at the Proceedings of the 4th International Conference on Smart City Applications, Casablanca, Morocco. https://doi.org/10.1145/3368756.3368962
8. Dorsey, E. R., & Topol, E. J. (2016). State of Telehealth. *New England Journal of Medicine*, *375*(2), 154–161. https://doi.org/10.1056/nejmra1601705
9. Feldner, A., & Jung, Y. (2019). *Security Issues in Mobile Healthcare Applications*. Paper presented at the Proceedings of the 21st International Conference on Information Integration and Web-based Applications Services, Munich, Germany. https://doi.org/10 .1145/3366030.3366106
10. Hau, Y. S., Kim, J. K., Hur, J., & Chang, M. C. (2020). How About Actively Using Telemedicine During the COVID-19 Pandemic? *Journal of Medical Systems*, *44*(6). https://doi.org/10.1007/s10916-020-01580-z
11. Huifeng, W., Kadry, S. N., & Raj, E. D. (2020). Continuous Health Monitoring of Sportsperson Using IoT Devices Based on Wearable Technology. *Computer Communications*, *160*, 588–595. https://doi.org/10.1016/j.comcom.2020.04.025
12 Lee, S. (2002). Stochastic Polling Interval Adaptation in Duty-cycled Wireless Sensor Networks - Sungryoul Lee, 2015. *SAGE Journals* Retrieved December 2, 2021, from https://journals.sagepub.com/doi/full/10.1155/2015/486908

13. Li, D. (2019). 5G and Intelligence Medicine: How the Next Generation of Wireless Technology Will Reconstruct Healthcare? *Precision Clinical Medicine, 2*(4), 205–208. https://doi.org/10.1093/pcmedi/pbz020

14. Liu, J. (2020). *Artificial Intelligence and Data Analytics Applications in Healthcare General Review and Case Studies.* Paper presented at the Proceedings of the 2020 Conference on Artificial Intelligence and Healthcare, Taiyuan, China. https://doi.org/10.1145/3433996.3434006

15. Lynch, M. E., Williamson, O. D., & Banfield, J. C. (2020). Covid-19 Impact and Response by Canadian Pain Clinics: A National Survey of Adult Pain Clinics. *Canadian Journal of Pain, 4*(1), 204–209. https://doi.org/10.1080/24740527.2020.1783218

16. Mahajan, A., Pottie, G., & Kaiser, W. (2020). Transformation in Healthcare by Wearable Devices for Diagnostics and Guidance of Treatment. *ACM Transactions on Computing for Healthcare, 1*(1), 1–12. https://doi.org/10.1145/3361561

17. Manal, R., Fatima, R., & Tomader, M. (2019). Authentication for e-health Applications in IoT Enabled 5G and Proposed Solution. Paper presented at the Proceedings of the 4th International Conference on Smart City Applications, Casablanca, Morocco. https://doi.org/10.1145/3368756.3369059

18. Melhem, A., AlZoubi, O., Mardini, W., & Yassein, M. B. (2019). Applications of Blockchain in Smart Cities. Paper presented at the Proceedings of the Second International Conference on Data Science, E-Learning and Information Systems, Dubai, United Arab Emirates. https://doi.org/10.1145/3368691.3368726

19. Reid, D. S., Weaver, L. E., Sargeant, J. M., & Allen, M. J. M. (1998). Telemedicine in Nova Scotia: Report of a Pilot Study. *Telemedicine Journal, 4*(3), 249–258. https://doi.org/10.1089/tmj.1.1998.4.249

20. Riva, G., & Gamberini, L. (2000). Virtual Reality in Telemedicine. *Telemedicine Journal and e-Health, 6*(3), 327–340. https://doi.org/10.1089/153056200750040183

21. Siriwardhana, Y., Gür, G., Ylianttila, M., & Liyanage, M. (2021). The Role of 5G for Digital Healthcare against COVID-19 Pandemic: Opportunities and Challenges. *ICT Express, 7*(2), 244–252. https://doi.org/10.1016/j.icte.2020.10.002

22. Stefano, G. B., & Kream, R. M. (2018). The Micro-Hospital: 5G Telemedicine-based Care. *Medical Science Monitor Basic Research, 24*, 103–104. https://doi.org/10.12659/msmbr.911436

23. Usman, M., Asghar, M. R., Granelli, F., & Qaraqe, K. (2018). Integrating Smart City Applications in 5G Networks. Paper presented at the Proceedings of the 2nd International Conference on Future Networks and Distributed Systems, Amman, Jordan. https://doi.org/10.1145/3231053.3231055

24. Xu, D., Zhou, A., Zhang, X., Wang, G., Liu, X., An, C., ... Ma, H. (2020). Understanding Operational 5G: A First Measurement Study on Its Coverage, Performance and Energy Consumption. Paper presented at the Proceedings of the Annual Conference of the ACM Special Interest Group on Data Communication on the Applications, Technologies, Architectures, and Protocols for Computer Communication, Virtual Event, USA. https://doi.org/10.1145/3387514.3405882

25. Yeole, A. S. S., & Kalbande, D. R. (2016, March 1). Use of Internet of Things (IoT) in Healthcare: A Survey. Use of Internet of Things (IoT) in healthcare | Proceedings of the ACM Symposium on Women in Research 2016. Retrieved December 1, 2021, from https://dl.acm.org/doi/10.1145/2909067.2909079

26. Nabbosa, V., & Kaar, C. (2020). Societal and Ethical Issues of Digitalization. Proceedings of the 2020 International Conference on Big Data in Management.

6 Energy Consumption in Smart City Projects in the Era of 5G
An Analysis of User-Generated Content

Yatish Joshi, Gaurav Kabra, and Abhishek Tripathi

CONTENTS

6.1 INTRODUCTION

The challenge of the present generation is the over-exploitation of resources and increased pollution. This consumption pattern is unsustainable, with the over-consumption of resources and unmanageable levels of hazardous waste [36]. There is a need to decrease over-consumption through lifestyle modification, including a radical reduction in natural resource use. Sustainable consumption is defined by the Norwegian Ministry of Environment (1994) as

> The use of goods and service that responds to the basic need and brings a better quality of life while minimizing the use of natural resources, toxic material, and emissions of waste and pollution over the life cycle, so as not to jeopardize the needs of future generations.

Increasing energy consumption is a vital concern, especially in infrastructure projects. While infrastructure development is beneficial for economic development, it

DOI: 10.1201/9781003227861-6

99

may lead to some issues for the environment. Energy needs are also prominent in smart city projects, which is paradoxical as the long-term objective of such projects is to decrease energy needs [1, 9, 10, 16, 17].

Consumers are also increasingly preferring energy-efficient infrastructure projects. Nielsen's (2019) survey on the global online climate and sustainability found that 86% of customers favor energy-efficient goods and appliances, followed by recycling processes (79%). According to the Greendex (2010; a green index) published by the National Geographic Society and the international polling firm GlobeScan, the top-scoring countries in terms of sustainability are India, Brazil, and China. Consumers' increased preference for green infrastructure projects was also indicated.

With the advent of 5G projects, it is clear that 5G can help in completing projects on time and can reduce energy consumption needs for smart city projects [34, 54]. The essential premise is that smart cities must adapt to their users' needs and requirements. There are several definitions of smart cities and many techniques necessary for their implementation. Although smart city technology supports multiple human-to-human, machine-to-machine, and combination interactions, the internet of things (IoT), an ecosystem of networked devices, is the primary smart city enabler with its ability to access large volumes of data. With IoT, physical things can be perceived and converted into a digitalized format [20, 21, 22, 23, 24, 28].

The unique feature helps us to postulate that consumer sentiment is necessary to be extracted to identify the respective concerns. However, the opinions are divided among consumers [49], and thus it is essential to understand consumer opinions and sentiments about the adoption of 5G in smart city projects. The primary concern of current work is the application of 5G in reducing energy consumption and transitioning towards smart cities. In light of this, this chapter aims to analyze consumer sentiments about 5G and energy consumption in smart city projects [2, 5, 8, 11–13, 59, 60].

The chapter is arranged as follows. A literature review is given in Section 6.2. Section 6.3 deals with the analysis of the results, and Section 6.4 concludes the chapter with comments about future scope and limitations.

6.2   LITERATURE REVIEW

The next generation of wireless telecommunications is evolving. The evolution of new services will enable connectivity. The first generation was introduced in 1980 and can only transmit voice by analog technology. The second generation, 2G, was released in 1990, using digital technology, which improved speech quality and increased data rate capability [25, 26, 29, 35, 37, 38, 39, 41, 43].

2G provides services such as SMS (short message service), MMS (multimedia message service), and WAP (wireless application protocol), which provide internet access. The third generation, 3G, appeared at the end of 2000 and brought truly wireless data, providing wide access to the internet [27, 30, 32–34].

There is a technological pause during which a number of services, including web surfing, email access, TV streaming, etc. 3G devices are expensive and consume a lot of electricity [61, 74].

The 4G internet protocol was launched in 2010 to provide high security, high quality, and a low-cost service [40, 42, 44, 45]. It has higher data speeds than previous generations [7, 31]. 4G was then superseded by 5G in 2019, bringing lower latency and greater ubiquity of network data rates around the world in this decade [51, 52, 55, 56, 58].

5G enables millions of connections per square kilometer, thereby enabling various IoT applications and consequently a variety of devices [5, 6, 14, 15, 17, 19, 29, 31, 50, 54, 57]. 5G supports a wide variety of business models and addresses the various requirements of different service providers [3].

Sentiment analysis has been defined as "a special type of text mining with the focus on identification of subjective statements and contained opinions and sentiments, particularly in consumer-generated content over the internet" [47]. Various depictions of sentiment analysis may be found in the literature. According to [46], opinion mining aims at "capturing users' attitude by investigating, analyzing and extracting subjective tests involving user opinion preferences and sentiment."

While many researchers have used a survey-based quantitative and qualitative approach to understand sustainable consumption behavior using well-established theories [39, 40], there is an increased focus on using IT analytical tools in understanding consumer behavior [4]. According to [61], sentiment and citation data from Twitter may hold the key to understanding consumer psychology. The task of recognizing positive and negative views, feelings, and assessments is known as sentiment analysis [18]. [46] explained sentiment analysis as

> judgment of the sentiment expressed in a subjective test, which is capable of disgusting positive, negative, or even more subtle sentiments, such as anger, grief, or joy. It involves two subsequent tasks: Identification of subjective/objective information and the sentiment classification of subjective information.
>
> [70–72];

Twitter is a popular microblogging service where a user creates a status message which is used for sharing an opinion about different things. According to recent social media industry statistics, Twitter is now one of the most popular social networks in the world, built on participative users [62, 63, 64, 67].

6.3 RESEARCH DEVELOPMENT AND FINDINGS

The data was gathered from Twitter, where the top search keywords were energy consumption, smart cities, and 5G. Figure 6.1 displays the analysis of the attributes found in the corpus. There are several steps to programming; the first is Twitter Application programming interface (API) generation, which entails token access, user code, and text corpus filtering that includes removing web-mail addresses, changing capitalization, and removing spaces. The next step is the generation of a

FIGURE 6.1   Word cloud of smart cities and 5G keywords

TABLE 6.1

Proposed Algorithm

Step 1	:	Identify the keyword for extraction
Step 2	:	Generate API for Twitter data extraction
Step 3	:	Analyze frequency of attribute and generate word clouds
Step 4	:	Generate sentiment score to analyze consumer sentiments

---

Term Document Matrix (TDM) matrix, which helps to identify attributes in the corpus. In the above process, we generate word cloud and sentiment scores which help to determine the sentiment of the consumer. The proposed method is depicted by an algorithm depicted in Table 6.1.

The algorithm is iterated for all the keywords as depicted in Table 6.1, and the method enables the use of attributes in any corpus and helps to identify associations with other words.

Results (Attribute in the Test) for Smart City and 5G

Analysis:

From the word cloud in Figure 6.1, it is evident that it refers to people mostly discussing the smart city and 5G. Keywords such as unconnected and connecting were prominent, which suggests that the advent of 5G will speed up requirements to connect, help to facilitate smart city projects, and could lead to a reduction in resource requirements (Figure 6.2).

Analysis

The majority of customers (more than 80%) are positive about the advantages of 5G in smart city initiatives, according to sentiment scores in Figure 6.2. In addition, consumers have faith that 5G would be crucial in advancing smart city initiatives.

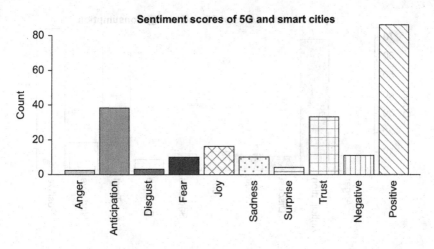

FIGURE 6.2   Sentiment score of 5G and smart cities

FIGURE 6.3   Word cloud of energy consumption and 5G keywords

Also, around 20% of consumers are happy about the prospect of more smart city initiatives as a result of 5G. Some consumers are unhappy with the effects of 5G, though. 15% of respondents are also concerned about how 5G would affect smart city initiatives.

Results (Attribute in the Test) for 5G and Energy Consumption

Analysis:

From the word cloud in Figure 6.3, it is evident that most people are sure that 5G will lead to energy consumption. Keywords such as energy, reducing, and sustainable were prominent, which suggests that the advent of 5G will help in reducing energy consumption requirements.

Analysis

Sentiment scores in Figure 6.4 highlight that most consumers (more than 60%) are positive about the benefits of 5G for the reduction of energy consumption. In addition, most consumers (more than 60%) believe that 5G will reduce energy consumption in smart city projects. Furthermore, around 70% of consumers anticipate that 5G will lead to energy consumption in smart city projects; around 10% are

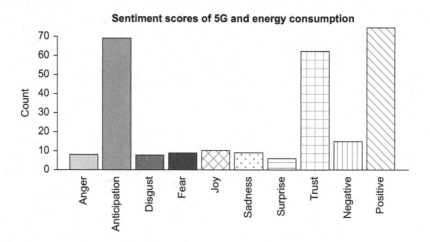

FIGURE 6.4 Sentiment score of 5G and energy consumption

joyful about it. However, some users (12%) feel negative about the impact of 5G. In addition, 10% are fearful about the impact of 5G on smart city projects.

6.4 DISCUSSION AND IMPLICATIONS

6.4.1 DISCUSSION

The paper uses sentiment analysis by which researchers can estimate sentiment over the web to convert user-generated content into insight. Sentiment analysis could help to overcome difficulties in the extraction and quantification of online data that consumers generate. The results of the sentiment analysis reveal that most people feel positive about the arrival of 5G and believe that 5G will lead to reducing energy consumption in smart city projects. In, addition, people feel joyful and believe that the arrival of 5G will be a boost in facilitating smart city projects. This positive sentiment of consumers indicates that they are inclined toward smart city projects during this Covid-19 era. However, some users have feelings of anger and fear, which are areas that could be investigated further [68–74]. Potential shortcomings could thereby be analyzed and overcome through various strategies. Sentiment analysis can be used for predictive purposes rather than descriptive purposes. This method has the requisite external validity to reveal the opinions of consumers.

6.4.2 THEORETICAL IMPLICATIONS

This study has major theoretical implications. The study focused on using sentiment tools to analyze consumer sentiments about the implication of 5G in reducing energy consumption in smart city projects. The identified sentiments enrich the literature in this area. The study outlines a positive transition in consumer sentiment and reflects a positive opinion about the arrival of 5G and the uses of 5G in reducing energy consumption in smart city projects. The findings reported more prevalent sentiments of joy and trust for smart cities. The findings highlight the need to understand consumer motivation, satisfaction, and psychological needs [65–72]. This research adds to the body of knowledge about this subject because it provides real-time analysis of consumers' opinions about the impact of 5G in connection to energy consumption requirements.

6.4.3 MANAGERIAL IMPLICATION

The study has major managerial implications. The study findings contribute to the literature by suggesting which emotions, when gratified, could foster the adoption of 5G in energy efficiency projects. Managers could use the study findings in mapping consumer minds and design suitable strategies to promote smart city projects. The significance of sentiment analysis could be useful in motivating consumers to adopt certain practices. This could also involve positive feedback and promoting customer relationships to enhance the promotion and adoption of smart city projects and thereby the reduction of energy use. Real estate companies could benefit from this trend by focusing on smart city projects [1–8]. The important tool of sentiment analysis could help practitioners to respond to consumer demands. The analysis of consumer opinions in real time through social media could help companies to identify changing patterns and take appropriate steps [47–49, 53]. The awareness of consumer sentiments could also help advertisers if specific sentiments were incorporated into various communication messages.

6.5 CONCLUSION

Social media is one of the best platforms to understand consumer opinions and awareness about any new technologies. This study utilized sentiment analysis of Twitter data and uncovered consumer emotions about the arrival of 5G and how it could impact energy consumption in smart city projects. The findings suggest a positive consumer mindset about smart city projects. The study helps in the analysis of this scenario and assesses when value can be enhanced by analyzing the language of Twitter users. There are certain limitations to this study that need to be addressed in the future. These limitations include the restriction of 1,000 tweets per keyword corpus. The corpus is, however, suitable for the study, as it indicates a point in time in a changing situation. Future studies might use a larger corpus size and tweet position identification in cluster analysis. In addition, this research only used consumer opinions from Twitter. Future research could explore other social medial platforms. Further, future research could comprise exploratory research with sentiment analysis.

REFERENCES

1. Abbasi-Moud, Z., Vahdat-Nejad, H., & Mansoor, W. (2019, December). Detecting tourist's preferences by sentiment analysis in smart cities. In 2019 IEEE Global Conference on Internet of Things (GCIoT) (pp. 1–4). IEEE.

2. Aboelmaged, M. (2021). E-waste recycling behaviour: An integration of recycling habits into the theory of planned behaviour. *Journal of Cleaner Production, 278,* 124182.

3. Adam, I., & Ping, J. (2018, August). Framework for security event management in 5G. In Proceedings of the 13th International Conference on Availability, Reliability and Security (pp. 1–7).

4. Aggarwal, P. & Vaidyanathan, R. (2003). Use it or lose it: Purchase acceleration effects of time-limited promotions. *Journal of Consumer Behaviour: An International Research Review, 2*(4), 393–403.

5. Ahmed, K. B., Bouhorma, M., & Ahmed, M. B. (2016a). Smart citizen sensing: A proposed computational system with visual sentiment analysis and big data architecture. *International Journal of Computer Applications, 152*(6), 20–27.

6. Ahmed, K. B., Radenski, A., Bouhorma, M., & Ahmed, M. B. (2016b). Sentiment analysis for smart cities: State of the art and opportunities. In Proceedings on the International Conference on Internet Computing (ICOMP) (p. 55). The Steering Committee of The World Congress in Computer Science, Computer Engineering and Applied Computing (WorldComp).

7. Alam, M., Abid, F., Guangpei, C., & Yunrong, L. V. (2020). Social media sentiment analysis through parallel dilated convolutional neural network for smart city applications. *Computer Communications, 154,* 129–137.

8. Alber, S., Reda, A., Shereen, A., Shofadekan, A. S., Ambrose, A. A., Akinwumi, H. ... Abouchabaka, J. (2021). Challenges and obstacle to implementing 5g in indonesia. *Journal of Theoretical and Applied Information Technology, 99*(21).

9. Albino, V., Balice, A., & Dangelico, R. M. (2009). Environmental strategies and green product development: An overview on sustainability-driven companies. *Business Strategy and the Environment, 18*(2), 83–96.

10. Alizadeh, T. (2018, May). Crowdsourced smart cities versus corporate smart cities. *In IOP Conference Series: Earth and Environmental Science, 158*(1), 012046. IOP Publishing.

11. Alkhammash, E. H., Jussila, J., Lytras, M. D., & Visvizi, A. (2019). Annotation of smart cities Twitter micro-contents for enhanced citizen's engagement. *IEEE Access, 7,* 116267–116276.

12. Alkhatib, M., El Barachi, M., & Shaalan, K. (2019). An Arabic social media based framework for incidents and events monitoring in smart cities. *Journal of Cleaner Production, 220,* 771–785.

13. AlKhatib, M., El Barachi, M., AleAhmad, A., Oroumchian, F., & Shaalan, K. (2020). A sentiment reporting framework for major city events: Case study on the China-United States trade war. *Journal of Cleaner Production, 264,* 121426.

14. Antonetti, P. & Maklan, S. (2014). Feelings that make a difference: How guilt and pride convince consumers of the effectiveness of sustainable consumption choices. *Journal of Business Ethics, 124*(1), 117–134.

15. Archetti, F., Giordani, I., & Candelieri, A. (2015). Data science and environmental management in smart cities. *Environmental Engineering & Management Journal (EEMJ), 14*(9).

16. Aryadinata, I. K. A., Pangesti, D., Anugerah, G. B., Aditya, I. E., & Ruldeviyani, Y. (2021, October). Sentiment analysis of 5G network implementation in Indonesia using twitter data. In 2021 6th International Workshop on Big Data and Information Security (IWBIS) (pp. 23–28). IEEE.

17. Azzari, M., Garau, C., Nesi, P., Paolucci, M., & Zamperlin, P. (2018, May). Smart city governance strategies to better move towards a smart urbanism. In International Conference on Computational Science and Its Applications (pp. 639–653). Springer, Cham.

18. Bermingham, A. & Smeaton, A. F. (2010). Classifying Sentiment in Microblogs: Is Breavity an Advantage? . *Proceedings of the 19th ACM International Conference on Information and Knowledge Management,* 1833–1836.

19. Brown, J. S., Collins, A., & Duguid, P. (1989). Situated cognition and the culture of learning. *Educational researcher, 18*(1), 32–42.
20. Buder, F., Feldmann, C., & Hamm, U. (2014). Why regular buyers of organic food still buy many conventional products. *British Food Journal.*
21. Chih-Lin, I., Han, S., & Bian, S. (2020). Energy-efficient 5G for a greener future. *Nature Electronics, 3*(4), 182–184.
22. Chiu, M. S. (2012). Gaps between valuing and purchasing green-technology products: Product and gender differences. *International Journal of Technology and Human Interaction (IJTHI), 8*(3), 54–68.
23. Dashtipour, K., Taylor, W., Ansari, S., Gogate, M., Zahid, A., Sambo, Y., ... & Imran, M. (2021). Public perception towards fifth generation of cellular networks (5G) on social media. *Frontiers in Big Data.*
24. de Oliveira, T. H. M., & Painho, M. (2021). Open geospatial data contribution towards sentiment analysis within the human dimension of smart cities. In *Open Source Geospatial Science for Urban Studies* (pp. 75–95). Springer, Cham.
25. Dilawar, N., Majeed, H., Beg, M. O., Ejaz, N., Muhammad, K., Mehmood, I., & Nam, Y. (2018). Understanding citizen issues through reviews: A step towards data informed planning in smart cities. *Applied Sciences, 8*(9), 1589.
26. Doran, D., Severin, K., Gokhale, S., & Dagnino, A. (2016). Social media enabled human sensing for smart cities. *AI Communications, 29*(1), 57–75.
27. Estévez-Ortiz, F. J., García-Jiménez, A., & Glösekötter, P. (2016). An application of people's sentiment from social media to smart cities. *Profesional de la Información, 25*(6), 851–858.
28. Fromhold-Eisebith, M., & Eisebith, G. (2019). What can smart city policies in emerging economies actually achieve? Conceptual considerations and empirical insights from India. *World Development, 123*, 104614.
29. Gaur, L., Afaq, A., Solanki, A., Singh, G., Sharma, S., Jhanjhi, N. Z., ... Le, D. N. (2021). Capitalizing on big data and revolutionary 5G technology: Extracting and visualizing ratings and reviews of global chain hotels. *Computers & Electrical Engineering, 95*, 107374.
30. Gleim, M. R., Smith, J. S., Andrews, D., & Cronin Jr, J. J. (2013). Against the green: A multi-method examination of the barriers to green consumption. *Journal of Retailing, 89*(1), 44–61.
31. Guevara, L., & AuatCheein, F. (2020). The role of 5G technologies: Challenges in smart cities and intelligent transportation systems. *Sustainability, 12*(16), 6469.
32. Herrera-Contreras, A. A., Sánchez-Delacruz, E., & Meza-Ruiz, I. V. (2019, December). Twitter opinion analysis about topic 5g technology. In International Conference on Applied Technologies (pp. 191–203). Springer, Cham.
33. Hilal, A. M., Alfurhood, B. S., Al-Wesabi, F. N., Hamza, M. A., Al Duhayyim, M., & Iskandar, H. G. (2022). Artificial intelligence based sentiment analysis for health crisis management in smart cities. *Computers, Materials and Continua*, 143–157.
34. Inamdar, M. A., & Kumaraswamy, H. V. (2020, September). Energy efficient 5G networks: Techniques and challenges. In 2020 International Conference on Smart Electronics and Communication (ICOSEC) (pp. 1317–1322). IEEE.
35. Jelonek, D., Stępniak, C., Turek, T., & Ziora, L. (2020). Planning cities development directions with the application of sentiment analysis. *Prague Economic Papers, 2020*(3), 274–290.
36. Joshi, Y., & Rahman, Z. (2019). Consumers' sustainable purchase behaviour: Modeling the impact of psychological factors. *Ecological Economics, 159*, 235–243.
37. Joshi, Y., Uniyal, D. P., & Sangroya, D. (2021a). Investigating consumers' green purchase intention: Examining the role of economic value, emotional value and perceived marketplace influence. *Journal of Cleaner Production, 328*, 129638.

38. Joshi, Y., Yadav, R., & Shankar, A. (2021b). The interplay of emotional value, trend affinity and past practices in sustainable consumption: An application of theory of reciprocal determinism. *Journal of Strategic Marketing*, 1–19.

39. Kumar, H., Singh, M. K., Gupta, M. P., & Madaan, J. (2020). Moving towards smart cities: Solutions that lead to the smart city transformation framework. *Technological Forecasting and Social Change*, *153*, 119281.

40. Li, M., Ch'ng, E., Chong, A., & See, S. (2016, July). The new eye of smart city: Novel citizen sentiment analysis in twitter. In 2016 International Conference on Audio, Language and Image Processing (ICALIP) (pp. 557–562). IEEE.

41. Malik, T., Tahir, A., Bilal, A., Dashtipour, K., Imran, M. A., & Abbasi, Q. H. (2021). Social sensing for sentiment analysis of policing authority performance in smart cities. *Frontiers in Communications and Networks*.

42. Marzouk, O. A. (2019). A qualitative examination of urban vs rural sustainable consumption behaviours of energy and water consumers in the emerging Egyptian market. *Journal of Humanities and Applied Social Sciences*.

43. Matharu, M., Jain, R., & Kamboj, S. (2020). Understanding the impact of lifestyle on sustainable consumption behavior: A sharing economy perspective. *Management of Environmental Quality: An International Journal*.

44. Mite-Baidal, K., Delgado-Vera, C., Solís-Avilés, E., Espinoza, A. H., Ortiz-Zambrano, J., & Varela-Tapia, E. (2018, November). Sentiment analysis in education domain: A systematic literature review. In International Conference on Technologies and Innovation (pp. 285–297). Springer, Cham.

45. Musto, C., Semeraro, G., de Gemmis, M., & Lops, P. (2015, May). Developing smart cities services through semantic analysis of social streams. In Proceedings of the 24th International Conference on World Wide Web (pp. 1401–1406).

46. Nanli, Z., Ping, Z., Weiguo, L., & Meng, C. (2012). Sentiment analysis: A literature review. *Proceedings of the International Symposium on Management of Technology (ISMOT)*, Hangzhou, IEEE, 572–576.

47. Naseem, U., Razzak, I., Musial, K., & Imran, M. (2020). Transformer based deep intelligent contextual embedding for twitter sentiment analysis. *Future Generation Computer Systems*, *113*, 58–69.

48. Pandey, H., & Sharma, A. (2018). Social big data analytics using sentiment learning algorithms for smart cities. *International Journal of Information Systems & Management Science*, *1*(1).

49. Praharaj, S., Han, J. H., & Hawken, S. (2018). Towards the right model of smart city governance in India. *Sustainable Development Studies*, *1*.

50. Psomakelis, E., Aisopos, F., Litke, A., Tserpes, K., Kardara, M., & Campo, P. M. (2016). Big IoT and social networking data for smart cities: Algorithmic improvements on big data analysis in the context of RADICAL city applications. *arXiv preprint arXiv:1607.00509*.

51. Pop, R. A., Săplăcan, Z., & Alt, M. A. (2020). Social media goes green: The impact of social media on green cosmetics purchase motivation and intention. *Information*, *11*(9), 447.

52. Pinto, G. E., Rosa, R. L., & Rodriguez, D. Z. (2021). Applications for 5G networks. *INFOCOMP Journal of Computer Science*, *20*(1).

53. Puri, S., Rai, R. S., & Saxena, K. (2018, August). Barricades in network transformation from 4G to 5G in India. In 2018 7th International Conference on Reliability, Infocom Technologies and Optimization (Trends and Future Directions) (ICRITO) (pp. 695–702). IEEE.

54. Rucinski, A., Garbos, R., Jeffords, J., & Chowdbury, S. (2017, September). Disruptive innovation in the era of global cyber-society: With focus on smart city efforts. In 2017 9th IEEE International Conference on Intelligent Data Acquisition and Advanced Computing Systems: Technology and Applications (IDAACS) (Vol. 2, pp. 1102–1104). IEEE.

55. Seçkin, T., & Kilimci, Z. H. (2020, October). The evaluation of 5G technology from sentiment analysis perspective in twitter. In 2020 Innovations in Intelligent Systems and Applications Conference (ASYU) (pp. 1–6). IEEE.

56. Sharma, S. (2018). Problems in implementing 5G IN India and solutions for it. *International Journal of Management and Applied Science, 4*(5).

57. Sharif, A., Li, J., Khalil, M., Kumar, R., Sharif, M. I., & Sharif, A. (2017, December). Internet of things: Smart traffic management system for smart cities using big data analytics. In 2017 14th International Computer Conference on Wavelet Active Media Technology and Information Processing (ICCWAMTIP) (pp. 281–284). IEEE.

58. Singh, M. (2021). Twitter opinion analysis about 5g technology. *Research Cell: An International Journal of Engineering Sciences, 34*, 14–27.

59. Song, H., Srinivasan, R., Sookoor, T., & Jeschke, S. (2017). *Smart Cities: Foundations, Principles, and Applications.* John Wiley & Sons.

60. Sun, J., Li, L., Li, W., Zhang, J., & Yan, C. (2020). Enabling 5G: Sentimental image dominant graph topic model for cross-modality topic detection. *Wireless Networks, 26*(3), 1549–1561.

61. Usama, M., Xiao, W., Ahmad, B., Wan, J., Hassan, M. M., & Alelaiwi, A. (2019). Deep learning based weighted feature fusion approach for sentiment analysis. *IEEE Access, 7*, 140252–140260.

62. Vakali, A., Chatzakou, D., Koutsonikola, V., & Andreadis, G. (2013, July). Social data sentiment analysis in smart environments-extending dual polarities for crowd pulse capturing. In International Conference on Data Management Technologies and Applications (Vol. 2, pp. 175–182). SCITEPRESS.

63. Van Zoonen, L. (2016). Privacy concerns in smart cities. *Government Information Quarterly, 33*(3), 472–480.

64. Visvizi, A., Lytras, M. D., Damiani, E., & Mathkour, H. (2018). Policy making for smart cities: Innovation and social inclusive economic growth for sustainability. *Journal of Science and Technology Policy Management.*

65. Vora, S., & Mehta, G. R. (2019). Investigating people's sentiment from twitter data for smart cities: A survey. *International Journal of Computational Intelligence & IoT, 2*(2).

66. Wang, J., & Wu, L. (2016). The impact of emotions on the intention of sustainable consumption choices: Evidence from a big city in an emerging country. *Journal of Cleaner Production, 126*, 325–336.

67. Yang, S., Li, L., & Zhang, J. (2018). Understanding consumers' sustainable consumption intention at china's double-11 online shopping festival: An extended theory of planned behavior model. *Sustainability, 10*(6), 1801.

68. Yu, H., Bae, J., Choi, J., & Kim, H. (2021). LUX: Smart mirror with sentiment analysis for mental comfort. *Sensors, 21*(9), 3092.

69. Yuan, Y., Lu, Y., Chow, T. E., Ye, C., Alyaqout, A., & Liu, Y. (2020). The missing parts from social media–enabled smart cities: Who, where, when, and what?. *Annals of the American Association of Geographers, 110*(2), 462–475.

70. Yuxue, Y., Huifeng, Y., Jing, W., Ruiying, L., & Xiangqian, N. (2021). A 5G network-oriented mobile edge computing offloading strategy and cloud computing network security. *International Journal of Engineering Intelligent Systems, 29*(2).

71. Zafar, A. U., Shen, J., Shahzad, M., & Islam, T. (2021). Relation of impulsive urges and sustainable purchase decisions in the personalized environment of social media. *Sustainable Production and Consumption, 25*, 591–603.

72. Zhang, Y., Lu, H., Jiang, C., Li, X., & Tian, X. (2021). Aspect-based sentiment analysis of user reviews in 5G networks. *IEEE Network, 35*(4), 228–233.

73. Zhao, J., Zhang, A., Rau, P. L. P., Dong, L., & Ge, L. (2020, July). Trends in human-computer interaction in the 5G era: Emerging life scenarios with 5G networks. In International Conference on Human-Computer Interaction (pp. 699–710). Springer, Cham.

74. Zhu, F., Li, Z., Chen, S., & Xiong, G. (2016). Parallel transportation management and control system and its applications in building smart cities. *IEEE Transactions on Intelligent Transportation Systems, 17*(6), 1576–1585.

7 The Role of 5G in Railway Applications

Ambar Bajpai, Manoj Tolani, Arun Balodi,
Sunny Sharma, and Lunchakorn Wuttisittikulkij

CONTENTS

7.1 INTRODUCTION

Fifth-generation (5G) telecommunication technology provides a very high speed of data communication with very low latency. Therefore, the demand for 5G is increasing for various applications [1–10]. The smart grid, smart shopping, high-speed video streaming, internet of things (IoT), IoT 4.0 industrial application, self-driven cars, health monitoring, and agriculture monitoring applications require low-latency high-speed data communication services. Thus, high-speed data communication is a basic requirement for future applications [11–20]. 5G provides various key enabling technologies to support all such applications, e.g. device-to-device (D2D) communication, massive multiple-input-multiple-output (massive MIMO), cognitive radio (CR), and software-defined wireless sensor network (SD-WSN) for 5G applications [11].

Due to the wide range of support of 5G cellular networks, 5G can also be utilized directly and indirectly in many other applications. The railway monitoring application is one of them. Railway monitoring can be classified into two broad categories. 5G-radio (5G-R) application for signaling operations and 5G railway track-condition

DOI: 10.1201/9781003227861-7

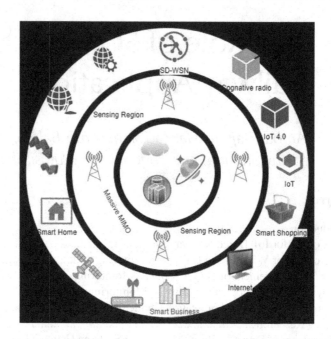

FIGURE 7.1   Application of 5G for WSN applications

monitoring (5G-RTCM) applications. In previous versions of cellular telecommunication technologies, e.g. 2G, 3G, and 4G applications, the cellular network is only utilized for signaling operations due to a lack of other technology interfacings [21–25]. In addition, the data communication rates and latency of traditional cellular networks are very limited. Thus, the traditional cellular network has not been utilized for other technologies. In the case of railway track-condition monitoring applications, wireless sensor network-based technology has previously been reported by various researchers. However, the SD-WSN and IoT interfacing features of 5G cellular communications enable the network to utilize high bandwidth wireless communication for all railway applications [11] (Figure 7.1).

In this chapter, we discuss the scope of 5G for railway monitoring applications. The 5G cellular network can be utilized for railway monitoring in the following ways:

1. IoT-based railway track-condition monitoring using 5G
2. WSN-based railway track condition monitoring using 5G
3. Railway signaling using 5G

7.2 SCOPE OF 5G FOR IOT-BASED RAILWAY MONITORING

5G requires a high data rate for continuous monitoring applications. To fulfill the demand of high data traffic conditions, previously, IEEE 802.15.4-based architecture was used in railway track-condition monitoring applications. The architecture defines both the contention access period (CAP) and contention-free period (CFP) for data transmission. In the CFP, the guaranteed time slot (GTS) is utilized for data traffic applications with time constraints. Researchers have reported the utilization of GTS for high data traffic load conditions. For low data traffic demand, the IoT network can be designed using 6LoWPAN or IEEE 802.15.4 standards. However, 5G can provide high-data-rate communication, and IoT devices can directly communicate with the internet. Therefore, 5G provides better usability for railway monitoring using IoT networks. The IoT is a newly evolved technology. There is no standard protocol suite designed yet for IoT. Manufacturers have used protocols based on their standards. The security protocols can also be classified based on the different operation layers [11, 26–30].

As per the previously reported works, the IoT model can be classified into four different layers, i.e., sensing layer/perception layer, network layer, transport layer, and application layer. The architecture of IoT-enabled 5G-RTCM is shown in Figure 7.2.

For IoT applications, sensor-based IoT devices can be distributed over the monitoring application. The IoT devices can transmit data to the IoT gateway as shown in Figure 7.2. The IoT gateway can transmit data to the mmWave base station. The mmWave base station can communicate with e-Node B and can process data over

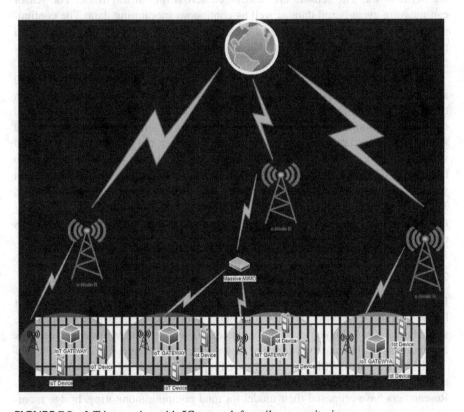

FIGURE 7.2 IoT integration with 5G network for railway monitoring

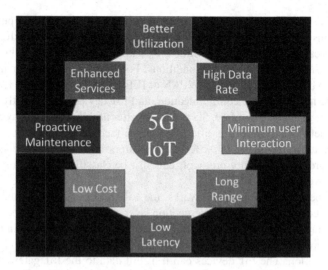

FIGURE 7.3   Advantages of 5G IoT for railway monitoring applications

the 5G network. The sensors are distributed across the railway track. The sensor can measure event-based data as well as continuous monitoring data. The continuous monitoring application generates high data traffic. The IoT integration with 5G provides various advantages for this high data traffic generation. The advantages of 5G-IoT for railway monitoring applications are shown in Figure 7.3 [11, 31–35].

The 5G network provides better reliability with good quality of service (QoS) and QoE. The throughput and available data rate of the 5G network are higher than traditional telecommunication technologies. Because of low latency, 5G can be used for real-time monitoring applications [36–40]. Also, this is an infrastructure-based system, therefore it requires less maintenance. However, the initial cost of 5G-based systems is higher, but the overall cost of the 5G-IoT system is lower compared to traditional IoT railway monitoring systems. Due to the importance of IoT integration with 5G, some local initiatives have been taken for integration. The United States, Japan, Korea, China, Europe, and the UK all have begun initiatives for the utilization of 5G in IoT applications. The spectrum requirement of 5G-IoT for RTCM is discussed in the next section.

7.3   SCOPE OF 5G FOR WSN-BASED RAILWAY MONITORING

Previously used telecommunication technologies were based on hardware systems that had very limited capability. The development of a software-defined network opens the scope for various technologies for development. 5G supports software-defined network communication. This can be integrated with various technologies [11].

The utilization of WSN has already been reported in railway monitoring applications. This method can be utilized for the efficient monitoring of the railway track. Researchers have proposed their model for mud pumping monitoring, bridge monitoring, track monitoring, vibration measurement, fish plate movement, alignment of the track, and many other applications. Researchers have also reported the efficient utilization of wireless channels for WSNs. Medium-access control protocols are proposed for railway monitoring applications. Both schedule-based and contention-based MAC protocols can be utilized for railway track monitoring applications. TDMA, EA-TDMA, BMA, EBMA, ASHMAC, EEHMAC, and many other schedule-based protocols have been reported for railway-condition monitoring applications. The biggest challenge is how to select the radio and bandwidth as per the application's requirements. Researchers have also analyzed the network for time-constraint applications. For these applications, wastage of bandwidth is a major challenge [41–45].

SD-WSN can be used as an integral part of the network. The software-defined WSN can also be used for efficient railway track monitoring applications. It can also be used to check the bogie condition as well as the operations of the engine. The comfort level of the bogies can also be monitored for railway track and railway bogie monitoring applications.

SD-WSN can be used for the effective tuning of the radio. The TDMA-based radio can be tuned for the selection of different applications. The integration of CR and SD-WSN can be used to fulfill all the requirements of railway monitoring. The low-latency feature of 5G can be utilized for traffic applications with time-constraint data. The independent control of the CAP and CFP in the IEEE 802.15.4 MAC protocol can also reduce the latency of the time-constraint data traffic applications. The integration of standard IEEE 802.15.4 can further be analyzed for 5G railway monitoring applications.

The aggregation method can also be used more efficiently with 5G technologies in WSN for railway monitoring applications. 5G provides a better data rate and bandwidth for 5G applications. Therefore, aggregation of the data can further improve the performance of the network. The integration of an aggregation protocol with IEEE 802.15.4 for WSN applications has already been reported for railway monitoring applications.

The integration of 5G technology with SD-WSN for railway monitoring applications has various challenges related to the mobility of high-speed trains. The back-end compatibility, front-end deployment, sensitivity of the measurements, coverage, and connectivity are a few of the major challenges of the railway monitoring application.

7.4 SPECTRUM REQUIREMENT OF 5G FOR RAILWAY MONITORING

Due to the increasing demand for bandwidth, 3GPP developed a new spectrum, i.e. new radio (NR) for 5G. There are two broadbands that can be utilized for 5G, i.e. the sub-6 GHz band and the mmWave band. The Federal Communications Commission (FCC) provides various operating ranges, including citizens' broadband radio range (CBRS) with 3.55–3.7 GHz, and C-band range of 3.7–4.2 GHz. It is intended that FCC will implement some new bands, e.g. 6–7 GHz for wider bandwidth requirements. In mmWave, a very wide bandwidth is available for 5G communication. The FCC has provided various bands for 5G communication: 24 GHz, 28 GHz, 37 GHz, 39 GHz, and 47 GHz. Up to now, railway telecommunication is based on a mix of generations. Many countries are still running 2G-based telecommunication systems for railway signaling operations. Therefore, the 5G-based system could be implemented to fulfill all the requirements of 5G-R signaling and telecommunication operations. For railway signaling operations, a dedicated sub-6 GHz band will be suitable for 5G-R operations.

7.5 5G PHYSICAL LAYER SUPPORT FOR RAILWAY MONITORING

The performance of the railway monitoring is analyzed for various telecommunication technologies. Previously, performance has been analyzed for 4G LTE and LTE-A. Features such as MIMO, D2D communication, cooperative communication, and carrier aggregation have already been analyzed for various applications. These technologies can also be utilized for the efficient performance of railway applications. In 5G, massive MIMO is used. Massive MIMO is an essential part of the overall 5G architecture. The utilization of large bandwidths for small cell architecture is an efficient method utilized in mmWave for high-data-rate applications. Many antenna elements are used for highly directional narrow beams. This feature can be utilized for a very high-capacity network for multiuser applications. This feature is very useful for railway monitoring with high mobility and short-range communication. The small base station size of the mmWave band can be installed in the railway coach, or one relay can be used to communicate with e-Node B for high-data-rate applications.

Different cellular sizes require different types of base stations. A heterogeneous network can be used for high-data-rate, low-range applications as well as low data rate, long-range applications. The heterogeneous network improves the spectral efficiency of the network. The feature can be used for heterogeneous applications.

Although the heterogeneous network is useful for low- to high-data-rate applications as well as for low-range to high-range communications, the efficiency of the protocol is not good enough for short-range applications. The railway application requires high mobility support and high efficiency of the network. However, the network performance for the heterogeneous network can't efficiently be utilized for railway applications. Device-to-device applications are also an integral part of IoT. They provide better efficiency, good QoS, better load balancing, and higher mobility for low-range applications. The load balancing feature of D2D applications can be used to increase the lifetime of the network. For short-range IoT applications, D2D can be used for railway monitoring.

7.6 5G RAILWAY MONITORING APPLICATION CHALLENGES

The challenges for the utilization of 5G technology for railway monitoring applications are as follows:

- The 5G network should be assessed for its capabilities under the huge network load of railway monitoring applications. This will ensure the performance of the network in the worst conditions.

- Suitable low-latency dedicated bandwidth for physical layer radio should be designed for better QoS.
- 5G technology should satisfy the requirement of the railway monitoring application.
- Integration of 5G with already existing lower-layer protocols for railway monitoring.
- The energy consumption reduction of the sensor devices is an important issue to be addressed for the 5G railway monitoring application.
- Issues related to the coverage and connectivity of the entire network should be addressed.
- Assessment of the possibility of reduction in the overall deployment costs of the network, as the railway is the largest sector of transportation of goods from one place to another.
- The dedicated networking layer protocol for 5G applications should be designed for the efficient performance of the network.
- The transport layer protocol is also important for 5G railway monitoring applications.
- Integrated energy harvesting using a wireless charging method can also improve the performance of the network.
- The mobility of high-speed trains should be examined for stable communication in 5G.

The above-mentioned challenges should be addressed before using the 5G network in railway monitoring applications. Previous research indicates that 5G can be utilized efficiently for railway monitoring applications.

7.7 TRENDING RESEARCH

Article	Challenges	Contribution	Reference
5G Communications in High Speed and Metropolitan Railways	Traditional telecommunication is not suitable for railway monitoring	Requirements, characteristics, and critical and non-critical transmissions are described in the paper	[1]
A Statistical mm-Wave Channel Modelling for Railway Communications Backhaul in 5G Networks	High bandwidth demand for video applications	The network is analyzed in an mmwave range of 28 to 60 GHz for high bandwidth demand applications	[2]
Towards Realistic High-Speed Train Channels at 5G Millimetre-Wave Band—Part II: Case Study for Paradigm Implementation	To address the issue of high bandwidth demand	The network is analyzed for tunnel environments as well as for outdoor environments	[3]

Article	Challenges	Contribution	Reference
28 GHz-Band Experimental Trial at 283 km/h Using the Shinkansen for 5G Evolution	To address the issue of high bandwidth and mobility	The network is analyzed at a high mobility environment of 283 Km/h for high-data-rate applications	[4]
Channel Modelling for Future High-Speed Railway Communication Systems: A Survey	Issues related to railway communication services for high-speed data operations	Both train operations and passenger services are analyzed for high-speed data traffic applications	[5]
Realistic Channel Characterization for 5G millimeter-Wave Railway Communications	5G railway network performance for realistic channels	The network is analyzed for the 60 GHz band with an 8 GHz bandwidth	[6]
Channel Analysis for Millimeter-Wave Railway Communications in Urban Environment	Analyzed for high mobility and high-data-rate environments	5G mmWave is analyzed for typical urban high-speed railway scenarios	[7]
Investigation of Power Delay Profiles for 5G Millimetre Wave Railway Communications	The demand for high data rates due to dense traffic	The network is investigated for power delay profile, RMS delay spread, received power, and different realistic HSR scenarios	[8]
Optimal Non-Uniform Steady mm-Wave Beamforming for High-Speed Railway	Challenges related to path loss and narrow beam coverage for high band frequencies	Optimal non-uniform steady mmWave beamforming is used	[9]
Characterization of Time-Variant Wireless Channels in Railway Communication Scenarios	The telecommunication network is analyzed for railway monitoring	The network is analyzed for T2I (train-to-infrastructure) and T2T (train-to-train) networks	[10]

7.8 REQUIREMENTS OF SMART RAILWAY MONITORING SYSTEMS USING 5G

The future requirements of 5G can be categorized into five different sections as follows [46, 47]:

1. **Physical infrastructure**
2. **Emerging technologies**
3. **System security**

4. **Software analytics**
5. **Research methodology**

7.8.1 Physical Infrastructure

The physical infrastructure of the network is dependent on three important parts of railway technology as shown in Figure 7.4. The smart railway system can be developed using 5G by connecting the stations, trains, and condition-monitoring systems to the IoT. The three parts of the development of railway technology are as follows:

1. Smart stations
2. Smart railway health monitoring systems
3. Smart trains

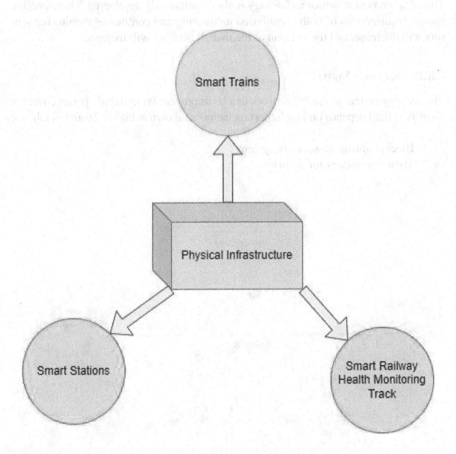

FIGURE 7.4   Physical infrastructure for smart 5G system

7.8.2 Emerging Technologies

Technology is changing day by day. From today's perspective, five major fields are growing rapidly, as shown in Figure 7.5 and as follows:

1. Core IoT technology for railway monitoring
2. 5G advancement
3. Cognitive radio
4. Continuous monitoring
5. Even-based monitoring

IoT and artificial intelligence (AI) are growing rapidly. An IoT-based cloud system with an effective machine-learning algorithm can be used for an advanced IoT platform. 5G is also advancing rapidly to meet user requirements. The bandwidth requirement can also be fulfilled by utilizing unutilized bands. For this, one can use cognitive radio. The advancement in sensor technology is also continuously developing. Therefore, the energy requirements of both event-based monitoring and continuous monitoring sensors will decrease, and the lifespan of the overall network will increase.

7.8.3 Security System

The security system of the 5G network can be improved. From today's perspective, the security system depends on four important factors as shown in Figure 7.6 and as follows:

1. Blockchain-based security system
2. Trust parameters for security

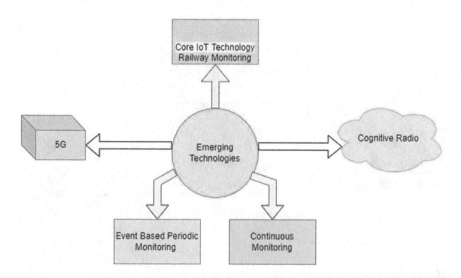

FIGURE 7.5 Emerging technologies for smart 5G system

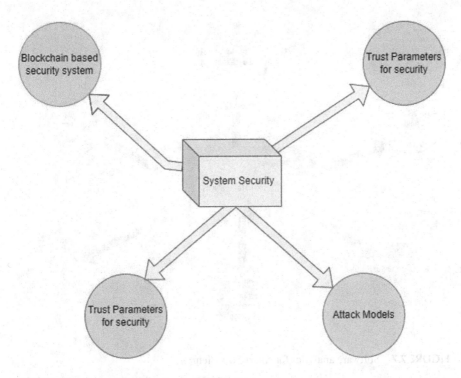

FIGURE 7.6   Security system for smart 5G system

   3. Other security parameter analysis
   4. Attack models

The blockchain-based security method follows a decentralized method for security. This improves the overall security of the system. System security is very important for railway monitoring applications. 5G security methods can be integrated with blockchain methods. To analyze the performance of the system, the 5G network can be analyzed for different attack models. An attack model is necessary to analyze the security of the protocol. The attack model is dependent on the trust parameters. Trust parameters with weight factors can be used to analyze and optimize important factors so that the security of the network can be improved without compromising the performance of the protocol (Figure 7.7).

7.8.4   SOFTWARE ANALYTICS

Efficient software can reduce the complexity of the system, improve its performance, and reduces security risks. For the compatibility of the software, there are six important requirements as follows:

   1. Analysis of applications
   2. Adaptive to emerging technologies

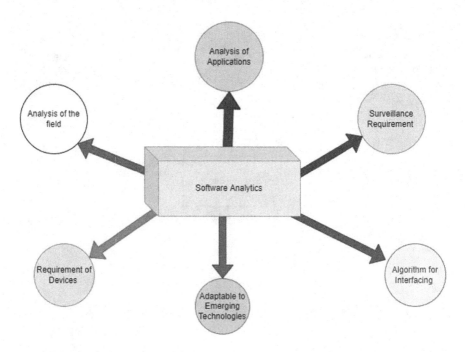

FIGURE 7.7   Software analytics for smart 5G system

3. Surveillance requirements
4. Analysis of the field
5. Algorithm for interfacing
6. Requirement of devices

Requirements for railways can be categorized for different applications. The requirements of the application are important factors in software design and development.
Efficient development of the software depends upon the requirements of the application.
The use of an application also depends on the environment and field. The requirements
of the application should also be adaptive to emerging technologies. Different modules
should also be adaptive to different levels of applications. Therefore, adaptive interfacing
of the software is also required for different interfacing applications. Hardware compatibility is also an important issue when developing software for a particular application.

7.8.5   RESEARCH METHODOLOGY

Research is a continuous process, and many research methods can be used to improve
5G to fulfill the requirements of railway monitoring. Research methods can be used
in two directions as shown in Figure 7.8 and as follows:

1. Data pre-processing
2. Analytical modeling

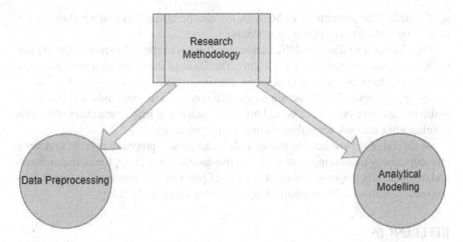

FIGURE 7.8 Research methodology for smart 5G system

For the efficient processing of the sensed data, the data should be processed by standard methods so that the monitoring station can make an informed decision. Efficient data pre-processing reduces prediction errors. A powerful algorithm can be designed with effective prediction methods. Future accidents can be avoided by prediction methods and alert signals. For the analysis of protocol and improvements within existing methods, research should focus on analytical modeling.

Research work has also focused on various channel coding techniques useful for forward error correction in ubiquitous channel models in ultra-high-speed railway networks [48–51].

5G can play a big role in the development of smart cities. The smart city can be developed with the help of smart buildings, smart homes, smart shopping malls, small grids, smart driving, and smart transportation. Most intercity, intra-city, inter-state, and intrastate transportation depend on the railway. Therefore, 5G integration for smart railway systems can improve railway services and avoid chances of accidents occurring. The advancement of IoT and AI can make the pilotless railway system more advanced and efficient. In addition, reinforcement learning and deep learning methods can be integrated, making the railway system more powerful and advanced. Machine-learning methods can enable devices to make decisions.

7.9 CONCLUSION

This chapter discussed the utilization of 5G telecommunication technologies for railway monitoring applications. The chapter also discussed the utilization of 5G services for high-load signaling operations. Monitoring of the field can be done using WSN and IoT methods. Advanced technologies, e.g. cognitive radio and software-defined radio, the software-defined network, can be integrated with WSNs. Software-defined WSN services can be utilized for railway monitoring applications. IoT utilization for 5G telecommunication technology has also been analyzed for railway monitoring applications. The integration of 5G with IoT can be utilized to make railway monitoring applications very powerful systems.

The chapter also discussed the various challenges in the utilization of the 5G network for railway monitoring applications. The focus of the discussion was to address issues for railway controlling operations, consumer data services, and railway monitoring applications. The possibilities of different channel demands and 5G bandwidth ranges have been discussed. This discussion could help researchers efficiently develop a 5G network for railway monitoring applications.

At the end of the chapter, the five-module structure was proposed in order to develop efficient railway monitoring systems. In the five-model architecture, future requirements and research directions are explained in terms of physical infrastructure, emerging technologies, system security, software analytics, and research methodology.

REFERENCES

1. A. Gonzalez-Plaza et al., "5G Communications in High Speed and Metropolitan Railways," 2017 11th European Conference on Antennas and Propagation (EUCAP), 2017, pp. 658–660, doi: 10.23919/EuCAP.2017.7928756.
2. H. B. H. Dutty, M. M. Mowla and M. A. Mou, "A Statistical mmWave Channel Modeling for Railway Communications Backhaul in 5G Networks," 2019 3rd International Conference on Electrical, Computer & Telecommunication Engineering (ICECTE), 2019, pp. 121–124, doi: 10.1109/ICECTE48615.2019.9303579.
3. K. Guan et al., "Towards Realistic High-Speed Train Channels at 5G Millimeter-Wave Band—Part II: Case Study for Paradigm Implementation," in *IEEE Transactions on Vehicular Technology*, vol. 67, no. 10, pp. 9129–9144, Oct. 2018, doi: 10.1109/TVT.2018.2865530.
4. N. Nonaka et al., "28 GHz-Band Experimental Trial at 283 km/h using the Shinkansen for 5G Evolution," 2020 IEEE 91st Vehicular Technology Conference (VTC2020-Spring), 2020, pp. 1–5, doi: 10.1109/VTC2020-Spring48590.2020.9129578.
5. T. Zhou, H. Li, Y. Wang, L. Liu and C. Tao, "Channel Modeling for Future High-Speed Railway Communication Systems: A Survey," in *IEEE Access*, vol. 7, pp. 52818–52826, 2019, doi: 10.1109/ACCESS.2019.2912408.
6. K. Guan et al., "Realistic Channel Characterization for 5G Millimeter-Wave Railway Communications," 2018 IEEE Globecom Workshops (GC Wkshps), 2018, pp. 1–6, doi: 10.1109/GLOCOMW.2018.8644076.
7. D. He, B. Ai, K. Guan, Z. Zhong, L. Tian and J. Dou, "Channel analysis for millimeter-wave railway communications in urban environment," 2017 XXXIInd General Assembly and Scientific Symposium of the International Union of Radio Science (URSI GASS), 2017, pp. 1–4, doi: 10.23919/URSIGASS.2017.8105416.
8. M. A. Mou and M. M. Mowla, "Investigation of Power Delay Profiles for 5G Millimeter Wave Railway Communications," 2019 5th International Conference on Advances in Electrical Engineering (ICAEE), 2019, pp. 763–768, doi: 10.1109/ICAEE48663.2019.8975589.
9. Y. Cui, X. Fang, Y. Fang and M. Xiao, "Optimal Nonuniform Steady mmWave Beamforming for High-Speed Railway," in *IEEE Transactions on Vehicular Technology*, vol. 67, no. 5, pp. 4350–4358, May 2018, doi: 10.1109/TVT.2018.2796621.
10. S. Zelenbaba et al., "Characterization of Time-Variant Wireless Channels in Railway Communication Scenarios," 2019 IEEE 2nd 5G World Forum (5GWF), 2019, pp. 536–541, doi: 10.1109/5GWF.2019.8911706.

11. K. Shafique, B. A. Khawaja, F. Sabir, S. Qazi and M. Mustaqim, "Internet of Things (IoT) for Next-Generation Smart Systems: A Review of Current Challenges, Future Trends and Prospects for Emerging 5G-IoT Scenarios," in *IEEE Access*, vol. 8, pp. 23022–23040, 2020, doi: 10.1109/ACCESS.2020.2970118.

12. E. Ahmed, I. Yaqoob, A. Gani, M. Imran and M. Guizani, "Internet-of-Things-based Smart Environments: State of the Art, Taxonomy, and Open Research Challenges," *IEEE Wireless Commun.*, vol. 23, no. 5, pp. 10–16, Oct. 2016.

13. *Co-OperationWith theWorking Group RFID of the ETP EPOSS, Internet of Things in 2020, Roadmap for the Future*, Version 1.1, INFSO D.4 Networked Enterprise RFID INFSO G.2 Micro Nanosystems, May 2008.

14. *The Internet of Things*, document ITU Internet Reports, Nov. 2005, J. Gubbi, R. Buyya, S. Marusic and M. Palaniswami, "Internet of Things (IoT): A Vision, Architectural Elements, and Future Directions," *Future Gener. Comput. Syst.*, vol. 29, no. 7, pp. 1645–1660, Sep. 2013.

15. K. Sha_que, B. A. Khawaja, M. D. Khurram, S. M. Sibtain, Y. Siddiqui, M. Mustaqim, H. T. Chattha and X. Yang, "Energy Harvesting Using a Low-cost Rectenna for Internet of Things (IoT) Applications," *IEEE Access*, vol. 6, pp. 30932–30941, 2018.

16. Q. Awais, Y. Jin, H. T. Chattha, M. Jamil, H. Qiang and B. A. Khawaja, "A Compact Rectenna System with High Conversion Ef_ciency for Wireless Energy Harvesting," *IEEE Access*, vol. 6, pp. 35857–35866, 2018.

17. B.-M. Pang, H.-S. Shi and Y.-X. Li, "An Energy-ef_cient MAC Protocol for Wireless Sensor Network," in *Future Wireless Networks and Information Systems*, vol. 143, Y. Zhang, Ed. Berlin, Germany: Springer, 2012, pp. 163–170.

18. S. Rani, S. H. Ahmed, R. Talwar, J. Malhotra and H. Song, "IoMT: A Reliable Cross Layer Protocol for Internet of Multimedia Things," *IEEE Internet Things J.*, vol. 4, no. 3, pp. 832–839, Jun. 2017.

19. N. Kushalnagar, G. Montenegro and C. Schumacher, *IPv6 Over Low-Power Wireless Personal Area Networks (6LoWPANs): Overview, Assumptions, Problem Statement, and Goals*, document RFC 4919, RFC Editor, Aug. 2007.

20. C. Perkins, *IP Mobility Support for IPv4*, document IETF RFC 3344, Aug. 2002.

21. A. Nilssen, "Security and Privacy Standardization in Internet of Things," in *Proc. Future Internet Workshop eMatch*, Oslo, Norway, Sep. 2009.

22. M. Feldhofer, S. Dominikus and J.Wolkerstorfer, "Strong Authentication for RFID Systems Using the AES Algorithm," in *Cryptographic Hardwareand Embedded Systems_CHES*, vol. 3156, M. Joye and J.-J. Quisquater, Eds. Berlin, Germany: Springer, 2004, pp. 357–370.

23. B. Calmels, S. Canard, M. Girault and H. Sibert, "Low-cost Cryptography for Privacy in RFID Systems," in *Smart Card Research and Advanced Applications*, vol. 3928, J. Domingo-Ferrer, J. Posegga and D. Schreckling, Eds. Berlin, Germany: Springer, 2006, pp. 237_251.

24. M. Weiser, "The Computer for the 21st Century," *ACM SIGMOBILE Mobile Comput. Commun. Rev.*, vol. 3, no. 3, pp. 3–11, Jul. 1999.

25. P. Kiss, A. Reale, C. J. Ferrari and Z. Istenes, "Deployment of IoT Applications on 5G Edge," in Proc. IEEE Int. Conf. Future IoT Technol. (Future IoT), Eger, Hungary, Jan. 2018, pp. 1–9.

26. R. Arridha, S. Sukaridhoto, D. Pramadihanto and N. Funabiki, "Classification Extension based on IoT-big Data Analytic for Smart Environment Monitoring and Analytic in Real-time System," *Int. J. Space-Based Situated Comput.*, vol. 7, no. 2, p. 82, 2017.

27. H. Uddin, "IoT for 5G/B5G applications in smart homes, smart cities, wearables and connected cars," in Proc. IEEE 24th Int. Workshop Comput. Aided Model. Design Commun. Links Netw. (CAMAD), Limassol, Cyprus, Sep. 2019, pp. 1–5.

28. M. Chen, S. Mao, Y. Zhang and V. C. M. Leung, "Related Technologies," in *Big Data*. Cham, Switzerland: Springer, 2014, pp. 11–18.

29. M. R. Palattella, M. Dohler, A. Grieco, G. Rizzo, J. Torsner, T. Engel and L. Ladid, "Internet of Things in the 5G Era: Enablers, Architecture, and Business Models," *IEEE J. Sel. Areas Commun.*, vol. 34, no. 3, pp. 510–527, Mar. 2016.

30. B. Khalfi, B. Hamdaoui and M. Guizani, "Extracting and Exploiting Inherent Sparsity for Efficient IoT Support in 5G: Challenges and Potential Solutions," *IEEE Wireless Commun.*, vol. 24, no. 5, pp. 68–73, Oct. 2017.

31. P. Annamalai, J. Bapat and D. Das, "Emerging Access Technologies and Open Challenges in 5G IoT: From Physical Layer Perspective," in Proc. IEEE Int. Conf. Adv. Netw. Telecommun. Syst. (ANTS), Indore, India, Dec. 2018, pp. 1–6.

32. J. Skold. (Feb. 2014). Research Trends and IMT Beyond 2020. [Online]. Available: https://www.itu.int/en/ITU-D/Regional-Presence/AsiaPacific/ Documents/

33. A. Al-Fuqaha, M. Guizani, M. Mohammadi, M. Aledhari and M. Ayyash, "Internet of Things: A Survey on Enabling Technologies, Protocols, and Applications," in *IEEE Commun. Surveys Tuts.*, vol. 17, no. 4, pp. 2347–2376, 4th Quart., 2015.

34. M. Song, "In-situ AI: Towards autonomous and incremental deep learning for IoT systems," in Proc. IEEE Int. Symp. High Perform. Comput. Archit. (HPCA), Vienna, Austria, Feb. 2018, pp. 92–103.

35. B. Chatterjee, N. Cao, A. Raychowdhury and S. Sen, "Context-aware Intelligence in Resource-constrained IoT Nodes: Opportunities and Challenges," *IEEE Design Test*, vol. 36, no. 2, pp. 7–40, Apr. 2019.

36. J. Guo, "A Deep Reinforcement Learning Based Mechanism for Cell Outage Compensation in Massive IoT Environments," in *Proceedings of the 15th International Wireless Communication Mobile Comput. Conf. (IWCMC)*, Tangier, Morocco, Jun. 2019, pp. 284–289.

37. X. Zhou, R. Li, T. Chen and H. Zhang, "Network Slicing as a Service: Enabling Enterprises' Own Software-defined Cellular Networks," *IEEE Commun. Mag.*, vol. 54, no. 7, pp. 146–153, Jul. 2016.

38. A. Ijaz et al., "Enabling Massive IoT in 5G and Beyond Systems: PHY Radio Frame Design Considerations," *IEEE Access*, vol. 4, pp. 3322–3339, 2016.

39. M. Wang, J. Chen, E. Aryafar and M. Chiang, "A Survey of Clientcontrolled HetNets for 5G," *IEEE Access*, vol. 5, pp. 2842–2854, 2017. [116] (Jan. 14, 2018). The Tech Wire Asia, 'The Next Generation of IoT'. Available: http://techwireasia.com/2017/08/next-generation-iot/

40. L. Vangelista, A. Zanella and M. Zorzi, "Long-range IoT Technologies: The Dawn of LoRaTM," in *Future Access Enablers for Ubiquitous and Intelligent Infrastructures*, vol. 159, V. Atanasovski and A. Leon-Garcia, Eds. Cham, Switzerland: Springer, 2015, pp. 51–58.

41. M. Tolani, A. Sunny and R. K. Singh, "Energy-efficient Adaptive GTS Allocation Algorithm for IEEE 802.15. 4 MAC Protocol," *Telecommunication Systems*, vol. 76, no. 3, pp. 329–344, 2021.

42. M. Tolani, A. Sunny and R. K. Singh, "A Markov model for IEEE 802.15. 4 MAC protocol with energy-efficient GTS utilization under saturated and unsaturated traffic conditions," *Ad Hoc Networks*, vol. 115, 2021.

43. M. Tolani, A. Sunny and R. K. Singh, "Energy Efficient Beacon-Enabled IEEE 802.15. 4 Guaranteed Time Slot-Based Adaptive Duty Cycle Algorithm for Wireless Sensor Network," *Journal of Circuits, Systems and Computers*, 2021.

44. M. Tolani, A. Sunny and R. K. Singh, "Energy-efficient Hybrid MAC Protocol for Railway Monitoring Sensor Network," *SN Applied Sciences*, vol. 2, no. 8, pp. 1–17, 2020.

45. M. Tolani, A. Sunny and R. K. Singh, "Lifetime Improvement of Wireless Sensor Network by Information Sensitive Aggregation Method for Railway Condition Monitoring," *Ad Hoc Networks*, vol. 87, pp. 128–145, 2019.

46. T. Anagnostopoulos et al., "Challenges and Solutions of Surveillance Systems in IoT-Enabled Smart Campus: A Survey," in *IEEE Access*, vol. 9, pp. 131926–131954, 2021, doi: 10.1109/ACCESS.2021.3114447.

47. M. Tolani, A. Bajpai, Sunny, R. K. Singh, L. Wuttisittikulkij and P. Kovintavewat, "Energy Efficient Hybrid Medium Access Control Protocol for Wireless Sensor Network," 2021 36th International Technical Conference on Circuits/Systems, Computers and Communications (ITC-CSCC), 2021, pp. 1–4, doi: 10.1109/ITC-CSCC52171.2021.9501482.

48. A. Kalsi, A. Bajpai, L. Wuttisittikulkij and P. Kovintaewat, "A Base Matrix Method to Construct Column Weight 3 Quasi-cyclic LDPC Codes with High Girth," 2016 International Conference on Electronics, Information, and Communications (ICEIC), 2016, pp. 1–4, doi: 10.1109/ELINFOCOM.2016.7562999.

49. A. Bajpai and A. Balodi, "Role of 6G Networks: Use Cases and Research Directions," 2020 IEEE Bangalore Humanitarian Technology Conference (B-HTC), 2020, pp. 1–5, doi: 10.1109/B-HTC50970.2020.9298017.

50. A. Bajpai, G. Srirutchataboon, P. Kovintavewat and L. Wuttisittikulkij. "A New Construction Method for Large Girth Quasi-cyclic ldpc Codes with Optimized Lower Bound Using Chinese Remainder Theorem." *Wireless Personal Communications*, vol. 91, no. 1, pp. 369–381, 2016.

51. G. Srirutchataboon, A. Bajpai, L. Wuttisittikulkij and P. Kovintavewat, "PEG-like Algorithm for LDPC Codes," 2014 International Electrical Engineering Congress (iEECON), 2014, pp. 1–4, doi: 10.1109/iEECON.2014.6925956.

8 Implications of Progressive Data Transfer Technologies for IoT-Based Wastewater Management in Smart Cities

Satyam and Payal Mukherjee

CONTENTS

DOI: 10.1201/9781003227861-8

8.1 INTRODUCTION

The breakthroughs in technology in recent years have allowed the evolution of solutions and devices that are helping stakeholders integrate cutting-edge innovations into smart cities. These innovations employ information and communication technologies in green energy, transport, health, waste, and water to ensure the best utility management. Smart cities across the globe aim for real-time monitoring, data collection, and efficient management of resources for sustainable living. One of the significant challenges for smart city developers is providing smart solutions for the purification, distribution, and remediation of water. Only 2–3% of fresh water on the entire planet is consumable, and it is a challenging task for stakeholders to meet the growing demand of a rapidly expanding population. In recent decades, there has been increasing demand for water. Emerging pollution challenges and severe water stress in many parts of the world are at an alarming stage. The fundamental and crucial role played by water in environmental sustainability has increasingly been acknowledged in terms of public perception and government priority in several nations [16].

The internet of things (IoT) can help optimize almost every step of water management, including real-time monitoring/sensing, distribution, and remediation. IoT is a network of connected devices/sensors that can control remote devices or provide valuable data over a network. One of the required dependencies of IoT-connected systems is network connectivity [12]. Conventional wired/fiber network offers lightning-fast data transfer rates but requires regular maintenance and leads to high operating costs. 5G is the fifth generation of mobile networks, succeeding earlier versions 2G, 3G, and 4G. The 5G network can provide significantly higher connection rates than previous networks. 5G networks, like previous cellular networks, rely on a network of cell sites that split their region into sectors and transmit encoded data over radio waves. Every cell unit is linked to a network backbone via a wireless backhaul. 5G data transfer technology uses orthogonal frequency division multiplexing (OFDM) encoding. This digital multi-carrier modulation scheme extends single-subcarrier modulation by using multiple subcarriers within the same single channel. Progressive data transfer technology with low latency and a high data transfer speed like 5G can boost IoT use in water management. A set of connected sensors can monitor vital parameters of water and wastewater in real time. The data gathered from these sensors can be used to optimize the remediation protocols at wastewater treatment plants [18].

Present water network components are constructed on massive, centralized systems with limited management choices. The monitoring systems in conventional water management depend on frequent sampling and analysis of variable water parameters. In the modern world, smart city plans will be critical in determining how cities will use technology to foster social and economic well-being. A sustainable water management technology in smart cities will ensure higher distribution and remediation efficiency through sensors and connected networks. This chapter delineates the role of modern data transfer technologies for IoT-integrated wastewater management in smart cities [1, 14].

8.2   CONVENTIONAL VS. SMART TECHNOLOGIES FOR WATER MANAGEMENT

Wastewater is produced when anthropogenic activities contaminate water. Growing industries across the globe, urban expansion, and intensive agriculture have placed a massive strain on our natural water bodies. Wastewater comprises a range of dissolved organic and inorganic compounds, as well as noxious elements. Discharging wastewater directly into natural water bodies can severely impact the aquatic ecosystem. Wastewater consumed by animals and humans living downstream of a natural water body can have severe irreversible health issues. Contaminated wastewater from industrial and municipal discharge used in the agriculture sector can lead to low yield and groundwater pollution. Hence, it is crucial to access wastewater parameters and treat wastewater before discharging it to natural water bodies. Furthermore, with the rising urbanization and paucity of drinking water, recycling and utilizing waste water for agricultural uses is essential [3].

8.2.1   CONVENTIONAL WASTEWATER MANAGEMENT

Conventional monitoring of natural water bodies is done by manual sampling and lab-based tests. These tests provide information regarding water quality, including the presence or absence of heavy metals, total organic carbon (TOC), biochemical oxygen demand (BOD), chemical oxygen demand (COD), total dissolved solids (TDS), pH, and inorganic and organic load. The distribution of water in conventional mode is done by high-power pumps. Traditional treatment of wastewater (CWWT) protocol relies on manual sampling and lab-based test results. There are four significant steps in CWWT – screening, primary treatment, secondary treatment, and tertiary treatment. Objects with a size greater than 20 mm are removed during the first screening process. In primary treatment, small suspended solid waste is separated from water by sedimentation. In order to clean the water further, the secondary procedure employs a biological process. Oxygen levels are raised, and foul odor is eliminated during tertiary treatment [27]. Figure 8.1 shows the steps in CWWT plants.

In the screening and pre-treatment process, visible insoluble solids are removed from wastewater which can block primary treatment tanks, block pumps, or harm sewage pipes. In the first step of the pre-treatment process, grit, i.e., heavy materials like plastic, sand, gravel, and cloth are removed. Fat and grease from wastewater are then separated using aeration-assisted skimmers. Primary treatment involves holding wastewater in large tanks, leading to the suspended solids settling down and low-weight pollutants floating on the tank. Sludge and floating items are then removed, and the remaining wastewater is then transferred to the next phase. In the secondary treatment phase, the biodegradable components in wastewater are removed using microbial action. This remediation step is carried out by microbes in an aerobic environment or, less frequently, in an anaerobic digester. In secondary treatment, microbes decompose all organic components like food waste, surfactants, fecal waste, sugar, fat, and short-chain organic carbon molecules. The tertiary phase is the last phase of wastewater remediation, which ensures disinfection and removal of

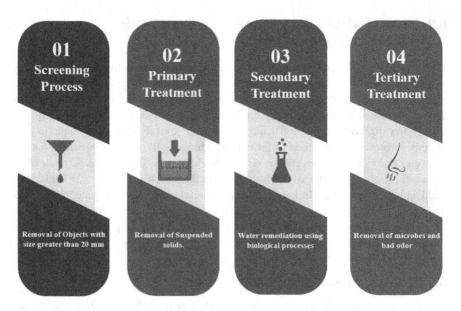

FIGURE 8.1   Steps in conventional wastewater treatment plants

micropollutants before the treated water can be discharged to natural water bodies. Disinfection in the tertiary step can be achieved by ultraviolet (UV) treatment, chlorination, or ozone treatment [30]. UV light disrupts the genetic material of microbes which renders them unable to reproduce. Chlorination kills microbes by disrupting the chemical bonds inside cellular components. Ozone can readily oxidize organic material; thus, it is used for the disinfection process. Nutrients like nitrogen are removed using nitrification (ammonia to nitrate) and denitrification (nitrate to nitrogen gas). Nitrogen gas evolves at the end of the reaction to reduce the nitrogen load of the wastewater. Phosphorus is removed by chemical precipitation method using ferric chloride, alum, or lime [22].

8.2.2   SMART WASTEWATER MANAGEMENT

Present supervisory control and data acquisition (SCDA) in conventional water management has several drawbacks like complicated installation, high operational cost, and high maintenance cost. IoT-integrated intelligent water management solutions provide insight into the demographics and tell us how vital water parameters are affected due to anthropogenic activities. The sensors installed at the point source (municipal and industrial waste discharge point) provide real-time COD, BOD, DO, TOC, TDS, pH, and turbidity-related data. These parameters define water quality and can alert stakeholders to take proper action in due course to formulate correct remediation measures. A set of connected sensors reduces the human effort for collecting data in a fixed interval of time. The water transmission line from the natural water body to the wastewater treatment plant is fully automated in intelligent water management infrastructure. The flow rate, water levels, energy consumption, and other water parameters are constantly monitored throughout the process [5, 10].

Smart wastewater treatment strategies are highly dependent on the real-time acquisition of wastewater parameters, and all the processes and steps are carefully monitored in each stage of treatment. Water level and float sensors limit the intake and outflow of water in each tank. The pumps that facilitate water movement from one tank to another are tightly controlled by monitoring and remediation stations. The entire remediation protocol of IoT-integrated wastewater remediation systems is curated by the software, which can accurately predict the correct formulation for efficiently cleaning wastewater. The dosage pumps that control inoculum volume (in secondary treatment), pH control, aeration, and flow rate can be controlled automatically from the monitoring and execution control room. Automatic dosage pumps and transmission pumps provide an energy-efficient water management experience. Post-processing sensors after tertiary treatment can trace chemicals and leftovers, which can provide feedback for process optimization. IoT technology is a remarkable notion that allows wastewater management systems and operators to communicate reliably. It provides an excellent balance of utility and cost reductions, which boosts total productivity [19]. Furthermore, it is a valuable tool for identifying possible sources of water waste and taking steps to reduce them. Figure 8.2 shows the processes involved in smart water management. IoT technology is an intelligent module that enables a proficient link between systems, sensors, and operators. It combines usability and productivity improvements to increase the overall performance

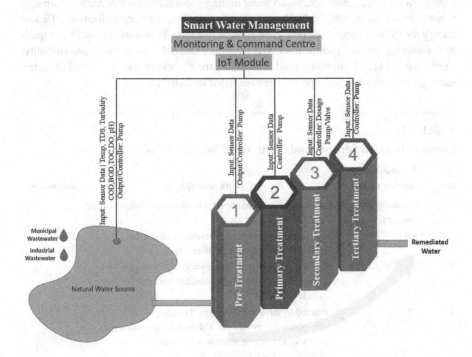

FIGURE 8.2   Processes in the smart water management system

of wastewater management invariably. It is also an excellent tool for detecting possible water wastage/leakage sites and taking steps to decrease water wastage [7]. Some of the perks of using IoT integration in water management are:

- IoT-integrated sensors that can detect multiple sewage discharge points. With smart solutions, we can establish threshold levels and receive real-time notifications when sewage water parameters fluctuate. Real-time monitoring helps keep an eye on wastewater sources and protect the dependent flora and fauna in good time.
- IoT-integrated water management systems can accurately monitor the end product from each remediation step for leftover chemicals/pollutants, which helps formulate a highly accurate remediation protocol customized for each batch.
- A distribution pipe equipped with leakage and pressure gauge prevents water leakage. Using analytics and algorithms, IoT-integrated sensors can sense pressure drops across the distribution network.

8.3 ROLE OF SENSORS AND SINGLE-BOARD COMPUTERS (SBCS) IN THE DEVELOPMENT OF SMART WATER MANAGEMENT INFRASTRUCTURE

Sensors have recognition elements and can produce a quantifiable signal when subjected to a particular interface. Smart water management is highly dependent on sensors. Sensors provide valuable feedback on a distribution line, resource utilization, efficient energy distribution, and water quality in each step of remediation/treatment. Water quality monitoring sensors include dissolved oxygen, TDS, pH, conductivity, and turbidity/clarity sensors [15]. Commonly used sensors and their working principles used for determining standard wastewater parameters are listed in Table 8.1.

TABLE 8.1
Commonly Used Sensors and Their Working Principles

Sl. No.	Standard water quality sensor	Working principle	Reference
1.	Conductivity, salinity, TDS	Potentiometric method using four-electrode setup	[9]
2.	pH	Measurement of potential difference between the reference electrode and pH electrode	
3.	Turbidity/clarity	Detected using measurement of backscattered light by photodetector when a light source illuminates the sample	
4.	DO	Detected by diffusion of oxygen through a semipermeable membrane. Diffused oxygen undergoes a chemical reduction reaction which produces quantifiable electric signals	

The quantifiable signal generated by sensors is generally in digital or analog form. The direct signal from a sensor is a raw signal that is then processed as per calibration data for final output. The bridge between the sensor(s) and the final output is mediated by SBC(s). SBCs have all the essential components present on a computer soldered on a single board. The size of these boards is significantly smaller when compared to a standard desktop or laptop. The emerging integrated circuit technology makes it possible to accommodate multiple transistors in a single chip, which drives an SBC. Portability, cross-platform support, simple programming language, open-source hardware/software, energy-efficient nature, and cost-effective accessories make SBCs user-friendly for both industries and academia. There are numerous SBCs available in the market, such as Raspberry Pi, Arduino, ASUS tinker board, Latte Panda, and Banana Pi, which can be programmed as per the requirements of the end-user. The most commonly used SBCs among these are Arduino and Raspberry Pi [8].

Arduino is an open-source SBC built on customizable software and hardware, allowing anybody to use a common schematic to create a board (SBC) of their choice. The hardware and software components of Arduino are licensed under CC-BY-SA (a type of creative commons license) and a lesser general public license (LGPL), respectively. Most Arduino boards have Atmel 8-bit AVR (Alf and Vegard's reduced instruction set computer processor). Arduino boards have varying amounts of input/output pins and flash memory. These boards can be programmed using a simplified version of the C++ programming language [4, 6].

Raspberry Pi has small SBCs designed by the Raspberry Pi foundation in collaboration with Broadcom. These SBCs have an onboard graphics processing unit (GPU) with an advanced RISC (reduced instruction set computer) machine (ARM)-based central processing unit. The amount of random-access memory (RAM) in Raspberry Pi ranges from 256 megabytes (MB) to 8 Gigabytes (GB) according to the type of model in use. Raspberry Pi supports a wide range of peripherals through input/output ports and has several networking options like Ethernet, Wi-Fi, and Bluetooth [17, 29].

8.4 FACTORS PROMOTING THE IMPLEMENTATION OF SMART TECHNOLOGIES IN WATER MANAGEMENT AND REMEDIATION

The definition of a smart city is focused on a city's capacity to respond to people's demands as soon as reasonably practicable. The basic systems of a smart city, such as transportation, government services, pedagogic institutes, law enforcement, and healthcare, significantly impact the quality of life and city growth. Water is at the heart of public health and safety; it requires a deliberate emphasis to provide clean water for everybody. Smart water technology now provides flexibility and enhanced power throughout the whole water distribution chain, from the natural water bodies to the collection and remediation of effluent. Several issues need to be addressed during the development and implementation of smart water and wastewater systems in smart cities. The strategy needs to be broad and resilient, ready to meet today's specific issues while preparing for tomorrow's demands and eventualities [11, 20]. The factors promoting the implementation of smart technologies in water management and remediation are listed as follows:

- **Optimum resource accessibility and use:** The fair and appropriate distribution of resources such as water and energy would be a fundamental feature of a smart city. This also involves access to proper sanitation and wastewater remediation. Smart cities need to guarantee resource access while sustaining a careful use of environmental assets to safeguard the availability of natural resources for future generations.
- **Perceive future demand:** The world population is growing each day. After one decade, the rate of urbanization will rapidly increase. Urban planning stakeholders must therefore consider future necessities to monitor and manage the use of resources today [25].
- **Smart and sustainable technologies:** Intelligent urban planning also involves implementing sustainable solutions that can enable the city to continue to stay "water-sufficient" throughout the year. Such solutions must be smart and integrated throughout the water monitoring, remediation, and distribution system.
- **Remediation and reuse:** Developing recycling services that promote the recurrent use of resources before their disposal is another significant aspect of smart cities.
- **Responsibility and individual obligations:** Smart cities can drive sustainable water use through sophisticated monitoring systems, and alert individuals to their usage patterns or predefined limitations when their usage exceeds their limits. An alert system can ensure increased responsibility for individuals and inculcates the conscientious use of resources.
- **Energy-efficient nature:** Smart water management solutions include energy-efficient motors, pumps, networking devices, and machines. These devices are strictly monitored for their energy consumption, making the whole smart water management system more energy efficient [24].

8.5   ROLE OF 5G IN SMART WATER MANAGEMENT

The fifth generation of mobile data transfer technology, also known as 5G, can offer speeds up to 599+ megabytes per second (theoretical download speed can range from 10 to 50 gigabytes per second). The latency of the 5G network is estimated to be as low as one millisecond (theoretical estimation), which is drastically lower than its predecessor 4G (50 milliseconds). 5G technology can perform various roles in developing fully automated and sustainable smart cities with low latency, higher data transmission rates, and enhanced reliability. With the rollout of 5G data transmission solutions, services of smart cities like virtual reality, 4K streaming, home automation, industrial automation, surveillance, automated vehicle, automation in the logistic sector, and efficient energy distribution system have leaped ahead [18, 23].

In the water management sector, 5G will aid in the development of autonomous framework operations, remote surveillance of water management infrastructures, accessing water/wastewater quality data remotely, monitoring processes, and process optimization using artificial intelligence. In innovative autonomous framework operations, the 5G data transfer technique with numerous IoT modules will send the live feed from sensors. 5G technology can connect and transmit digital data from millions of connected devices. 5G data transmission requires less power than its predecessor, which enhances the sustainability of mobile IoT modules. The security of water management infrastructures can also be ensured with the help of motion detection and night vision cameras. The data gathered from various water parameter sensors are logged into software that can accurately enhance water quality. Dosage pump regulation and inoculum formulation in a secondary water treatment plant can be efficiently managed using artificial intelligence-based algorithms. 5G and automation will reduce anomalies based on human behavior and error. Apart from a few limitations of 5G technology, there are immense possibilities for sustainable development using high-speed data transfer technologies [2].

8.6 LIMITATIONS AND FUTURE PERSPECTIVES

Connectivity with IoT is progressively evolving. In progression with a smart solution, there are often many ethical, technical, and operational challenges. Some of these challenges include the compatibility of sensors with IoT modules, data breaches, and network reliability and speed. One of the prime reasons for the popularity of smart solutions is their cost-effectiveness. The sensors developed for SBCs and IoT modules must be compatible with sensors developed by third-party companies. Compatibility reduces the expense of any fault in the sensor installed at a natural water source or treatment plant. Any anomaly in the production of patented technology operational only with selected sensors can significantly impact the market and increase operating costs [13, 21, 26].

Apart from the government, many private firms are also investing in the field of smart water management. Therefore, processed data from sensors, actionable insight data, and reagents/inoculum formulation data must be protected. Any unencrypted data transmission can lead to data breaches, which can impact the intellectual property rights of the stakeholders. The whole concept of a smart city is highly dependent on the network. The network can be of wired or wireless type. Wired/fiber optic data communication is fast, has low latency, and provides consistent results but requires high investment and maintenance costs. Conversely, wireless data transmission technology requires less maintenance and can be accessed from a remote location [28].

Despite many challenges, smart water management technology is the only way to provide a sustainable solution to global wastewater challenges. The compatibility issues of IoT modules and sensors can be overcome by using an open-source license to develop software and hardware-compatible third-party sensors. End-to-end encryption technologies can protect intellectual property-related digital data transmitted over a network. Research and development in data transfer technology can help penetrate 5G over a large area and provide low latency and high data transfer rates.

8.7 CONCLUSION

Technology is a boon in today's world. It has made resource management much more accessible and efficient, provided implemented accurately. Because water is an essential part of all life, it is critical that strategies to protect this vital resource are developed. Our community's water distribution system is a well-designed blueprint bequeathed from our forefathers during the dawn of human civilization and has progressed due to technological advancements. Water distribution and management systems continue to be hampered by leakage or contamination of water pipelines, inefficient distribution due to shortage of energy and resources, and mainly due to high treatment costs. To address these constraints, a new water management strategy that allows for real-time monitoring is desired. The technology of IoT combinedly operated through 5G networks can be a viable solution in near-future innovative city establishments. Smart cities, when strategically planned, can achieve tangible economic, social, and urban development outcomes. Smart city strategies are critical in determining how cities will use technology to promote innovation networks, healthy societies, and dynamic economies. They also aim to address a wide range of rapid urbanization and sustainability issues. This is established by addressing concerns such as natural resource use, allowing for healthy living. Although visionary, the strategies represent genuine and meaningful urban development policies that include significant investments and long-term consequences. Therefore, in terms of policy design and implementation, it is critical to study them methodically and cohesively for sustainable water resource management.

IoT technology has immense potential to provide necessary data during real-time monitoring strategies for water management because the data can be transferred at the fastest possible rate with 5G speed, assisting in improving human living standards and upgrading the environment. Sensors and gateways already used for small-scale systems have immense potential to be upscaled for better living in the future. Through further research and development, the depletion of non-renewable resources can be prevented for better global survival through the use of IoT. Apart from connecting millions of devices simultaneously, 5G can improve sensor quality and lifetime. This will not only reduce the overall cost of sensory networks but also exhibit improved security protocols against cybercrimes. Rapid data transfer and alerts through 5G networks can expedite decision-making during emergencies. Operators of critical infrastructure will be able to use network slicing to construct their own network infrastructure. Governments must also assign enough wireless spectrum to fulfill the requirements of new technologies and set relevant standards for which frequencies will carry 5G communications to pave the path for the adoption of 5G.

Consequently, an increasing number of technology vendors and consultants are vying for a spot on the market for smart city services. There are various ways that IoT may be utilized to alter city development provided different cities accept the technology. The prediction of patterns of utilization of valuable resources can be tracked and managed to maintain equality and sustainability. Water utilization per individual can be conserved through 5G-based IoT water management tactics. Processing wastewater and making it fit for consumption is one of the effective methods of reusing water. Water utilities could leverage IoT-enabled sensors and communication gateways to improve wastewater management and treatment in the future, promoting water distribution and consumption. Citizens should be made aware of the benefits of adopting technology and know where they are wasting more water with actionable intelligence.

According to technology and business experts, 5G can transform production and, over time, increase efficiency simultaneously. Specific engineering issues must be addressed before 5G will be known as an all-conquering cure, including spectrum allocation, security concerns, upscaling limitations, and edge analytics. Industry must better understand the data types being transferred, their sensitivity to propagation delay, and whether the data must be processed independently or in comparison to past data. The data obtained will show whether a firm needs to deploy a smart manufacturing solution based on 5G topologies or whether alternative protocols are more suited to the specific solution.

ACKNOWLEDGMENTS

Satyam and Payal Mukherjee acknowledge the Department of Biosciences and Bioengineering, Indian Institute of Technology, Guwahati and MHRD.

CONFLICT OF INTEREST

The authors declare that there is no conflict of interest.

REFERENCES

1. Angelidou, M. (2015). Smart cities: A conjuncture of four forces. *Cities*, *47*, 95–106. https://doi.org/10.1016/J.CITIES.2015.05.004
2. Boursianis, A. D., Papadopoulou, M. S., Damantoulakis, P., Karampatea, A., Doanis, P., Geourgoulas, D., Skoufa, A., Valavanis, D., Apostolidis, C., Babas, D. G., Baltzis, K. B., Kaifas, T. N., Siozios, K., Siskos, S., Samaras, T., Siakavara, K., Nikolaidis, S., Goudos, S. K., Liopa-Tsakalidi, A., ... Maliatsos, K. (2019). Advancing rational exploitation of water irrigation using 5G-IoT capabilities: The AREThOU5A project. In 2019 IEEE 29th International Symposium on Power and Timing Modeling, Optimization and Simulation, PATMOS 2019, 127–132. https://doi.org/10.1109/PATMOS.2019.8862146
3. Crini, G., & Lichtfouse, E. (2018). Advantages and disadvantages of techniques used for wastewater treatment. *Environmental Chemistry Letters*, *17*(1), 145–155. https://doi.org/10.1007/S10311-018-0785-9
4. D'Ausilio, A. (2011). Arduino: A low-cost multipurpose lab equipment. *Behavior Research Methods*, *44*(2), 305–313. https://doi.org/10.3758/S13428-011-0163-Z
5. Dong, J., Wang, G., Yan, H., Xu, J., & Zhang, X. (2015). A survey of smart water quality monitoring system. *Environmental Science and Pollution Research*, *22*(7), 4893–4906. https://doi.org/10.1007/S11356-014-4026-X

6. Evans, B. (2011). *Beginning Arduino Programming* (D. Shakeshaft (ed.); Vol. 6). Springer.

7. Farah, E., & Shahrour, I. (2017). Leakage detection using smart water system: Combination of water balance and automated minimum night flow. *Water Resources Management, 31*(15), 4821–4833. https://doi.org/10.1007/S11269-017-1780-9

8. Ferdoush, S., & Li, X. (2014). Wireless sensor network system design using raspberry Pi and Arduino for environmental monitoring applications. *Procedia Computer Science, 34*, 103–110. https://doi.org/10.1016/J.PROCS.2014.07.059

9. Gangar, T., Satyam, K., & Patra, S. (2021). Monitoring/sensing techniques to address pollutant heterogeneity assessment in wastewater. *Microbial Ecology of Wastewater Treatment Plants*, 279–314. https://doi.org/10.1016/B978-0-12-822503-5.00014-X

10. Goel, D., Chaudhury, S., & Ghosh, H. (2017). Smart water management: An ontology-driven context-aware IoT application. *Lecture Notes in Computer Science (Including Subseries Lecture Notes in Artificial Intelligence and Lecture Notes in Bioinformatics), 10597 LNCS*, 639–646. https://doi.org/10.1007/978-3-319-69900-4_81

11. Hartley, K., & Kuecker, G. (2020). The moral hazards of smart water management. *45*(6), 693–701. https://doi.org/10.1080/02508060.2020.1805579

12. Jan, F., Min-Allah, N., & Düştegör, D. (2021). Iot based smart water quality monitoring: Recent techniques, trends and challenges for domestic applications. *Water, 13*(13). https://doi.org/10.3390/W13131729

13. Kumar, S. A., Vealey, T., & Srivastava, H. (2016). Security in internet of things: Challenges, solutions and future directions. *Proceedings of the Annual Hawaii International Conference on System Sciences, 2016-March*, 5772–5781. https://doi.org/10.1109/HICSS.2016.714

14. Lee, S. W., Sarp, S., Jeon, D. J., & Kim, J. H. (2014). Smart water grid: The future water management platform. *Desalination and Water Treatment, 55*(2), 339–346. https://doi.org/10.1080/19443994.2014.917887

15. Manjare, S. A., Vhanalakar, S. A., & Muley, D. V. (2010). Analysis of water quality using physicochemical parameters Tamdalge tank in Kolhapur district, Maharashtra. *International Journal of Advanced Biotechnology and Research, 1*(2), 115–119.

16. Mohammed Shahanas, K., & Bagavathi Sivakumar, P. (2016). Framework for a smart water management system in the context of smart city initiatives in India. *Procedia Computer Science, 92*, 142–147. https://doi.org/10.1016/J.PROCS.2016.07.337

17. Molano, J. I. R., Betancourt, D., & Gómez, G. (2015). Internet of things: A prototype architecture using a raspberry Pi. In International Conference on Knowledge Management in Organizations, 618–631.

18. O'Connell, E., Moore, D., & Newe, T. (2020). Challenges associated with implementing 5G in manufacturing. *Telecom 2020, 1*(1), 48–67. https://doi.org/10.3390/TELECOM1010005

19. Perera, C., Zaslavsky, A., Christen, P., & Georgakopoulos, D. (2014). Sensing as a service model for smart cities supported by Internet of Things. *Transactions on Emerging Telecommunications Technologies, 25*(1), 81–93. https://doi.org/10.1002/ETT.2704

20. Radhakrishnan, V., & Wu, W. (2019). IoT technology for smart water system. In Proceedings - 20th International Conference on High Performance Computing and Communications, 16th International Conference on Smart City and 4th International Conference on Data Science and Systems, HPCC/SmartCity/DSS 2018, 1491–1496. https://doi.org/10.1109/HPCC/SMARTCITY/DSS.2018.00246

21. Radoglou Grammatikis, P. I., Sarigiannidis, P. G., & Moscholios, I. D. (2019). Securing the Internet of Things: Challenges, threats and solutions. *Internet of Things, 5*, 41–70. https://doi.org/10.1016/J.IOT.2018.11.003

22. Sangave, P. C., Gogate, P. R., & Pandit, A. B. (2007). Combination of ozonation with conventional aerobic oxidation for distillery wastewater treatment. *Chemosphere*, *68*(1), 32–41. https://doi.org/10.1016/J.CHEMOSPHERE.2006.12.053

23. Shafi, M., Molisch, A. F., Smith, P. J., Haustein, T., Zhu, P., De Silva, P., Tufvesson, F., Benjebbour, A., & Wunder, G. (2017). 5G: A tutorial overview of standards, trials, challenges, deployment, and practice. *IEEE Journal on Selected Areas in Communications*, *35*(6), 1201–1221. https://doi.org/10.1109/JSAC.2017.2692307

24. Soares, R. B., Memelli, M. S., Roque, R. P., & Gonçalves, R. F. (2017). Comparative analysis of the energy consumption of different wastewater treatment plants. *International Journal of Architecture, Arts and Applications*, *3*(6), 79–86.

25. Soboll, A., Elbers, M., Barthel, R., Schmude, J., Ernst, A., & Ziller, R. (2010). Integrated regional modelling and scenario development to evaluate future water demand under global change conditions. *Mitigation and Adaptation Strategies for Global Change* *16*(4), 477–498. https://doi.org/10.1007/S11027-010-9274-6

26. Tang, S., Shelden, D. R., Eastman, C. M., Pishdad-Bozorgi, P., & Gao, X. (2019). A review of building information modeling (BIM) and the internet of things (IoT) devices integration: Present status and future trends. *Automation in Construction*, *101*, 127–139. https://doi.org/10.1016/J.AUTCON.2019.01.020

27. Vakula, D., & Kolli, Y. K. (2018). Waste water management for smart cities. Proceedings of the International Conference on Intelligent Sustainable Systems, ICISS 2017, 275–279. https://doi.org/10.1109/ISS1.2017.8389414

28. Wang, W. (2020). Data analysis of intellectual property policy system based on Internet of Things. *14*(9–10), 1475–1493. https://doi.org/10.1080/17517575.2020.1712744

29. Zhao, C. W., Jegatheesan, J., & Loon, S. C. (2015). Exploring iot application using raspberry pi. *International Journal of Computer Networks and Applications*, *2*(1), 27–34.

30. Zinicovscaia, I. (2016). Conventional methods of wastewater treatment. *Cyanobacteria for Bioremediation of Wastewaters*, 17–25. https://doi.org/10.1007/978-3-319-26751 -7_3

9 Smart Grid Design with Hybrid Renewable Energy Management Systems for Smart Cities

S. Pravinth Raja, B. Vidhya Banu, and R. Sapna

CONTENTS

9.1 INTRODUCTION

Smart city development systems focus on energy demand reduction, health, education, road infrastructures, and various schemes for improvement. Energy demand in today's world is increasing day by day. An energy management system reduces this demand by utilizing various renewable energy resources such as solar, wind, fuel cells, and battery storage systems. The energy management system is conducted on a grid-connected system for supplying to various distributors. The distribution generation system is based on blockchain technology. Blockchain technology improves the result of the grid system by managing various power sources and customers. The energy system is mainly used in applications of industrial, domestic, and commercial areas. Demand response management approaches use various algorithms, design models, and technologies. Recently, increased efforts have been made to use blockchain and its mix in different application spaces. Blockchain is an advanced appropriated record, which is updated and refreshed by a decentralized system working using general conventions. Assembly of innovations dealing with the arrangements, information, agreement, personality, and computerization of the board is fundamental for the effective creation and execution of blockchain technology for smart city applications. The more advancement in the various structured

DOI: 10.1201/9781003227861-9

applications in the blockchain, the more value we can obtain [1]. By connecting various innovations, the smart city could then start to mechanize fundamental city processes. For instance, IoT sensors could, in a split second, sense an issue and caution the suitable city office's artificial intelligence (AI) to dispatch a specialist. The AI may enable the expert to evaluate the problem using augmented reality (AR) glasses, send layouts for parts to the 3D printer in the specialist's truck, pay the supplier the part through a smart financial agreement, guide the person using the AR glasses, and finally informing the city organization and landowner when the repair has been done. Envision a city having computerized records of every home, where all information about the home is contained, such as property ownership details, home loan repayment details, and additional information such as energy use, property charge evaluation, and past and current contractual worker connections [2]. The city could access these and could perform regulatory undertakings identified with the property more productively and precisely, which would be beneficial. The homeowner would have a confirmed, dependable method of performing activities such as the leasing of a room, recruiting contract workers to do garden work, or selling power produced by solar panels to the matrix [3]. For large urban communities, steps should be taken to consolidate innovations and progress urban planning, where the current energy and transportation within a neighborhood should be considered. The innovations could lead to new systems of urban planning being implemented. Since the necessities and prerequisites of every city are diverse, it is up to urban planners to characterize the best and most innovative arrangement for their area. It is here that blockchain can be of use, as it can undoubtedly provide connections between fundamental innovations [4].

Blockchain is an advanced record of monetary exchanges that can be customized to record money-related exchanges as well as other items of significant value. A framework, where exchanges made in bitcoin or other digital currencies are recorded, is maintained using a number of PCs that are connected in a shared system [5]. The utilization of blockchain in fully functioning frameworks is a subject of great interest in research, particularly because the further improvement of these frameworks by the use of new and imaginative developments would be very beneficial. The energy management system for smart city applications is depicted in Figure 9.1.

Blockchain, because of its specific characteristics, can allow various smart energy applications. One use is where energy prosumers can exchange surplus energy with their neighbors [6]. With blockchain, there is no need for an intermediary because information recorded on the blockchain is confirmed by a disseminated system of hubs. Mechanization can be accomplished through PC programs known as smart contracts, which are saved on the blockchain, and are reliable, secure, and beneficial [7]. A purchaser of energy can check the sustainable power source of the prosumer using blockchain. These models indicate the general idea of blockchain and its utilization in smart energy frameworks. However, current blockchain arrangements to connect these applications are not clear. Blockchain innovation is quite recent, and even though it has great potential, the quantity and execution of blockchain arrangements are still being discussed. How blockchain can be used

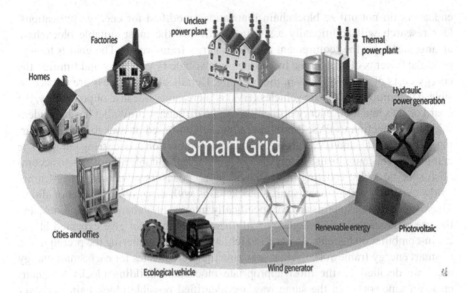

FIGURE 9.1   Energy management system for smart city applications

to satisfy the necessities of various smart energy applications isn't clear. In this chapter, we survey blockchain-building algorithms and show how blockchain can assist with the requirements of different smart energy frameworks. For instance, blockchain can be classified as public, private, or consortium. Additionally, information can be on-chain (all information is kept on the blockchain) and off-chain (just information hashes are kept on the blockchain) [8]. A mix of how blockchain is executed is possible, with different benefits and possibilities. Smart energy systems can use grids of blockchain for activities of energy distribution, green activities, and energy management. In our research, we discovered that blockchain is not very suitable for smart energy frameworks. Blockchain is a decentralized, advanced, and large system that has a variety of applications. Exchanges that move or trade currencies or computerized resources, for example, data, administration, or products, are created and gathered by a system of processing hubs [9]. A time-interval algorithm (containing these exchanges) is created by a decentralized contract between the hubs as indicated by pre-defined conventions. The recently made algorithm additionally contains a reference to the algorithm that preceded it (parent block) as a cryptographic hash, consequently setting up a connection between the algorithms [10].

9.2   MATERIALS AND METHODS

Connections between blockchain and smart energy frameworks could be useful. Please note that in this chapter, we will not give a complete overview of blockchain incorporation in smart energy frameworks. We will simply present specific stages and activities in each smart energy area to show that a large proportion of these endeavors do not utilize blockchain innovations modified for energy applications. Our research will additionally assist in identifying the most suitable blockchain arrangements for the requirement of smart energy frameworks. The goal is to augment the benefits of each home by selling photovoltaic (PV) energy and limiting the energy costs of shared offices in the building. Details of this process are not accessible. The number of electric vehicles (EVs) is increasing. Because of portability, the board of EVs and their energy utilization can be difficult. CareWallet has been identified in connection to EVs. It provides a blockchain-based answer for vehicle sharing, vehicle rental, and EV charging. Blockchain innovation is occurring but it can be complicated because its use in any area requires using suitable algorithms to accomplish specific tasks. Existing mixed blockchain endeavors in smart energy frameworks generally utilize open-source blockchains with programmed functionalities. These types of blockchains are not specifically intended for energy applications, and the use of blockchain-based energy with these types may not give expected blockchain-combination benefits. In our research, we began by gathering the prerequisites of smart energy frameworks. After itemizing the prerequisites for each smart energy area, we decided on the most appropriate blockchain-building blocks for smart energy frameworks. In the same way, we identified possible blockchain improvements that could meet these prerequisites. We further tweaked blockchain uses for different smart energy applications in the smart infrastructure (SI), energy trading (ET), green initiatives (GI), and energy management (EM). This research could help in the development of adaptable types of blockchains reconfigured for smart energy frameworks and procuring further benefits for using blockchain in combination with smart energy frameworks. A sustainable power source is an important area where we can utilize the blockchain-based framework. It can help improve the development of different evaluation models to minimize energy use. Such models can advance individual self-sufficiency with regard to reliance on energy. It can likewise help in dealing with energy demand and evaluation requirements. Additionally, records of energy utilization and charging can be produced and stored. Residents can use resources sustainably, monitor how much energy is required daily, and sell the remaining energy back to the grid. In a distributed energy system, microgrids work freely from an incorporated grid. However, microgrids are restricted in the number of activities they can manage, and blockchain systems are progressively becoming more significant for overseeing exchanges inside the microgrid. For instance, LO3 Energy, a New York-based company, has collaborated in the development of the Brooklyn Microgrid, which is empowered by blockchain innovation to oversee inward energy exchanges.

9.2.1 System Design

The electrical management system for smart city applications is performed by adopting solar and wind modules. Incorporating solar and wind turbines gives continuous supply to the consumer that is controlled by using various approaches and algorithms. Wind turbines are utilized to remove power from a wind stream to create mechanical or electrical force. This innovation was developed in a wide

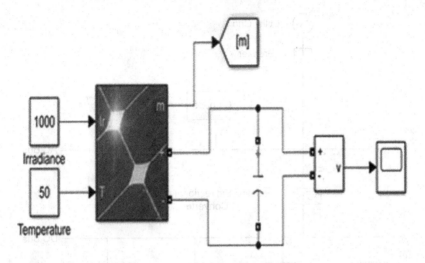

FIGURE 9.2 A basic PV module power generation unit

assortment of sizes, creating a reasonable amount of useable energy. However, it can be costly because of the possibility of the turbine stopping operation in certain weather. Therefore, wind turbines would perform better if connected to other energy sources. Here the power generation system with a grid-connected system performed effectively for energy distribution [11–13]. The basic model of the PV generation system is given in Figure 9.2.

A description of smart city energy-related components and possible uses as well as the possibilities of connecting energy management systems has been discussed. It should be noted that a system demonstrating these connections has not been found thus far in the literature. Frameworks could be custom-made to incorporate various innovations to access various energy markets. To the best of the authors' knowledge, such a smart city energy model has not been developed yet, and it could be left up to analysts, speculators, and strategy creators to examine smart city plans, plans of action, and strategies. This has been a concern to numerous scientists in the field. To our knowledge, there has been no research in this area. With regard to distributed energy resources (DER) framework development, the greater part of the available research looks at assessing value, and some research looked at value producers. The energy management of smart cities has just been concerned with current activities. Subsequently, a proposed value-producer model contributed to the research on this topic, providing a significant examination of the changes in value delivered by DER frameworks. Up until this point, scientists have focused on DER frameworks, for example regarding EVs (however principally demonstrating their use in connection to batteries). Other significant energy frameworks have been disregarded. Another study included metro frameworks other than the EVs and DER, and it was indicated that such a plan could be truly beneficial to all included frameworks, and it presented energy cooperatives that do not play a part when frameworks are overseen autonomously (Figure 9.3) [14–17].

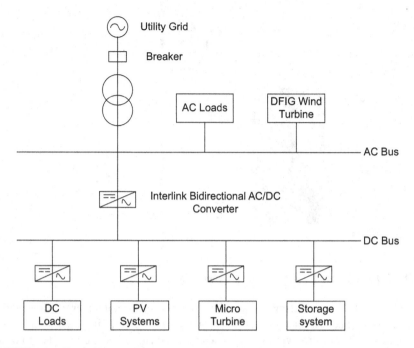

FIGURE 9.3   Single line diagram for grid-connected PV and wind for AC load

In the future smart city, new data and communication innovations will empower a superior administration of accessible assets. Smart grid foundations are developing as intricate frameworks where detailed observation and control of energy creation to identify possible energy-wasting elements inside the arrangement is conceivable. This will result in better methodologies that will help energy productivity. To make this vision a reality, (public) blockchains giving access to smart meter information along with necessary administrative functions and ways to assess value are required [18, 19]. These will offer essential energy benefits that can be regularly utilized by energy engineers. Maximum power could be obtained from the renewable energy system with various sources connected, using maximum power point tracking (MPPT). By changing the values of irradiance and temperature, the PV module can be used for the grid. The solar module generates power mainly during the daytime. It also can access nighttime power from wind generators. Various controlling and switching activities are performed to improve the grid system by reducing demand. The grid-connected system uses traffic lights, streetlights, and energy management systems for household and office demands. A smart city is a maintainable and effective urban system that gives a high standard of living to residents through the superior administration of urban assets [20]. Energy management is one of the most demanding issues within the urban environment, attributable to the intricacy of the energy frameworks and their essential job. Hence, consideration and effort should be given to this issue. Specific instruments are normally used to evaluate the innovative and strategical effects of smart arrangements, and to design the most ideal methods of moving from the current setup in urban communities to smarter ones. This chapter provides details of the arrangement, activity, and management of the smart grid inside the smart city by characterizing five primary areas: age, stockpiling, framework, offices, and transport. Further innovative urban energy models that coordinate with more than one of the above areas are additionally inspected, and an overview of their specifications, restrictions, existing patterns and difficulties, and some significant applications is provided.

9.2.2 ENERGY MANAGEMENT SYSTEM IN SMART CITY APPLICATIONS

It is clear from the overview provided in this chapter that an overall urban energy management framework is an intricate undertaking. Some parts in each of the various stages are significant. This section provides a few rules for the satisfactory demonstration of such a framework and depicts the components that ought to be considered. In the consideration of arrangements and activity, numerous methodologies can be utilized, for example, expository, iterative, and hybrid techniques. With regard to parameters and asset accessibility, performance boundaries (for example electric productivity, warm effectiveness, power ratings, and errors) and accessibility of the asset when necessary (for example with EV and distributed generator (DG) activity). Considering system costs, all the relevant costs to financially assess the possibility of such frameworks (for example cost per introduced kW, activity, and upkeep costs) should be calculated. Geolocation attributes include characteristics of the sources of data (for example solar power, wind speed, and precipitation). The area of energy costs covers energy expenses for similar purposes (for example retail energy taxes, fuel expenses, and value-added tax). Regulatory requirements refer to every obligation and potential outcome for the ideal area. Energy requests are an attribute of the ideal system. The possibilities of energy management in smart city applications are smart meters, charging systems, street lighting, smart parking, smart buildings, smart grid distribution systems, and EVs [21–23].

9.2.3 TECHNIQUES AND POSSIBILITIES

There are various possibilities for smart city applications, such as streetlights, battery charging, EV charging, etc. Smart lighting in streets is one of the application-based framework ideas that could perceivably influence the quality of life in smart urban areas. The first stage of assessing smart lighting is to guarantee appropriate light inside the city while saving energy. This new smart light innovation upgraded with sensor systems will measure light levels on streets and turn the lights off as necessary. The limitless possibilities of sustainable power, such as solar and wind, have led to another idea known as the "hybrid system", where customers are additionally energy makers. With this approach, power can be sold back to the grid if excess energy is produced. Consequently, the use of sustainable power sources and the assessment of energy use become important. This will shape microgrids, which can be portrayed as limited grids that can interface and detach from the main grid if "islanding" should be necessary. Smart city applications can have a small-scale grid known as islanding, which is when power supplies come from an external power source in the city, such as a DG, when connection to the main grid is not possible. The administrators of microgrids can create a new plan of action with the conveyance framework administrator who is accountable for serving continuous power. Improved and novel approaches would be helpful for a better energy management system. Here the smart grid circuit uses AI, optimization, and various control process (switch) [24–26].

9.3 DISCUSSION

Because of its size and population, India has great potential for experimentation and improvement in the smart energy sector. We are able to provide data on which kind of energy is least expensive at a particular point in time by estimating and investigating various sources of energy, such as wind, solar, and battery power. This offers great potential for households to begin to use more powerful types of energy management systems. Smart energy systems have been already implemented in India, but there needs to be approved information sources and control of access during investigations, which would be achievable. Outsourcing information will not help and advise neighborhoods and local governments; more control would be given to residents themselves if information was available locally. Through investigation of the information available, we can improve the administration and roll out genuine improvements to local residents. Thus, an ideal energy management system in a complex framework like a smart city, not exclusively its energy components, should be identified and contemplated, and the connections within this system should also be considered. Moreover, experimentation would be useful to improve existing and new frameworks. In smart urban areas, appropriate energy data from different urban administrations can influence households' energy use to improve urban ecological sustainability. The reason for smart urban areas is that with improved access to data on energy use, households can properly manage energy use, thereby bringing about improved management of the city. As per social learning and social psychological speculations, the management of smart cities is emphatically focused on energy preservation [27, 28].

9.4 CONCLUSION

Energy management systems for smart city applications have the possibility to reduce the demand and improve applications. The utilization of renewable energy is a basis for smart structures and smart urban communities. Advances like smart metering, smart lighting, smart grids, energy internet, renewability, portability, net metering, LED, energy management systems, insulation, daytime lighting, and smart frameworks are significant innovations being utilized to accomplish smart building design. The Simulink design model is mostly utilized on microgrid circuits, which is helpful to smart city application models; here the hybrid energy system uses integrates solar and wind modules, and continuous supply can meet demand. Control strategies such as the pulse generation model, PI controller, and fuzzy logic are used for this kind of approach. Input data like irradiance, temperature, wind speed, and pitch angles are used in the renewable energy system. In this way, the maximum power is stored and utilized on the demand grid circuits. This chapter has discussed using an energy management system so demand is continuously met. The hybrid system improves performance and reduces demand. This chapter has shown that various control strategies and better energy supply can be improved, and the smart grid system used in energy management systems has been effectively analyzed and discussed.

REFERENCES

1. Karale, S., & Ranaware, V. (2019). Applications of blockchain technology in smart city development: A research. *International Journal of Innovative Technology and Exploring Engineering, 8,* 556–559..
2. Li, S. (2018, August). Application of blockchain technology in smart city infrastructure. In 2018 IEEE International Conference on Smart Internet of Things (SmartIoT) (pp. 276–2766). IEEE.
3. Chang, S. E., & Chang, C. Y. (2018, July). Application of blockchain technology to smart city service: A case of ridesharing. In 2018 IEEE International Conference on Internet of Things (iThings) and IEEE Green Computing and Communications (GreenCom) and IEEE Cyber, Physical and Social Computing (CPSCom) and IEEE Smart Data (SmartData) (pp. 664–671). IEEE.
4. Biswas, K., & Muthukkumarasamy, V. (2016, December). Securing smart cities using blockchain technology. In 2016 IEEE 18th International Conference on High Performance Computing and Communications; IEEE 14th International Conference on Smart City; IEEE 2nd International Conference on Data Science and Systems (HPCC/SmartCity/DSS) (pp. 1392–1393). IEEE.
5. Hassan, N. U., Yuen, C., & Niyato, D. (2019). Blockchain technologies for smart energy systems: Fundamentals, challenges, and solutions. *IEEE Industrial Electronics Magazine, 13*(4), 106–118.
6. Mika, B., & Goudz, A. (2021). Blockchain-technology in the energy industry: Blockchain as a driver of the energy revolution? With focus on the situation in Germany. *Energy Systems, 12,* 285–355.
7. Livingston, D., Sivaram, V., et al. (2018). *Applying Blockchain Technology to Electric Power Systems.*
8. Andoni, M., Robu, V., et al. (2019). Blockchain technology in the energy sector: A systematic review of challenges and opportunities. *Renewable and Sustainable Energy Reviews, 100,* 143–174.
9. Palop, J. J., Mucke, L., & Roberson, E. D. (2010). Quantifying biomarkers of cognitive dysfunction and neuronal network hyperexcitability in mouse models of Alzheimer's disease: Depletion of calcium-dependent proteins and inhibitory hippocampal remodeling. In *Alzheimer's Disease and Frontotemporal Dementia* (pp. 245–262). Humana Press, Totowa, NJ.
10. Calvillo, C. F., Sánchez-Miralles, A., & Villar, J. (2016). Energy management and planning in smart cities. *Renewable and Sustainable Energy Reviews, 55,* 273–287.
11. Sampathkumar, A., Murugan, S., et al. (2020). Advanced energy management system for smart city application using the IoT. *Internet of Things in Smart Technologies for Sustainable Urban Development,* Book Series, EAISICC, 185–194, Springer, ISBN 978-3-030-34328-6 . https://doi.org/10.1007/978-3-030-34328-6_12
12. Navidi, A., & Al-Sadat Khatami, F. (2017). Energy management and planning in smart cities, *CIRED – Open Access Proceedings Journal, 1*(10), 2723–2725.

13. Mahapatra, C., Moharana, A. K., & Leung, V. (2017). Energy management in smart cities based on internet of things: Peak demand reduction and energy savings. *Sensors*, *17*(12), 2812.

14. Rahiman, R., Yenneti, K., & Panda, A. (2019). Making Indian Cities Energy Smart. TERI-UNSW Policy Brief, The Energy and Resources Institute.

15. Francisco, A., Mohammadi, N., & Taylor, J. E. (2020). Smart city digital twin–enabled energy management: Toward real-time urban building energy benchmarking. *Journal of Management in Engineering*, *36*(2), 04019045.

16. Karunakaran, K., Shanmugasundaram, N., & Pradeep-Kumar, S. (2018). Analysis of smart energy supply to smart city. *International Journal of Pure and Applied Mathematics*, *118*, 757–762.

17. Pokhrel, A., Katta, V., & Colomo-Palacios, R. (2020, June). Digital twin for cyber-security incident prediction: A multivocal literature review. In Proceedings of the IEEE/ACM 42nd International Conference on Software Engineering Workshops (pp. 671–678).

18. Song, H., Srinivasan, R., Sookoor, T., & Jeschke, S. (2017). *Smart Cities: Foundations, Principles, and Applications*. John Wiley & Sons.

19. Ioannis, A., Prashant, A, et al. (2020). *Securing Smart Cities, Modeling and Design of Secure Internet of Things –Wiley*. IEEE Press, 185–215.

20. Atasoy, T., Akınç, H. E., & Erçin, Ö. (2015, November). An analysis on smart grid applications and grid integration of renewable energy systems in smart cities. In 2015 International Conference on Renewable Energy Research and Applications (ICRERA) (pp. 547–550). IEEE.

21. Şerban, A. C., & Lytras, M. D. (2020). Artificial intelligence for smart renewable energy sector in europe: Smart energy infrastructures for next generation smart cities. *IEEE Access*, *8*, 77364–77377.

22. Prasad, R. (2020, April). Energy efficient smart street lighting system in Nagpur smart city using IoT: A case study. In 2020 Fifth International Conference on Fog and Mobile Edge Computing (FMEC) (pp. 100–103). IEEE.

23. Patel, S., & RY, U. K. (2016, July). Role of smart meters in smart city development in India. In 2016 IEEE 1st International Conference on Power Electronics, Intelligent Control and Energy Systems (ICPEICES) (pp. 1–5). IEEE.

24. Ghosh, S. (2018, March). Smart homes: Architectural and engineering design imperatives for smart city building codes. In 2018 Technologies for Smart-City Energy Security and Power (ICSESP) (pp. 1–4). IEEE.

25. Bhutta, F. M. (2017, November). Application of smart energy technologies in building sector: Future prospects. In 2017 International Conference on Energy Conservation and Efficiency (ICECE) (pp. 7–10). IEEE.

26. Mehdi, L., Ouallou, Y., Mohamed, O., & Hayar, A. (2018, June). New Smart Home's energy management system design and implementation for frugal smart cities. In 2018 International Conference on Selected Topics in Mobile and Wireless Networking (MoWNeT) (pp. 149–153). IEEE.

27. Akshatha, Y. and Raja, S.P. (2021). Certain Investigations on Different Mathematical Models in Machine Learning and Artificial Intelligence. In *Simulation and Analysis of Mathematical Methods in Real-Time Engineering Applications* (eds T.A. Kumar, E.G. Julie, Y.H. Robinson and S.M. Jaisakthi). https://doi.org/10.1002/9781119785521.ch127

28. Sumbul Alam, Pravinth Raja, Yonis Gulzar, "Investigation of Machine Learning Methods for Early Prediction of Neurodevelopmental Disorders in Children", Wireless Communications and Mobile Computing, vol. 2022, Article ID 5766386, 12 pages, 2022. https://doi.org/10.1155/2022/5766386

10 MIMO-NOMA With mmWave Transmission

Sunita Khichar, Pruk Sasithong, Htain Lynn Aung,
Abhishek Sharma, Sushank Chaudhary, Wiroonsak
Santipach, and Lunchakorn Wuttisittikulkij

CONTENTS

10.1 INTRODUCTION

Internet of things (IoT) and internet of everything (IoE) technologies have been widely deployed and implemented. In addition, mobile users will soon reach up to 13.1 billion users. To support these increasing demands, the ability to provide a massive number of connections becomes essential. Multiple-access technologies have been developed to serve enormous numbers of devices/users efficiently and flexibly for given wireless radio resources. Multiple-access technologies can be divided into two types: non-orthogonal and orthogonal. Orthogonal multiple-access (OMA) schemes have been employed in the current and the past generation of wireless technology: frequency division multiple access (FDMA) in the first generation (1G) cellular network, time division multiple access (TDMA) in 2G, code division multiple access (CDMA), in 3G, and orthogonal frequency division multiple access (OFDM) in 4G and 5G. These orthogonal schemes allocate users with orthogonal frequency/time/code resources to avoid interference with relatively low configuration complexity.

However, orthogonal transmission has limitations to the number of users/ demands and low spectral efficiency. In contrast to OMA, non-orthogonal multiple access (NOMA) allocates more than one user to the same resource block and, thus, can serve more users. But interference is introduced. Therefore, the transmitter and receiver in NOMA need to be redesigned to manage multiplexing and interference, and are more complex. By scheduling multiple user equipment (UE) in the same radio resources, NOMA achieves massive connectivity and high spectral and energy efficiency [1]. NOMA has gained much attention recently and is a candidate for transmission techniques beyond the 5G network.

By using the non-orthogonal mode, NOMA allows the user to interfere with other user (interference allowed between the users who are sharing same resources) for a certain limit, leading to the benefit that users can use all resources at the same time. To deal with interference due to non-orthogonality, different transmitting and receiving techniques are instigated. In Section 10.2, the different types of NOMA will be discussed: power domain NOMA and code domain NOMA. Power domain NOMA users are differentiated on the basis of their power allocation, but in the code domain, users are allocated a different code. Code domain NOMA can be further divided into different types: low-density spread (LDS), sparse code multiple access (SCMA), pattern division multiple access (PDMA), and interleave division multiple access (IDMA).

The research shows that NOMA is the most promising technique for high spectrum sharing, more user handling, better efficiency, and high mobility, and NOMA is also compatible with other techniques like multi-input multi-output (MIMO) and mmWave (millimeter-wave). The mmWave-NOMA is considered the future of communication generations (6G). The mmWave-NOMA reduces the requirement of channel state information of each user to the base station. It allows denser user connection in a small area. The different kinds of beamforming techniques affect the performance of MIMO, NOMA, and mmWave-NOMA. MIMO supports the delay and sum, null steering, and beamforming using reference signals. At the same time, hybrid beamforming is preferable with mmWave to gain the benefit of both analog and digital beamforming.

In the sixth generation (6G) wireless network, there are demanding key requirements such as having at least one terabit per second peak data rate, 0.01 to 0.1 milliseconds air interface latency for users, 10 times larger connectivity density than 5G, 5–10 times higher spectral efficiency, 10–100 times energy efficiency, and 99.99999% higher reliability [2]. A multiple-access scheme that can provide a large number of connections is crucial in the smart city of the future, which requires measured data from sensors deployed in buildings, streets, public areas, drainage systems, and utility systems. Since NOMA is able to serve more users with limited orthogonal resources, it has an important role in 6G and smart cities [3].

10.2 TYPES OF NOMA

NOMA can support a higher number of users than OMA by allocating multiple users in a radio resource block. As a result, NOMA can lead to interference for all users sharing the same resource block, and a more complex receiver is required to decode the intended message. Compared to OMA, NOMA's advantages are higher cell-edge throughput, improved spectral efficiency, low transmission latency with lower signaling costs, massive connectivity, and relaxed channel feedback [3]. The need for channel state feedback will be minimized in the RCF. This is because in the RCF the received signal strength is required instead of exact channel state information. Channel state information (CSI) is only needed for power allocation. There are two main categories of existing NOMA, which are the power domain and code domain. Power domain (PD) NOMA streamlines the principle of concurrent power allocation to multiple users based on channel gain. When the channel gain increases, the user's allocated power level decreases. Thus, cell-center users will be allocated higher transmission power than cell-edge users. For the transmission of information, messages for cell-center and cell-edge users with different power allocations can be multiplexed onto the same time-frequency-code resource [4]. At the receiver, demultiplexing of the signal is achieved by exploiting the difference of power level allocated at the transmission side using multi-user detection (MUD) algorithms like successive interference cancelation (SIC) [5]. Code domain (CD) NOMA allocates different code assignments to multiple users for concurrent information transmission. This section gives an overview of power domain and code domain NOMA.

10.2.1 POWER DOMAIN

Power domain NOMA (PD-NOMA) recognizes users based on different power levels. The main reason behind this technique is to serve the same or all resources (time, frequency, code). Power domain multiplexing is performed in PD-NOMA. Signals are allocated by different power levels from different users and superimposed at the transmitter, and by using the same subcarrier, the ensuing signal is transmitted. The transmission and reception are done by superposition coding (SC) and SIC respectively. There are two basic requirements users for power allocation: one is fairness, and another is quality of service (QoS).

The user compared and paired together on the basis of channel correlation matrix. The user with bad channel gain is allocated high power, and low power is assigned to the user with good channel gain. Similarly, for the second requirement (QoS), the need for QoS defines the power allocation pattern or level. To meet the desired QoS, power allocation is adapted.

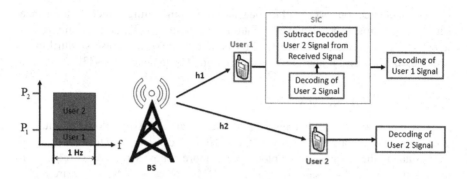

FIGURE 10.1(A)   Power domain NOMA in downlink

SIC is employed at reception to perform MUD and message decoding successively from each user. The main point is that the information from other users is considered interference and treated accordingly.

As mentioned previously, PD-NOMA allocates different power levels to multiple users based on their channel strength. Figures 10.1(a) and (b) show the uplink and downlink of a PD-NOMA cellular network consisting of a base station with two users for transmitting information between them. For downlink NOMA, x_1 and x_2 refer to the transmitted symbols for User 1 and 2 from the base station, respectively. Then the base station outputs a coded signal expressed as [6]

$$s = \sqrt{P_1}x_1 + \sqrt{P_2}x_2 \tag{1}$$

where $P_i, i = 1, 2$ is the transmitted power for User i with the total power $P = P_1 + P_2$. For User i, the received signal is

$$y_i = h_i s + n_i \tag{2}$$

where h_i is the channel gain between User i and the base station, and n_i is the added white Gaussian noise and may account for interference from other cells.

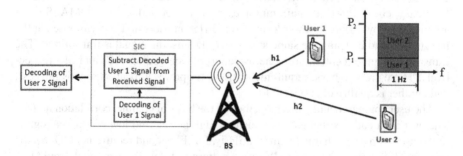

FIGURE 10.1(B)   Power domain NOMA in uplink

In order to distinguish the signals transmitted from the two users, SIC is applied at User 1's receiver. User 2's message is decoded first, as User 2 is allocated with higher power. The receiver then uses the message and reconstructs the signal for User 2 and subtracts that from the received signal. If the decoding of User 2's message is correct, only User 1's message is left (with noise) after the cancelation. Then, User 1's message can be decoded. The order of SIC follows the decreasing order of the power of the user channels. By using this order, interference from other users can be eliminated, and signals can be easily separated. This operation of SIC ordering is carried out by the base station, which depends on the user feedback of CSI. The base station provides updated SIC ordering information to users. At User 2, SIC is not required since the base station allocates higher power to User 2, and, thus, it can decode its own message and regard User 1's signal as additional noise. To achieve the increase in the signal-to-interference-plus-noise ratio (SINR), the user having weak channel strength must be allocated higher power than the users having strong channel strength. As shown in Figure 10.1, User 1 has higher signal strength than User 2. Therefore, the power allocation of User 2 must be higher than User 1. In this case, only User 1 needs to perform the SIC operation. The signal of User 2 is decoded first (x_2) and is deducted from the received signal by User 1, denoted by y_1. Then x_1 can be decoded. For User 2, the signal of User 1 (x_1) can be regarded as additional noise. The receiver for User 2 can directly decode its own signal y_2 without SIC.

Thus, for User i with a transmission bandwidth of 1 Hz, the achievable data rate is given by

$$R_1^{DL} = \log_2\left(1 + \frac{P_1|h_1|^2}{N_{f,1}}\right) \tag{3}$$

$$R_2^{DL} = \log_2\left(1 + \frac{P_2|h_2|^2}{P_1|h_2|^2 + N_{f,2}}\right) \tag{4}$$

where $N_{f,i}$ is the noise power for User i. The sum rate is given by $R^{DL} = R_1^{DL} + R_2^{DL}$.

Figure 10.2 shows the NOMA uplink where User 1 and User 2 are sending the signal simultaneously toward the base station. At the base station, the received signal is

$$y = \sum_{i=1}^{2} \sqrt{P_i} h_i x_i + n \tag{5}$$

where n is Gaussian noise with power spectral density N_f. In this scenario, User 1 is again assumed to have strong channel strength compared to User 2. User 1 and User 2 transmit the superimposed signal toward the base station (BS), which will perform SIC to differentiate the signals. By treating User 2's signal as noise, BS decodes User 1's signal. After that, the signal of User 1 (x_1) will be deducted from the received signal (y). Then, the signal of User 2 (x_2) will be decoded from the remaining signal.

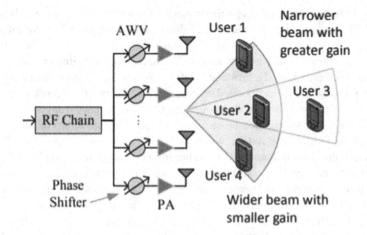

FIGURE 10.2 mmWave-NOMA with analog beamforming

Thus, for uplink, User 2 interferes with User 1, but User 1 does not interfere with User 2. User i's achievable data rate is given by:

$$R_1{}^{UL} = \log_2\left(1 + \frac{P_1|h_1|^2}{P_2|h_2|^2 + N_f}\right) \tag{6}$$

$$R_2{}^{UL} = \log_2\left(1 + \frac{P_2|h_2|^2}{N_f}\right) \tag{7}$$

and the sum achievable data rate is given by $R_1{}^{UL} + R_2{}^{UL}$.

10.2.2 CODE DOMAIN

The idea of code domain (CD) NOMA originates from CDMA in which users can utilize unique code sequences while sharing the same frequency-time resource. However, code domain NOMA is different from CDMA with the use of cross-correlation sequences that are of low density and are non-orthogonal. Low-density spreading CDMA (LDS-CDMA) is one of the basic forms of the CD-NOMA technique. CD-NOMA utilizes unique spreading sequences for users which are sparse counterparts of the spreading sequences used in CDMA. Only a fraction of sparse sequences is filled with non-zero entities [7]. These LDS sequences utilized in LDS-CDMA NOMA schemes can significantly increase system performance compared to traditional CDMA. LDS-OFDM is another example of CD-NOMA and utilizes OFDM and LDS-CDMA [8]. In this technique, each user has a signature sequence that is known by the receiver; this means signature sequences are fully transparent. The LDS scheme spreads the data of each user over a small number of chips, but in CDMA, the non-zero N chip arrangement depends on auto/cross-correlation. After finishing the zero padding, the interleaving of chips is the last step before transmission. The optimal message-passing algorithm (MPA) detection is used at the receiver for detection. The number of interferers should be smaller than the total users per chip.

In the LDS-OFDM code domain NOMA scheme, spreading sequences are first assigned to original data streams and then transmitted to various subcarriers similar to OFDM. LDS-OFDM code domain NOMA also has the same advantage as OFDM, such as a reduction in inter-symbol interference with lower complexity. The basic characteristics of both LDS-CDMA and LDS-OFDM are almost identical. The mapping of subcarriers can be done in the subcarriers. At the receiver, a low complex-based MPA algorithm is used for detection. LDS-OFDM is more appropriate for wideband communication because of the multicarrier transmission. The frequency diversity in LDS-OFDM helps to achieve overloading. It provides high user capacity and also reduces Inter Symbol Interference (ISI).

Researchers also use SCMA, which is one of the existing code domain NOMA schemes. SCMA looks like a better version of LDS-CDMA. SCMA is developed by a sparse sequence structure inherited from LDS [9]. SCMA looks like a better version of LDS-CDMA. SCMA is developed by a sparse sequence structure inherited from LDS. The output from quadrature amplitude modulation (QAM) is combined with the spreading sequence. The resultant output is a SCMA codebook set which is mapped from incoming bits. In SCMA, bits from a predefined multidimensional codebook can be mapped to multidimensional code words directly. MPA algorithm detection is proposed for SCMA, but it is an impractical solution due to being extremely complex with respect to the codebook size. The other possible detectors are the expectation propagation algorithm (EPA) detector and the SIC-MPA detector.

SCMA performs better than the LDS-CDMA code domain NOMA scheme by reducing receiver side complexity.

10.3 NOMA WITH MULTIPLE-ANTENNA TRANSMISSION

Multiple antennas at the transmitter and/or the receiver result in a MIMO channel in which reliability and achievable rate can be increased without increasing transmission power and bandwidth. In this section, we consider NOMA in which the base station has more than one transmit/receive antennas; and UE may have single or multiple transmit/receive antennas. We will focus on the downlink channel and communication system. There are many aspects to consider as follows.

10.3.1 DOWNLINK CHANNEL

Downlink channel for NOMA has been investigated in various aspects such as user pairing, power allocation, and reducing implementation complexity. In Islam et al. [10], a survey was conducted regarding resource allocation, specifically user pairing and power allocation, for downlink NOMA. User pairing or device pairing can achieve high capacity gain with the knowledge of the user's channel gain. On the other hand, power allocation can achieve fairness for the user and a balanced system throughput by allocating power judiciously among weak and strong users.

10.3.2 USER PAIRING

Generally, pairing users with different channel quality such as cell-center and cell-edge users is desirable. Examples of pairing methods in single-input single-output (SISO) NOMA are random pairing, next-largest-difference-based, and next-best diversity [10]. In random pairing, users are chosen randomly by the BS to form a group (more than two users) or pair (two users). Since random pairing is simple and not complex, the sum-rate gain obtained is not significant. For the next-largest-difference-based pairing, the strongest user and the weakest user are formed as a group, and then the user after the strongest user is paired with the second-weakest user. The pairing is iterated until all users are paired. This method is the most common and can give the best performance gain. The pairing method known as the next-best-diversity pairing is used in cognitive radio (CR)-inspired NOMA. For this method, the first and the second strongest users are paired, and then the third strongest with the fourth strongest are paired. This process repeats until all pairs are obtained. In this way, the next-best-diversity pairing assures the QoS of weak users while serving the strong user. In Islam et al. [10], a hybrid approach was proposed to determine whether there were enough strong users to be paired with weak users. The remaining weak users left from the pairing will be in OMA mode instead of NOMA. The complexity of the user-pairing algorithm in NOMA should be low to reduce hardware complexity. An efficient user pairing can produce a better sum-rate gain for MIMO-NOMA.

10.3.3 POWER ALLOCATION

The most important role in NOMA is played by power allocation due to multiplexing users in the power domain. Power allocation takes into consideration the availability of CSI, channel condition of users, power constraints, QoS, and other performance metrics. Since power allocation has a direct effect on rate distribution, rate management, and user admission, improper power allocation can lead to unfairness among users and system interruption. The effectiveness of power allocation can be measured by the number of simultaneously served users, sum rate, fairness among users, total power usage, and outage of the system. Early work for power allocation in NOMA leads to user unfairness and fewer served users because the water-filling approach is applied, resulting in all the powers allocated to users in the best channel condition. To overcome unfairness to users and increase system throughput, the user with a poor channel is given more power than the one with a strong channel. The strong user will perform SIC to deal with the interference of the weaker user. However, the other user, who is a weak user, has higher transmission power and will forego SIC and decode the intended message directly.

10.3.4 mmWave Transmission

With the abundance of very large bandwidth, the mmWave band 3–300 GHz is utilized for current generations of mobile technology and will also be used in future generations. The challenge is large path loss and signal blockage due to large objects. However, the small wavelength in the millimeter range allows a huge number of antenna arrays with a huge number of antennas, which produce high beamforming (BF) gain. This BF gain keeps the balance between the increased path loss and satisfactory performance. NOMA in a mmWave range can accommodate hundreds of user connections in a small area with a high data rate.

Beamforming on a transmission side with a large number of antennas can achieve high-quality communication links by realigning the antennas to focus the power in the desired direction. Beamforming techniques can be classified into analog, digital, or hybrid. Hybrid beamforming is favorable for mmWave-NOMA. Application of NOMA in mmWave transmission improves beam gain and increases coverage and, hence, improves system capacity [11]. The downside is complex hardware with high costs.

10.4 TRANSMISSION BEAMFORMING

Beamforming can achieve a high data rate and reduce path loss. There are digital and analog beamforming techniques. Digital BF is a signal processing approach in baseband (BB). Each radio-frequency (RF) chain drives an independent antenna and can transmit multiple bitstreams simultaneously. Digital BF is more flexible and can give high performance with an increase in complexity and cost. It requires a large number of analog-to-digital converters (ADC), digital-to-analog converters (DAC), power amplifiers, and mixers [11]. The other BF technique is analog BF, which consists of a phase shift network with less complex beam steering. Only single-stream transmission is possible with analog BF. Analog BF can generate high BF gain, but it is less flexible than digital BF. Analog BF can be implemented with more efficient transceiver hardware.

Hybrid beamforming is a combination of both analog and digital beamforming and can improve performance with a cost-effective approach. Joint optimization over a transmit precoding at differently configured sub-arrays can be performed for hybrid BF. By applying Spatial Division Multiple Access (SDMA), it is possible to transmit multi-streams with hybrid BF. It is shown that hybrid BF provides higher spectral efficiency than digital BF [12].

10.4.1 mmWave Analog Beamforming

Due to hardware constraints, each RF chain in the transmitter can only form a single beam. For NOMA to serve multiple users in a single slot, the beam must be wide enough to include all users who are served in that time slot. The relative angle between these users affects beam width and can reduce beam gain. Beam gain and width are roughly inversely proportional to each other. The reduction in beam gain can reduce the performance of NOMA. To understand the relationship between beam width and beam gain, we consider a mmWave-NOMA system with four users in Figure 10.2. The system needs to serve two users at a time. When the system is serving User 2 and User 3, the relative angle between them is small. Therefore, the BS can generate a beam small in width but high in gain. On the other hand, when the system is serving User 1 and User 4, the relative angle between them is large. BS needs large beam width, which reduces beam gain. This can cause the performance to suffer.

10.4.2 HYBRID BEAMFORMING IN MMWAVE

mmWave will be a very important technique for future networks. Effective beam-forming is very important to significantly reduce path loss. By using a small number of RF chains, hybrid beamforming reduces the cost of hardware and power consumption. The concept of hybrid beamforming was proposed in the 2000s. The most important factor is to improve system performance considering hardware constraints. These hardware constraints are as follows: limited RF chain and high dimensional phase shifter-based analog beamformer.

There are two kinds of mapping strategies for hybrid beamforming: fully connected and partially connected. For fully connected hybrid beamforming mapping, all RF chains and antennas are connected, or all antennas are connected to every RF chain. However, partially connected structures have different mapping strategies. There are antenna subsystems that are connected to the RF chain which do not overlap each other. In the case of hardware implementation, the classical single-phase shifter (SPS) implementation takes this into account. The SPS will work as a link between the RF chain and antenna pair. There is a very important role of the analog network in hybrid beamforming. All users and subcarriers share the analog network. Therefore, the channel state of users should match single analog beamforming on different subcarriers.

As per a performance comparison of both fully and partially connected structures, we found that fully connected provides better spectral efficiency, but partially connected structures are cost-effective. Fully connected structures also suffers from computational complexity and hardware complexity.

10.4.3 MULTI-BEAMFORMING

To resolve the problem of a single beam, BS is proposed to generate multiple narrow beams with a single RF chain to cover multiple NOMA users simultaneously. To generate multi-BF, there is a predefined number of antennas to create sub-arrays from the array of antennas in the RF chain, and each sub-array will steer in a different direction. Each sub-array will generate a beam with a different beam gain to generate multiple BF. There are some techniques that use optimal solutions to find the optimal antenna-weight vector (AWV) in a desired direction or optimal phases of beam gains, since, for mmWave, the dimension of AWV is very large and it is also limited by strict constraints like constant modulus and beam gain. According

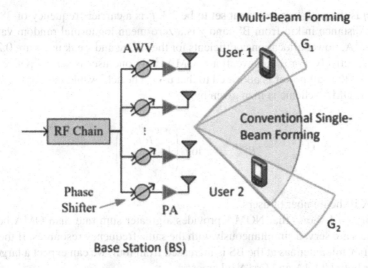

FIGURE 10.3   Single and multi-beamforming comparison

to these criteria, there are a few methods to generate multi-BF, such as the sub-array technique, optimization technique, and intelligent search technique.

In Figure 10.3, a BS in the same time slot serves User 1 and User 2 with two narrow beams. Due to narrow-range coverage, the beam gain can be high. If the relative angle between users is increased in this case, the beam gain will not be reduced. Different users will experience different beam gains: G_1 for User 1 and G_2 for User 2. Beam gain for User i depends on the AWV denoted by w and steering vector $a(\phi_i)$ in the desired direction ϕ_i and is given by

$$G_i = \left| w^H a(\phi_i) \right|. \tag{8}$$

These two factors in the beam gain provide extra degrees of freedom for beamforming in mmWave-NOMA in addition to power allocation. To generate multi-BF, there are a few methods that can be used, such as sub-array, optimization, and intelligent search [13].

10.5   SIMULATION RESULTS

In this section, some numerical results are presented to compare the performance of OMA and NOMA for a two-user system. We obtain the individual user rate and the sum rate from the simulation with increasing signal-to-noise ratio (SNR) from −10 to 30 dB, assuming the distance of strong and weak users from BS is 20 and 50 meters, respectively. Path loss in dB in mmWave transmission is modeled as follows [14]

$$PL = 32.4 + 10\eta \log(f_c) + 20\log(d) + \chi. \tag{9}$$

where η is the path loss exponent set to be 3.3, f_c is a carrier frequency of 28 GHz, d is the distance in km from BS, and χ is a zero-mean lognormal random variable. For NOMA, power allocation coefficients for the strong and weak users are 0.25 and 0.75, respectively. For the conventional OMA, only one user is served per resource block, and thus all power is allocated to that user. The achievable rate for the kth user under the OMA scheme is then given by

$$R_k^{OMA} = \frac{1}{K} \log_2 \left(1 + \frac{P|h_k|^2}{N_f} \right) \tag{10}$$

where K is the number of users.

Figure 10.4 shows that NOMA provides a greater sum rate than OMA because both users are served simultaneously with the same frequency resources. If the number of transmit antennas at the BS is increased from four, we can expect a larger rate gain for both NOMA and OMA schemes.

In Figure 10.5, we examine the rate of each user and note that the rate for the weak user in NOMA saturates when SNR is larger than 10 dB. The rate saturation for the weaker user is due to interference since SIC is not applied. The rate of the weaker user can be increased by optimizing power allocation instead of fixing the power coefficients at 0.25 and 0.75. The rate saturation does not occur with OMA since there is no interference between the two users. However, the sum rate of the two users in NOMA is larger than that in OMA.

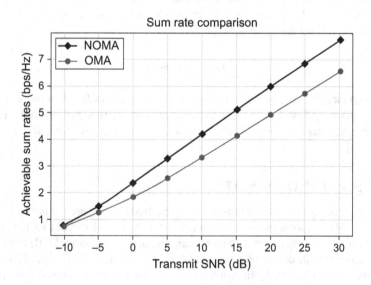

FIGURE 10.4 Sum rate for downlink NOMA and OMA with four-antenna BS and two single-antenna users

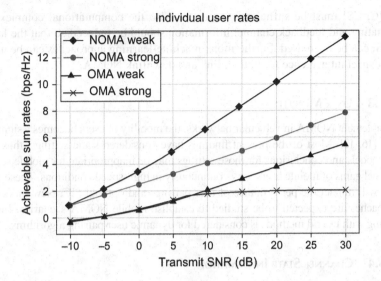

FIGURE 10.5 Comparison of the achievable rate for the stronger and weaker users in NOMA and OMA schemes

10.6 DEPLOYMENT AND PRACTICAL ISSUES FOR SMART CITY

Although NOMA is a promising multiple-access strategy for 6G and has smart applications, there are still a few challenges to be addressed. The critical issues that must be addressed are highlighted in the following section.

10.6.1 APPLICATION OF PAIRING GREATER THAN THREE USERS

One of the theoretically proven key benefits of NOMA is its ability to accommodate several users in an individual resource block. However, most reported studies believe that a three-user, at most, pairing scheme is achievable in practice. This constraint is to ensure effective successive interference cancelation (SIC) at the receivers. As the demand for connected devices increases, particularly for machine-to-machine (M2M) and massive machine-type communication (mMTC) in addition to the IoT , new multi-user pairing methods need to be developed to provide these comprehensive diverse networks with their imminent wireless network needs [15, 16].

10.6.2 SUCCESSIVE INTERFERENCE CANCELATION (SIC)

Nearly all the investigation of NOMA is conducted with a notion of perfect SIC [16, 17]. Users with distinct channel gains are grouped to share a resource block and distinguished by different power allocations. An optimal decoding order must be applied for SIC to decode the intended message. If CSI is not correct or delayed, SIC will not be perfect and there will be residual interference. As a result, the performance of the stronger user will suffer. To improve the efficiency and accuracy of SIC, CSI must be sufficiently accurate. Also the computational complexity of estimating and feedback channel information should be reduced so that the latency of CSI can be decreased. Furthermore, machine-learning approaches can be used to help cancel interference for both uplink and downlink NOMA.

10.6.3 USER MOBILITY

To implement NOMA in vehicular networks, the mobility of users becomes a significant issue [16, 18]. Most of the present findings have considered static settings, thus available models and conclusions for those settings may be inappropriate for mobile settings. Channel gains of mobile users vary continuously in high-speed conditions. These conditions will impact the performance of user pairings and optimal SIC. New models and approaches are expected to be studied to establish mobile NOMA scenarios. Instance caching with hybrid methods is considered for dynamic user-pairing algorithms.

10.6.4 CHANNEL STATE INFORMATION

CSI is required for user grouping, optimal SIC order, and detection at the receivers [, 16, 19, 20]. Most research work has assumed perfect CSI. The assumptions of limited feedback channels or high mobility in some settings may not be pragmatic. In Mamat and Santipach [22], the effect of limited CSI on the performance of NOMA was studied. Optimal feedback-rate allocation was also proposed to maintain the max-min fairness among users in a cell. More recently, learning methods are applied to estimate and relay CSI.

10.6.5 MULTIPLE-CELL NOMA

There are a limited number of studies on multiple-cell NOMA, which is deployed in smart cities [16, 21]. In multiple cells, there exists inter-cell interference (ICI) that further reduces user performance. However, ICI as well as inter- and intra-group interference can be tackled by small-cell or coordinated multipoint (CoMP) schemes. CoMP improves spectral efficiency and cell-edge performance. CoMP has adopted different transmission schemes, such as zero-forcing coherent joint transmission, non-coherent joint transmission, and coordinated scheduling.

10.7 CONCLUSION

We have introduced NOMA and its implementation with MIMO and mmWave by providing some basics, the technical background, and the limitations. We have also discussed transmit beamforming in multiple-antenna settings and some implementation issues. User pairing based on channel strength has been discussed. via simulation results, NOMA is shown to have a larger sum rate than OMA. Some implementation issues for NOMA and its deployment have been discussed. Future work that solves these issues will make NOMA a strong candidate for next-generation wireless communication.

REFERENCES

1. Liu , Y., et al. "Evolution of NOMA toward next generation multiple access (NGMA) for 6G." *IEEE Journal on Selected Areas in Communications* 40 (4): 1037-1071. 2022.
2. Zhang, Zhengquan, et al. "6G wireless networks: Vision, requirements, architecture, and key technologies." *IEEE Vehicular Technology Magazine* 14.3: 28-41. 2019.
3. Dai, Linglong, et al. "A survey of non-orthogonal multiple access for 5G." *IEEE communications surveys & tutorials* 20.3: 2294-2323. 2018.
4. S. R. Islam, N. Avazov, O. A. Dobre, and K.-S. Kwak, "Power-domain non-orthogonal multiple access (NOMA) in 5G systems: Potentials and challenges," *IEEE Communications Surveys & Tutorials*, vol. 19, pp. 721–742, 2016.
5. M. Mohammadkarimi, M. A. Raza, and O. A. Dobre, "Signature-based nonorthogonal massive multiple access for future wireless networks: Uplink massive connectivity for machine-type communications, " *IEEE Vehicular Technology Magazine*, vol. 13, pp. 40–50, 2018.
6. S. R. Islam, M. Zeng, O. A. Dobre, and K. S. Kwak, "Nonorthogonal multiple access (NOMA): How it meets 5G and beyond," *Wiley 5G Ref: The Essential 5G Reference Online*, pp. 1–28, 2019.
7. R. Hoshyar, F. P. Wathan, and R. Tafazolli, "Novel low-density signature for synchronous CDMA systems over AWGN channel," *IEEE Transactions on Signal Processing*, vol. 56, pp. 1616–1626, 2008.
8. R. Hoshyar, R. Razavi, and M. Al-Imari, "LDS-OFDM an efficient multiple access technique," in 2010 IEEE 71st Vehicular Technology Conference, 2010, pp. 1–5.
9. H. Nikopour and H. Baligh, "Sparse code multiple access," in 2013 IEEE 24th Annual International Symposium on Personal, Indoor, and Mobile Radio Communications (PIMRC), 2013, pp. 332–336.
10. S. R. Islam, M. Zeng, O. A. Dobre, and K.-S. J. I. W. C. Kwak, "Resource allocation for downlink NOMA systems: Key techniques and open issues," vol. 25, pp. 40–47, 2018.
11. "Millimetre wave massive MIMO technology," in *5G Physical Layer Technologies*, Abu-Rgheff, Mosa Ali. *5G physical layer technologies*. John Wiley & Sons, 2019., pp. 189–239.
12. J. Zhang, X. Yu, and K. B. Letaief, "Hybrid beamforming for 5G and beyond millimeter-wave systems: A holistic view," *IEEE Open Journal of the Communications Society*, vol. 1, pp. 77–91, 2020.
13. L. Zhu, Z. Xiao, X.-G. Xia, and D. O. Wu, "Millimeter-wave communications with non-orthogonal multiple access for B5G/6G," *IEEE Access*, vol. 7, pp. 116123–116132, 2019.
14. M. N. Kulkarni, S. Singh, and J. G. Andrews, "Coverage and rate trends in dense urban mmWave cellular networks," in 2014 IEEE Global Communications Conference, 2014, pp. 3809–3814.
15. S. M. R. Islam, M. Zeng, O. A. Dobre, and K. Kwak, "Resource Allocation for Downlink NOMA Systems: Key Techniques and Open Issues," *IEEE Wireless Communications*, vol. 25, pp. 40–47, 2018.
16. A. Akbar, S. Jangsher, and F. A. Bhatti, "NOMA and 5G emerging technologies: A survey on issues and solution techniques," *Computer Networks*, vol. 190, p. 107950, 2021.
17. S. Li, M. Derakhshani, and S. Lambotharan, "Outage-constrained robust power allocation for downlink MC-NOMA with imperfect SIC," in 2018 IEEE International Conference on Communications (ICC), 2018, pp. 1–7.
18. J. Tang, L. Jiao, N. Wang, P. Wang, K. Zeng, and H. Wen, "Mobility improves noma physical layer security," in 2018 IEEE Global Communications Conference (GLOBECOM), 2018, pp. 1–6.

19. O. Maraqa, A. S. Rajasekaran, S. Al-Ahmadi, H. Yanikomeroglu, and S. M. Sait, "A survey of rate-optimal power domain NOMA with enabling technologies of future wireless networks," *IEEE Communications Surveys & Tutorials*, vol. 22, pp. 2192–2235, 2020.

20. M. Vaezi, Z. Ding, and H. V. Poor, *Multiple Access Techniques for 5G Wireless Networks and Beyond* vol. 159: Springer, 2019.

21. W. Shin, M. Vaezi, B. Lee, D. J. Love, J. Lee, and H. V. Poor, "Non-orthogonal multiple access in multi-cell networks: Theory, performance, and practical challenges," *IEEE Communications Magazine*, vol. 55, pp. 176–183, 2017.

22. K. Mamat and W. Santipach, "On optimizing feedback-rate allocation for downlink MIMO-NOMA with quantized CSIT," *IEEE Open Journal of the Communications Society*, vol. 1, pp. 1551–1570, 2020.

11 Traditional and Modern Techniques for Visible Light Positioning Systems

*Muhammad Saadi, Ambar Bajpai, and
Demóstenes Zegarra Rodríguez*

CONTENTS

DOI: 10.1201/9781003227861-11

11.1 INTRODUCTION: AN OVERVIEW OF VISIBLE LIGHT POSITIONING TECHNIQUES

Navigation-based services utilize a positioning system to estimate the user's location. Currently, out of multiple available positioning approaches, the global positioning system (GPS) is widely deployed to provide positioning and navigation in real-time, especially in aircraft, vehicles, mobile phones, and other equipment of communication [1]. GPS performance can be disrupted when subjected to the environment, especially in an overcrowded urban area and indoors. Signals transmitted by the satellite are interrupted and degraded by clouds, ceilings, walls, and other obstacles, due to which navigation becomes inaccurate and discontinued [2, 3]. Indoor applications demand immeasurably more accurate positioning than outdoors, and this problem became an active topic known as the "last meter" problem. To fill this gap of GPS inaccuracies, the indoor positioning system (IPS) was proposed, which utilizes indoor wireless signals like Wi-Fi [4, 5], Bluetooth [6, 7], radio frequency identification (RFID) [8, 9], and ZigBee [10] to increase the performance of indoor positioning. During the last decade, Wi-Fi and Bluetooth have been widely employed in smart devices for positioning, but indoor positioning systems based on LEDs emerged as important areas of research, giving leverage over radio frequency (RF), as using visible light as the source fulfills the requirement to provide light indoors while providing services of communication. LED is known for its positioning application services in the communication field known as visible light communication (VLC) [11] and encompasses the following features:

- Utilizes high bandwidth of 100s of MHz for secure, safe, and high-speed wireless transmission with a sampling rate of 10s of MHz [12]. VLC reduces interference, as it uses visual light to communicate indoors, where penetration through opaque objects is not possible, enabling more secure wireless communication.
- Low consumption of power (100 mW for 10 Mbps) makes LEDs more efficient hence promoting green technology.
- LEDs have a lifespan of up to a decade with reliable illumination [13] and are cost-efficient.
- The positioning system has proved to be more accurate (by a few mms) than Wi-Fi (1 to 7 m) and Bluetooth (2 to 5 m) [14].

A clear comparative analysis is shown in Table 11.1, which compares VLC with other technologies used for wireless communication, thus highlighting the significance of LED-based indoor positioning [10–15].

11.2 LOCALIZATION PROCESS AND OPERATIONAL FRAMEWORK

Figure 11.1 shows the general framework of VLC, which is infrastructure on the positioning of LEDs for efficient delivery of data to the user. The transmission point encloses the controller and the signal modulator along the optical drive, which

TABLE 11.1

A Comparative Analysis of Various Wireless Technologies

Wireless technique	Transmission range	Omni-directional	Interference with	Passes through opaque surface	Power consumption	Range of accuracy
RFID	Long	Yes	RF signal	Yes	Low	cm
Acoustic	Short	Yes	Acoustic	Yes	Medium	cm
Bluetooth	Short	Yes	RF Signal	Yes	Low	cm
Wi-Fi	Long	Yes	RF Signal	Yes	Medium	cm
UWB	Short	Yes	Immune to interference	Yes	Medium	cm
Visible light	Long	No	Light	No	Low	mm

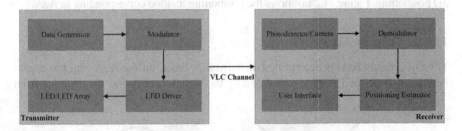

FIGURE 11.1 Localization process and operational framework

modulates the data and is transmitted in terms of flickering of the LED array over the channel toward the receiver junction. At the receiver end, after receiving the data through a camera or a photodiode, the packets are interpolated and demodulated along with the positioning information using the positioning estimator unit, and the localized information is expressed to the user with the help of the user interface (UI).

The localization process consists of a number of stages. In the first stage, the access point forwards the data to the processor for the encoding of data to a particular binary sequence which is generally operated by altering the voltage level through switching termed on-off keying (OOK) modulation, but since VLC is intensity sensitive, modulation referred to as "intensity modulation" (IM) is generally used. Other possible modulation options are color shift keying (CSK) [16], pulse positioning modulation (PPM) [17], orthogonal frequency division multiplexing (OFDM) [18], which have been used in the literature. Indoor localization is dependent upon multiple LEDs or transmitters which require multiplexing. Many multiplexing techniques are considered dependent on the condition, which mainly includes frequency division multiplexing and time-division multiplexing. In the next stage, the location of the receiver is calculated to deliver the data to the receiver. After the reception of the signal, one of the parameters can be determined, such as time of arrival (ToA), angle of arrival (AoA), time difference of arrival (TDoA), received signal strength (RSS), and received signal strength intensity (RSSI), which are interpolated by the localization module over which positioning algorithms are implemented to attain the exact location. LED-based visible light positioning (VLP) is dependent on the light intensity along with other parameters such as LED power, angle of incidence, and PD area at the receiver.

11.3 TRADITIONAL METHODS FOR POSITIONING

11.3.1 ANGLE OF ARRIVAL (AoA)

The angle of arrival refers to the calculated angle and distance following the multiple reference points and the intersecting lines. In VLP, measured angle and distance are required for the estimation and positioning of the transmitter involved in communication, and retrieved data is consumed to navigate or keep a track of the communication path. Incorporating AoA assists in determining the position with a few sensors in both 2D and 3D positioning. Figure 11.2 (a) shows the positioning method corresponding to AoA.

11.3.2 TIME OF ARRIVAL (ToA)

Time of arrival (ToA) is determined on a distance basis, unlike AoA which is angle-based and is defined as time consumed by the signal in covering the distance from

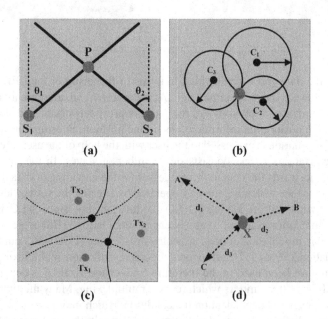

FIGURE 11.2 (a) Angle of arrival; (b) time of arrival; (c) time difference of arrival; (d) received signal strength

the stationary transmitter to the receiver while the transmitter is considered as a reference point. Time of flight (ToF), also known as the time taken by the flight of signal from a transmitter to a receiver where the receiver is a reference point, is the key to this technique. Since ToA utilizes the absolute time instead of calculating the time difference between arrival and departure of signal, the distance in between the transmitter and receiver can be retrieved directly from ToA while position can be estimated with the retrieved data. However, for an indoor positioning system, this is not a popular choice, as the distance between the transmitter and the receiver is short, and highly precise and specialized devices are required to estimate the time of flight. The time of arrival is demonstrated in Figure 11.2 (b).

11.3.3 Time Difference of Arrival (TDoA)

TDoA is also based on the distance which estimates the relative position of a transmitter accompanying mobility by determining the difference in time during propagation between the transmitter and multiple sensors or established reference points. TDoA reduces complexity, since it calculates the ToA at sensors positioned at two different locations, thus eradicating the necessity for estimating after the signal has been propagated. In addition, TDoA provides results with high accuracy. The TDoA positioning method is shown in Figure 11.2 (c).

11.3.4 Received Signal Strength (RSS)

RSS provides the measures for the signal strength in terms of power, regardless of distance or angle, and assists in determining the distance between mobile devices especially radio-based infrastructure. The RSSI method calculates attenuation induced in a signal to analyze the loss in signal strength of the transmitted signal, through which the distance between the devices can be determined. In an open wireless infrastructure, RSSI presents the relative RSS while good signal strength ensures the higher RSSI and vice versa. However, indoor environments are less adaptable as it is difficult to attain a line of sight (LOS), thus reducing the accuracy by directly affecting the RSSI and positioning due to the shadow and multipath effect. Figure 11.2 (d) shows the RSSI-based method.

A comparison table (Table 11.2) with the positioning method based on signal properties implemented on different systems is shown and analyzed.

Summarizing the signal properties based on the workings and analysis in Table 11.2, effectiveness is then demonstrated in Table 11.3.

11.4 POSITIONING ALGORITHMS – AN OVERVIEW

In the previous section, different positioning algorithms utilizing various techniques were presented, which focused on the techniques, characteristics, and accuracy of IPSs such as ToA/TDoA, received signal strength (RSS), and angle of arrival (AoA). Broadly speaking, we can classify the IPS into three different categories, namely mathematical/probabilistic methods, sensor assistive methods, and positioning

TABLE 11.2

Comparison of Wireless Technology Applications with Known Positioning Algorithm

System	Wireless technologies	Positioning algorithm	Accuracy	Complexity	Scalability/ dimension	Robust-ness	Cost
Microsoft Radar [19, 20]	RSS, WLAN	K-NN Viterbi-like algorithm	3–5 m	Moderate	Good/2D, 3D	Good	Low
Horus [21, 22]	RSS, WLAN	Probabilistic method	2 m	Moderate	Good/2D	Good	Low
LAC [23, 24]	RSS, WLAN	MLP, SVM	3 m	Moderate	Good/2D, 3D	Good	Low
Beamforming [25]	RSSI, WLAN	Probabilistic	1 m	Moderate	Good/2D	Good	Low
Snaptrack [26]	Assisted GPS, TDoA		5 m–50 m	High	Good/2D, 3D	Poor	Medium
WhereNet [27]	UHF TDoA	Least square/ RWGH	2 m– 3m	Moderate	Very Good/ 2D, 3D	Good	Low
Ubisense [28]	Unidirectional UWB TDoA	Least square	15 cm	Real-time response	24– sensors per cell/ 2D, 3D	Poor	Medium to high
Smart LOCUS [29]	RSS, WLAN + ultrasound	N/A	2–15cm	Medium	Good/2D	Good	Medium to high
EIRIS [30]	IR+UHF (RSS)+LF	PD-dependent	< 1 m	Medium to High	Good/2D	Poor	Medium to high
SpotON [31]	RFID RSS	Ad-hoc lateration	Depends on cluster size	Medium	Cluster at least two tags/ 2D	Good	Low
LANDMARC [32]	RFID RSS	K-NN	< 2m	Medium	Dense node placement required-	Poor	Low

(Continued)

TABLE 11.2 (CONTINUED)
Comparison of Wireless Technology Applications with Known Positioning Algorithm

System	Wireless technologies	Positioning algorithm	Accuracy	Complexity	Scalability/dimension	Robustness	Cost
TOPAZ [33]	Bluetooth	Based on PD	2 m	Positioning delay 15–30 sec	Nodes placed every 2–15 m	Poor	Medium
MPS [34]	QDMA	Ad-hoc lateration	10 m	1 s	Excellent/2D, 3D	Good	Medium
GPPS[35]	DECT cellular system	Gaussian process, k-NN	7.5 m	Medium	Good/2D, 3D	Good	Medium
Robot-based [36]	WLAN (RSS)	Bayesian approach	1.5 m	Medium	Good/2D	Good	Medium
MultiLoc [37]	WLAN (RSS)	SMP	2.7 m	Low	Good/2D	Good	Medium
TIX [38]	WLAN (RSS)	TIX	5.4 m	Low	Good/2D	Good	Medium
PinPoint 3D-ID [39]	UHF(RTOF)	Bayesian approach	1 m	5 s	Good/2D, 3D	Good	Low
GSM fingerprinting [40]	GSM cellular network (RSS)	Weighted k-NN	5 m	Medium	Excellent/2D, 3D	Good	Medium

TABLE 11.3

Pros and Cons of Various Indoor Positioning Techniques

Signal property	Measurement metric	Advantages	Disadvantages
AoA	Angle-based	High accuracy at room level	This technique is expensive as well as complex with low accuracy and wider coverage
ToA	Distance-based	High accuracy	Expensive and complex hardware requirements
TDoA	Distance-based	High accuracy	Expensive
RSSI	Signal-based (RSS)	Low cost, easy to implement/less complex	Medium accuracy

optimization methods. In addition, many RF-based algorithms are also applicable to VLC. The positioning algorithm is based on trilateration (mathematical method) comprised of a minimum of three LEDs. Each LED acts as a transmitter and locates the receiver based on the intensity and the distance between them; a circle can be drawn with radii equivalent to distance. Three circles emerge with the help of three LEDs, and thus the location is determined by finding the intersection point over the intersection area.

The algorithms are classified on the specific technology method adopted, whether the sensor-assisted method, mathematical method, or positioning optimal method, as shown in Figure 11.3. A brief description of algorithms based on the method is given in the next section.

11.4.1 MATHEMATICAL METHOD:

The mathematical method encompasses proximity, triangulation, and fingerprint-based algorithms. Proximity offers characteristics relevant to the information and is based on the location and range of a particular station or access point (AP). If there are multiple beacons, then the user is allocated based on the strength of the signal received by the mobile device that plays a role in positioning accuracy. For the optimization of costs, VLC comprises LED lamps as beacons [41], LEDs, and mobile devices, and the user derives the exact location when data from a lamp is received that sends ID or coordinates repeatedly.

The triangulation method is designed based on the properties (geometric) of the triangle for the estimation of the mobile device's location. Different positioning estimation methods led to the classification of triangulation into three classes> RSS, AoA, and ToA. AoA detects the location by considering the angle between the mobile device and the base station. The functionality of positioning is structured on the intersection of multiple directions of wireless signals that locate the mobile device, which means that at least two base stations are required for AoA so that a

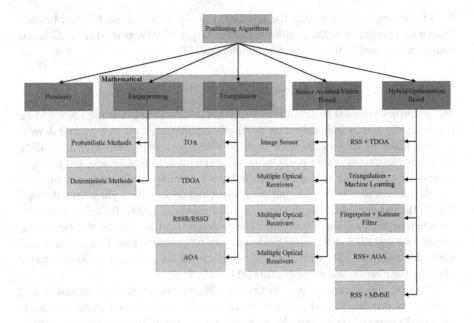

FIGURE 11.3 Positioning methods classification

user can be located. AoA is easily affected by the environment, hindering the accuracy of positioning, which can become lower with the increased distance between the mobile and base station. The maximum accuracy is around 0.1m, [42] and it requires external hardware which results in increased costs. Apart from the distance, AoA has an advantage over ToA by avoiding time synchronization and non-consideration of path losses and disturbance due to the particular light source.

In practical situations, the distance between the transmitter and receiver keeps changing, therefore distance is calculated according to the time taken by the signal to reach the base station; this approach is referred to as ToA. The location of an object can be found in a 2D plane when the distance between the targeted object and the non-collinear reference point is known. This method demands the accurate time synchronization of transmitter and receiver and hence is dependent on hardware for synchronization, resulting in increased costs. A system based on ToA utilizes white LEDs for illumination and signal transmission while considering the ideal scenario of perfect time synchronization [43]. TDoA was proposed to improve ToA by reducing the need for critical time synchronization and being based on the time at which transmitter and receiver get synchronized. The propagation time is measured as the difference in TDoA between the base station and mobile device and converting it into distance by multiplying it by the speed of propagation.

RSS provides an alternative approach that uses the attenuation property of emitted signal strength to determine the distance between the mobile device and the base station [44, 45, 46]. The increment in the distance leads to the weakening of the signal strength that is fundamental in measuring distance. Many systems-based models have been proposed, including the utilization of signal path loss, but this has not proven to be efficient in the positioning of the target. OFDM is used in VLC-based positioning to nullify the effect of multipath loss [47].

11.4.2 SENSOR-ASSISTED METHOD

Many sensors are used to attain high precision in positioning and are known to be efficient. The sensor is installed on the user's equipment, such as a mobile device. Various kinds of sensors are used in VLC-based positioning, but four are widely used that encompass image positioning, an accelerator, a light sensor, and multiple optical sensors. Image sensors, generally known as image positioning sensors, utilize the camera to take images and then detect and decode the light source through lenses, further demodulating the position information of LEDs. By using geometrical relations, the position of the device can be determined. A minimum of two image sensors are installed at the same place and can be extended based on situation and range. Four single LEDs with different colors can be used for transmission because of easier installation and cheaper costs [48].

Received power can be used to find the distance between the transmitter and receiver but can be affected by the distance, incidence angles, and irradiance, leading to a decrease of power that ultimately affects accuracy. To avoid this, an accelerometer is embedded in smartphones and is used for positioning [49]. For this system, accuracy is around 0.5 m in a simulative environment. A light sensor that can measure sensitivity for both angle of incidence and distance is therefore suitable for VLC-based communication [50], since it can retrieve information from the beacon, estimate RSS, and determine the position [51].

11.4.3 OPTIMIZATION METHOD

For the improvement of performance and accuracy, researchers have proposed methods, other than sensor-assisted or mathematical models, that involve modification in positioning methods to make them adaptable for VLC-based IPS. The optimization method considers filtering techniques, normalization methods, and spring models to achieve a better accuracy rate and tractability.

The filtering techniques are classified as the Kalman filter (KF) and particle filter (PF). KF is used for the measurements in positioning and tracking the mobile user's location. KF required the system measurement models to be dynamic and linear. For non-linear systems, the extended Kalman filter (EKF) is proposed, which can linearize the non-linear model. Rahaim et al. [52] refer to this model and present the recursive KF method in four steps: initialization, prediction, measurement, and update.

The PF algorithm is based on particles that are simply a set of random samples that are independently collected through proposal distribution. These particles then go through well-defined processes and rules to update the weight. This scheme allows the adoption of a non-linear model of Gaussian noise without consideration of the Gaussian hypothesis of the system.

The Gaussian mixture sigma-point particle filter (GM-SPPF) combines the Gaussian mixture model (GMM) and sigma-point approach (SPA) to attain higher accuracy and lower the computational costs [53]. GMM is based on the probability density formula (PDF) in which a set of particles is represented through the weighted sum of Gaussian components. SPA refers to the sampling based on the posterior distribution of a set of points. A localization algorithm based on a spring model (LASM) has been proposed to reduce the computational complexity while retaining the same accuracy, as per Chen et al. [54].

11.5   REVIEW OF MACHINE LEARNING AND ARTIFICIAL INTELLIGENCE

Artificial intelligence (AI) refers to the intelligent/rational agents that perceive and perform in an environment to maximize the performance parameters through learning [55]. Search algorithms and optimization theory are fundamentals in the AI field, due to which they are extensively employed in optical networks. By incorporating knowledge, planning, and reasoning, agents are made more intelligent so that they can play their roles more efficiently. Intelligent agents keep a knowledge base (KB) in which relevant environmental information is stored to determine the impact of their decisions or actions. KB is used by the agents while making a decision or making a plan and determining how to make decisions, which can be adapted to the changing conditions of the environment. Since optical networks are continuously subjected to uncertainty, intelligent agents must develop inference algorithms for temporal models to perform tasks like filtering, prediction, or smoothing, using techniques such as hidden Markov models (HMM) [56] and the Kalman filter [57]. The second fundamental element is the use of decision-making algorithms for the maximization of the expected utility, where the utility function is defined for the assignment of a single number to present the desirability of a state [58]. Realistic networking environments are subjected to uncertainty more often, and utility is directly dependent on the sequence of decisions rather than on a single one. Optical network agents are modeled on sequential decision problems in an uncertain environment. The third key factor in AI is learning, which enables an agent to improve performance based on its prior experience. A learning-capable agent is more adaptable to environmental changes and unforeseen scenarios that couldn't be predicted while designing the agent.

Machine learning (ML) techniques have been widely deployed for a variety of problems and in the context of telecommunication networks. Research based on the application of ML over a wireless network includes multiple-input and multiple-output (MIMO) communications [59], opportunistic spectrum access [60], channel estimation and signal detection in OFDM systems [61], and dynamic frequency reuse [62]. Machine learning techniques can be characterized into three categories: supervised learning, unsupervised learning, semi-supervised learning, and reinforcement learning [63, 64].

11.5.1 SUPERVISED LEARNING

Supervised learning is applicable in various applications, including spam detection, speech recognition, and object recognition. The main purpose of this algorithm is to predict one or more variables of output while providing the input variables x. A training data set contains N samples of the input variables and N samples for the output variables correspondingly. Different learning algorithms build a function $y(x)$ that enables the prediction of output variables based on new input variables. Supervised learning can be categorized into two classes: parametric models and non-parametric models.

Parametric models have a fixed number of parameters and represent the function y as a combination of a fixed number of parametric basis functions. Such models use training data to predict a fixed set of parameters w. The data set can be removed after the learning process. The simplest parametric model is a linear model that consists of a linear combination of fixed non-linear basis functions. Neural networks (NNs) are the most efficient models, which apply a series of functional transformations to the inputs [65–67]. NN represents a network of units or neurons, and each neuron has a bias parameter that permits any fixed offset in the data. Non-parametric models have parameters that are dependent on the training set. In this method, a subset or the entire training data is kept to utilize it for the prediction process. Widely used approaches include k-nearest neighbor models [68] and support vector machines (SVMs) [65, 66].

11.5.2 UNSUPERVISED LEARNING

Unsupervised learning methods are broadly used in social network analysis, market research, and gene clustering. In this method, the training data set is composed of only a set of input vectors x. Clustering refers to the process of grouping data and is of two types: intra-clustering and inter-clustering. The similarity for intra-clustering is high compared to inter-clustering where similarity is described in terms of distance function [69]. Multiple clustering approaches exist, out of which two methods are commonly known that include the k-means method (portioning approach) and the Gaussian mixture method (model-based approach). k-means is an iterative algorithm that starts with the partition of data into k clusters, and then the center of each cluster is determined, and data points are assigned to the cluster that has the closest center. This procedure is repeated until the assignment doesn't change or iterations exceed the predefined limit where K can be computed automatically [70]. The Gaussian mixture model (GMM) is a linear superposition of Gaussian distributions and is a probabilistic approach for clustering. This model exhibits parameters that include the mixing coefficient of each Gaussian component, the mean, and the covariance for each Gaussian coefficient.

11.5.3 SEMI-SUPERVISED LEARNING

Semi-supervised learning methods are a combination of supervised and unsupervised learning methods that take attributes from both. Semi-supervised methods are deployed especially when labeled points are not so unique or expensive to determine based on the availability of unlabeled data. Semi-supervised learning can be applied for all those applications in which supervised learning methods can be applied. Self-training is the oldest version of semi-supervised learning methods [71] and is an iterative process in which labeled data points are used by supervised learning algorithms initially, then unlabeled points are labeled at each step according to the predicted results for the training data.

11.5.4 Reinforcement Learning

Generally, the main objective of reinforcement learning (RL) is to learn a policy that maps states of the environment for which an action has to be performed while interacting with the environment. The RL method permit agents to learn by exploiting the available actions and improving their behavior based on evaluative feedback so that long-term performance can be ultimately improved. The RL method is applied under Markov decision processes (MDP), and the main purpose of the agent is to find a sequence of state-action pairs that maximize the evaluated feedback (reward) that is the optimal policy. Q-learning is the type of RL algorithm that is widely employed and is based on a model-free algorithm that determines the optimal action-value function [72].

11.5.5 Deep Learning

Deep learning adopts various methods and techniques. A few of the main methods are listed below.

11.5.5.1 Dense Neural Networking (DNN)

The fundamental module of the dense neural network is a neuron based on input weight and a function for activation, such as tanh and Relu, to attain output. DNN doesn't allow direct interaction within hidden network layers, and the invoked input is modified layer after layer according to the requirements.

11.5.5.2 Convolutional Neural Networking (CNN)

In convolutional neural networks, layers assigned for convolutional functions and pooling functions are considered to be the fundamental parts for the maximization of pooling. CNN can learn complex infrastructures comparatively more efficiently and encloses abstraction subjected to progression with the assistance of these two layers stacked alternatively. CNN can learn local patterns and spatial-based hierarchal patterns.

11.5.5.3 Recurrent Neural Networking (RNN)

The hidden layers in the recurrent neural network's architecture are interconnected, and in the time domain, the output is dependent not only on the current input but also on previous inputs, as demonstrated in Figure 11.4, which ensures the memory in RNNs and enables the remembering capacity.

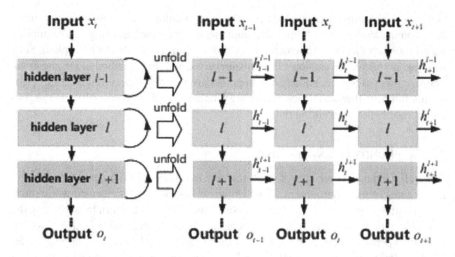

FIGURE 11.4   RNN architecture [73]

11.5.6   AUTO-ENCODERS

These are unsupervised neural networks that deliver the required output based on the type of input, and their functioning is implemented in different forms such as sparse encoders and de-noising auto-encoders. These networks can learn the vigorous compressed input to regenerate the constructive input as a required output. The prerequisite for training in auto-encoders is that the dispersal of input must be similar to the training set, which has proven to be a disadvantageous aspect for deploying auto-encoders. In addition, the working procedure is very complex to understand, and the setting of hyper-parameters, such as analyzing the number of neurons present in the hidden layer, is considered to be difficult.

11.5.7   EXTREME LEARNING MACHINE

This is infrastructure on one or multiple layers with a forwarded feed NN for which parameters need to be generated randomly by deploying probabilistic distribution. The error is minimized by mitigating the difference in value generated at the output and the true output value.

11.6   MACHINE LEARNING AND ARTIFICIAL INTELLIGENCE-BASED POSITIONING ALGORITHMS

In recent years, machine learning has been given attention due to remarkable achievements in different sectors using it to solve complex problems without integrating the external module, especially in the fields of computer vision and processing of natural language [74]. The successful integration of machine learning-based applications in the real world has not only influenced the industry but has also ignited researchers to focus on the directories of machine learning, especially in wireless communication for networking, management of resources, and positioning [75, 76]. ML techniques have been explored for integration into indoor positioning by incorporating LIFI technology, including the support vector machine (SVM), k-nearest neighbor (k-NN) [77], and extreme machine learning (EML) [78, 79].

Deep learning is one of the most well-known techniques that can integrate learning with the assistance of artificial neural network (ANN) and has advantages over other techniques particularly when there is a lot of data to be trained [80]. The services provided by deep learning provoke innovations in multiple scientific areas, including image recognition, recognition of text, speech identification, robotics, and processing of audio, video, and languages [80]. Deep learning (DL) can assist with challenges in wireless communication, especially in 5G, including complex circumstances to address high speed, accuracy, and models with non-identified channels. Influenced by the mentioned categories, it also has been deployed in wireless communication for the allocation of resources [81, 82], efficient traffic control [83], communication between physical layers [84], and indoor positioning [85].

There has been a rapid increase in its use for location-dependent services, particularly where efficiency is directly dependent on accuracy and preciseness while positioning. GPS is considered to be a reliable channel for outdoor localization, but when it comes to indoor positioning, results are not reliable due to the subjected attenuation and obstacles like furniture or wardrobes. Under such circumstances, many wireless technologies like WLAN, Bluetooth, or visible light have been integrated with an advanced approach for precise indoor localization. Different scenarios associated with localization have been studied and addressed by deploying machine learning. A few of them are discussed as follows.

11.6.1 INDOOR LOCALIZATION WITH SUPERVISED LEARNING APPROACHES

The k-nearest neighbor algorithm is based on the classifier method, which estimates the difference between values utilized in visible light positioning (VLP), particularly for fingerprinting. Comparison is made between the RSS value estimated online while storing the RSS value by deploying the distance metric and the k-nodes with the minimum distance considered as k-nearest neighbors. The average of the coordinates of these nodes assists in determining the position. Further improvement is made in attaining accuracy by assigning weightage to each node based on the distance, usually known as the weighted k-nearest neighbor (Wk-NN). According to a study, both Wk-NN and k-NN have shown 50% better results in terms of accuracy when compared to the conventional trilateration method based on RSS [86], but the time required for simulation was much higher due to the extensive computation. Another study deployed relatively small data sampling to build a compact database [87, 88], but this approach showed less robustness.

Feature scaling k-NN (FS-k-NN) was proposed to avoid the conventional localization technique of distancing, since the measured signal deviations and the geometric positioning is directly linked with measured RSS [89]. While estimating the distance for the fingerprint corresponding to the RP and RSS vector, the square of difference is multiplied by a weightage which is a function of the calculated RSS value. For the identification of parameters influencing the weightage function, a training procedure conducted with iterations and performance analysis is done on the test set of which the metric is deployed in the form of an objective function while tuning parameters. After the completion of model training, the difference is calculated between the recently captured RSS and estimated fingerprints, and then the user is positioned with the assistance of the calculated mean of weightage assigned to the locations with k-nearest RPs.

The regular training initiated from the starting phase incorporated in the positioning model may increase time consumption and complexity; to avoid this, a study has proposed the integration of an online independent support vector machine (OIVSM), which can learn online while keeping a balance in terms of accuracy and size of the model, making it adaptable for mobile devices [90]. There are generally two phases for the constructive model, which include the online phase and offline phase. The offline phase is categorized for the selection of kernel parameters, the sampling of data to overcome the issue of unbalanced data problems, and offline training incorporating the initially collected set of RSS data. The online phase provides the services of position determination for the new samples of RSS, and learning is done as soon as the training set is received and can be accessed through crowdsourcing; this method minimizes the estimation error up to 0.8 m while implementing indoor localization along with the reduction in time for the training data set and predicting time.

The blockage due to non-line of sight (NLOS) can minimize accuracy during positioning estimations, thus hindering the overall performance of VLC. The same scenario for radio is handled by Van Nguyen et al. in their study by proposing a relevance vector machine (RVM)-based model, which was specified for ToA-based localization subjected to ToA bandwidth [91]. The identification of the line-of-sight signal and the non-line-of-sight signal is made with the help of an RVM-based classifier which acquires data from the agent accompanying an unknown location that has been accessed by the anchor with the identified location. The fringe benefit of deploying RVM is less computation compared to SVM, due to the few numbers of support vectors adopted. On the other hand, a study proposes SVM with direct learning capable of withdrawing features from a received signal and the error corresponding to range, thus having the advantage of eradicating the need to distinguish LOS and NLOS signals [92]. An extreme learning machine (ELM) has been proposed to eradicate the time cost during training [93]. The output weights are trained according to the fingerprints of RSS and physical position and based on training; it can suggest the new coordinates for the newly arrived RSS vector.

A study incorporated an extreme learning machine to overcome the cost of the training procedure [94]. The training of output weight is done with the assistance of RSS-based fingerprints and their physical locations, and after completion of training, the location of a new RSS vector can be suggested. A deep neural network is integrated for indoor localization without considering path loss. The overall procedure is categorized into three steps, transformation, de-noising, and positioning, where prerequisite training is done for transformation and de-noising by integrating auto-encoders.

11.6.2 Indoor Localization with the Deep Learning Approaches

The artificial neural network (ANN) is one of the most deployed machine learning methods for both PD-oriented and sensor-oriented positioning for indoor localization in visible light communication because of its self-learning competence, which is maintained by keeping a balance between the input in terms of RSS or imaging and the output in the form of location information. A study proposed the integration of an artificial neural network to build a relationship between measured RSS and location information, considering the error in measured RSS occurs due to the multipath effect or diffuse reflation in optics [95]. The study has depicted that the larger the data training set, the greater the positioning accuracy, and the average error demonstrated is around 6.39cm. The light source image featuring and parameters regarding positioning which include angle of arrival and 3D position estimation can be revealed by integrating ANN in sensor-oriented techniques [96]. The study provides good results in terms of accuracy in centimeters, and the error induced due to the tilt in the angle of the camera has been calibrated effectively. Camera-based positioning is demonstrated in Polasek and Nemecek [97], where a neural network is implemented for the determination of a mutually positioned light source captured via the beacon received.

Recent work incorporating the ANN approach for indoor localization has presented effective robustness, providing evidence for the reliability of adaption in different positioning environments. However, there is a need for a large amount of real data for training purposes, but with this larger data, there is a drastic decrease in time for determining the location when compared to conventional positioning algorithms, having the advantage of being utilized for real-time purposes, especially for tracked positioning. DL has also been implemented into the physical layer to make it adaptable to adopting the advancement in architecture by deploying auto-encoders [1]. Another study incorporated deep learning for a Li-Fi-based system, where a joint estimation is made of the position of the user in a 3D model and user equipment within an indoor environment [98]. Fingerprinting and SNR are integrated to attain estimation metrics, and the ANN model based on multilayer perceptron (MLP) and conventional neural network (CNN) are implemented for UE and location of user positioning. Results compared with k-NN demonstrated the effectiveness with high gains and robustness.

11.6.3 Indoor Localization with Unsupervised Learning Approaches

Clustering is considered to be an unsupervised learning approach that is categorized for classifying the elements with the same attributes into a group due to similarities when compared to elements from other groups. This approach is incorporated in the literature to overcome the complexity involved in computation while plotting steps in the fingerprinting method. A two-step cluster method is proposed to determine the centers of the cluster by utilizing values of RSS and location coordinates [99]. The final location is determined after mitigating the Euclidean error for the provided LED-based RSS value subjected to the cluster centroids. This approach is needed to calculate the distance between measured RSS and estimated centroid only, thus providing the advantage of less computational time. Although the accuracy is limited to 0.31m, which is comparatively less than other machine learning approaches such as ANN, it has highlighted a way to achieve high precision. Another study used a conventional trilateration algorithm iteratively for estimating the positions of N candidates, and later, the DBSCAN cluster algorithm was deployed to distinguish precise position information from the deviated data to retrieve final location coordinates [100]. Experimental results show that this approach provided higher accuracy with a root mean square error of 3.5 cm and is capable of eradicating the outliers subjected to errors regarding measurements or natural occurrences in the operational environment

Clustering can acquire high accuracy even when provided with less computation as demonstrated from the above literature, but it is subjected to multiple factors affecting the efficiency, which include the adopted algorithms for clustering, amount of centroids, and characteristics selection, which provoke multiple complexities when considering the design for positioning algorithm. Gradim et al. [101] proposed indoor positioning for the VLC model by providing a fusion of two algorithms that enclose the k-means and random forest algorithm, which infer information from the parameters required in a model like RSS and provided strong robustness to the outer intrusions. In addition, the study introduced the VLP kernel concept to compact the database of fingerprinting while reducing the training time, which was validated by implementation in the real scenario of VLP. Another study proposed fingerprinting-based indoor positioning and neural networks for predicting the coordinates of a device placed in the 3D model [102]. It integrated three neural networks for three coordinates, and the model's infrastructure on RSS datasets originated from a grid with different source points. Results demonstrated an average distance error of up to 0.4mm with 99% claimed accuracy.

Determining the lower coordinated traits retrieved from the raw data of RSS measurements is done according to the linear distinguished analysis, as demonstrated in Yoo et al. [103]. The auto-encoder networking is deployed in the offline phase for the reconstruction of gathered information of CSI, and the assigned weights are noted to avoid high random probability and weak correlation corresponding to the distance covered [104]. To retrieve a new location during an online phase, a probabilistic approach is implemented which gathers information by estimating the weightage based on an average of the provided locations; the whole procedure is demonstrated in Figure 11.5. To reduce complexity, the amplitude responses of CSI are invoked as input to the deep neural network, which is trained by implementing a greedy learning algorithm on subsequent layers [105], and after the completion of training, the estimated weights are saved as fingerprints which assist the positioning process during the online assessment. A similar approach was applied by Wang et al. [106] along with the integration of deep auto-encoder-based networking for the extraction of the channel characteristics from the CSI-based bi-model. As in the previous study, average amplitudes measured, along with the angle of arrival and weights assigned while implementing deep auto-encoder, are considered to be the required characteristics

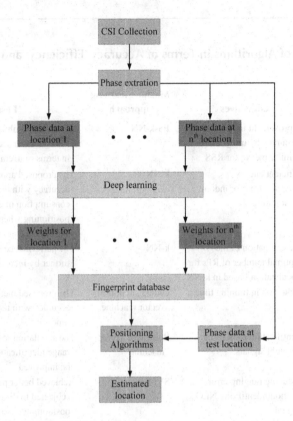

FIGURE 11.5   Architecture of deep learning (DL) for position estimation

that need to be retrieved as fingerprints; this approach achieved localization with high accuracy compared to other approaches presented in the literature.

11.7   COMPARISON OF MACHINE LEARNING-BASED POSITIONING ALGORITHMS

Conclusive literature has been shown in Table 11.4 for better comparative analysis in terms of accuracy, efficiency, and achievement.

11.8   CONCLUSION AND FUTURE WORK

This article presented a comprehensive overview that includes understanding the requirement of positioning. In addition, we covered various machine learning and artificial intelligence aspects related to VLP. Due to increased machine learning and artificial intelligence applications, the research community has been working on various algorithms used in AI/ML techniques to enhance VLP. We believe the use of ANN, RSS, and k-NN in VLP system development will increase positioning

TABLE 11.4
Comparison of Algorithms in Terms of Accuracy, Efficiency, and Achievement

Literature	Objectives	Machine learning approach	Results
[89]	Improvement in positioning accuracy by integrating a similar metric for RSS	FS-k-NN	Simulated results predicted that FS-k-NN can accomplish 1.93m in terms of average distance error
[106]	Efficient energy consumption for indoor positioning	k-NN	The proposed approach attains accuracy with the efficient consumption of energy while positioning when compared to the Wi-Fi-based approach
[107]	The estimation of the optimal number of RPs for localization-based in k-NN	k-NN	The performance can be enhanced further by increasing parameters k
[90]	Reduction in training time	Online support of vector machine	The proposed method attains high accuracy with reduced training time
[91]	Identification of non-line-of-sight signals	Relevance vector machine	The simulation results show that range identification of NLOS can be improved
[92]	Reducing ranging error without identifying NLOS signals	SVM	Achieved better performance when subjected to different indoor positioning environments
[103]	Extraction of RSS characteristics with low dimensions	PCA and LCA	Showed good results in terms of accuracy, especially in floor mapping
[93, 94]	Reduction in training time for positioning	ELM	Parallel ELM provides better performance in terms of accuracy, cost, and robustness when compared to centralized ELM
[108]	Reduction in computation time	Dense neural network (DNN)	The proposed approach achieves an error distance of 6 m for indoor positioning
[104]	Improvement in accuracy while deploying CSI-based data for fingerprinting	Auto-encoders	The proposed approach outperforms the estimation by integrating RSS-based neural network and fingerprinting
[105]	Overcoming the fallback of RSS-based method by integrating CSI-based model	Deep auto-encoder network	Performs well in two different scenarios while implementing three distinguishing benchmarks based on CSI
[106]	Accomplishing better accuracy by utilizing CSI amplitudes and AoA	Deep auto-encoder network	Outperforms compared to other techniques such as FIFS

(Continued)

TABLE 11.4 (CONTINUED)
Comparison of Algorithms in Terms of Accuracy, Efficiency, and Achievement

Literature	Objectives	Machine learning approach	Results
[109]	Achieving 3D localization in vast indoor places	Deep auto-encoder network	Positioning can be improved by deploying 3D-based fingerprinting
[86]	A single classifier-based weighted k-nearest model for VLP	k-NN	Accuracy was less than 0.1 m with less efficiency, thus subjected to improvements for efficient performance
[87]	3D indoor positioning for VLC	k-NN	Results show an accuracy of 4 cm, which is relatively high and provides a better performance
[88]	3D positioning for VLC based on fingerprinting and k-NN	k-NN	The presented approach provides an accuracy of up to 2.7 cm, thus there is a need for more improvements
[95]	ANN-based VLP with diffused channel	ANN	Results demonstrated an accuracy of 6.39 cm and high efficiency with enough data sampling and training
[97]	Optical positioning by the integration of neural network	ANN	The proposed approach achieves accuracy in centimeters with better performance
[96]	Tilt receiver correction method for VLP	ANN	The efficiency estimated in the proposed study is relatively high after training the dataset
[99]	LED-based positioning using clustering	Clustering	The proposed approach demonstrated good efficiency in VLP although accuracy is 0.31 m
[100]	Improvement in accuracy for VLC using machine learning	Clustering	The accuracy achieved up to 3.5 cm with a medium level of efficiency comparatively
[110], [111]	VLP based on the fusion of multiple classifiers	Fusion of multiple classifiers	The accuracy achieved approx. 5 cm with a medium-level efficiency comparatively but with high computational complexity
[112], [113]	Indoor localization with two-layer fusion network for VLC	Fusion of multiple classifiers	The proposed approach attained an accuracy of 5 cm with high robustness but is subjected to high computation complexity

efficiency. This chapter covers applications of VLP, a comparison of machine learning positioning techniques, and future trends of VLP research work.

The machine learning algorithm in a particular merging of supervised and unsupervised learning will be of research interest in VLP accuracy modeling. Many clustering approaches exist in the literature. k-means clustering in particular has proven its importance in terms of accuracy. Recently, in unsupervised clustering techniques, the DBSCAN-based method shows a 35% improvement in positioning estimation systems [86]. With the advancement of micro-electromechanical systems (MEMS), sensor fusion techniques, where the combination of smaller-size sensors can be used for positioning, can be considered a promising positioning technique. A singular value decomposition-based sensor fusion (SVD-SF) algorithm was proposed, having less complexity. It will lead to further enhancements in fusion-based positioning systems. There will be communication constraints in VLP systems for indoor positioning, and cost and complexity will play a significant role in algorithm modeling. By considering these constraints, the use of deep learning methods, such as ANN and neuromorphic computing architectures, will be useful VLP research and development.

REFERENCES

1. Saadi, Muhamamd, Touqeer Ahmad, M. Kamran Saleem, and Lunchakorn Wuttisittikulkij. "Visible light communication: An architectural perspective on the applications and data rate improvement strategies." *Transactions on Emerging Telecommunications Technologies* 30, no. 2 (2019): e3436.
2. Ward, N. "Understanding GPS: Principles and applications. Elliott D. Kaplan (Editor).£ 75. ISBN: 0-89006-793-7. Artech House Publishers, Boston & London. 1996." *The Journal of Navigation* 50, no. 1 (1997): 151–152.
3. Saadi, Muhammad, and Lunchakorn Wuttisittikulkij. "Visible light communication: The journey so far." *Journal of Optical Communications* 40, no. 4 (2019): 447–453.
4. Kalsi, A., Bajpai, A., Wuttisittikulkij, L. and Kovintaewat, P. "A base matrix method to construct column weight 3 quasi-cyclic LDPC codes with high girth." In 2016 International Conference on Electronics, Information, and Communications (ICEIC) (pp. 1–4). IEEE, 2016, January.
5. Bajpai, A. "A novel two dimensional visible light positioning system based on received signal strength and bi-literation." In The 29th international technical conference on circuits/systems, computers and communications (ITC-CSCC 14), pp. 1–4. 2014.
6. Hossain, AKM Mahtab, and Wee-Seng Soh. "A comprehensive study of bluetooth signal parameters for localization." In 2007 IEEE 18th International Symposium on Personal, Indoor and Mobile Radio Communications, pp. 1–5. IEEE, 2007.
7. Zhuang, Yuan, Jun Yang, You Li, Longning Qi, and Naser El-Sheimy. "Smartphone-based indoor localization with bluetooth low energy beacons." *Sensors* 16, no. 5 (2016): 596.
8. Wijayasekara, Sanika K., Muhammad Saadi, Warakorn Srichavengsup, Robithoh Annur, Suvit Nakpeerayuth, Hung-Yun Hsieh, and Lunchakorn Wuttisittikulkij. "Frame size analysis of optimum dynamic tree in RFID systems." *Engineering Journal* 24, no. 1 (2020): 239–249.
9. Yang, Po, and Wenyan Wu. "Efficient particle filter localization algorithm in dense passive RFID tag environment." *IEEE Transactions on Industrial Electronics* 61, no. 10 (2014): 5641–5651.

10. Bajpai, A. Performance analysis of non-binary low-density parity-check code and its future applications. *IEIE Transactions on Smart Processing & Computing*, 7, no. 1 (2018): 8–15.

11. Saadi, Muhammad, L. Wattisuttikulkij, Yan Zhao, and Paramin Sangwongngam. "Visible light communication: Opportunities, challenges and channel models." *International Journal of Electronics & Informatics* 2, no. 1 (2013): 1–11.

12. Saadi, Muhammad, Thiti Sittivangkul, Yan Zhao, Lunchakorn Wuttisittikulkij, and Paramin Sangwongngam. "System demonstration for visible light communication using adaptive threshold detection for low data rate applications." In 2012 IEEE International Conference on Electron Devices and Solid State Circuit (EDSSC), pp. 1–3. IEEE, 2012.

13. Saadi, Muhammad, Lunchakorn Wuttisittikulkij, Yan Zhao, Kittisak Panlek, Kampol Woradit, and Paramin Sangwongngam. "Performance analysis of optical wireless communication system using pulse width modulation." In 2013 10th International Conference on Electrical Engineering/Electronics, Computer, Telecommunications and Information Technology, pp. 1–5. IEEE, 2013.

14. Chi, Nan, Yingjun Zhou, Yiran Wei, and Fangchen Hu. "Visible light communication in 6G: Advances, challenges, and prospects." *IEEE Vehicular Technology Magazine* 15, no. 4 (2020): 93–102.

15. Saadi, Muhammad, Paramin Sangwongngam, S. Nakpeerayuth, P. Vanichchanun, Y. Zhao, and L. Wuttisittikulkij. "Global efforts in realizing visible light communication systems and its comparison with other short range wireless communication networks." In NTBC End Year Conference. 2011.

16. Delwar, Tahesin Samira, Abrar Siddique, Manas Ranjan Biswal, Ahmed Nabih Zaki Rashed, Anindya Jana, and Jee-Youl Ryu. "Novel multi-user MC-CSK modulation technique in visible light communication." *Optical and Quantum Electronics* 53, no. 4 (2021): 1–16.

17. Das, Sandip, and Soumitra Kumar Mandal. "Dimming controlled multi header hybrid PPM (MH-HPPM) for visible light communication." *Optical and Quantum Electronics* 53, no. 2 (2021): 1–18.

18. Adnan, Assaidah, Yang Liu, Chi-Wai Chow, and Chien-Hung Yeh. "Demonstration of non-hermitian symmetry (NHS) IFFT/FFT size efficient OFDM non-orthogonal multiple access (NOMA) for visible light communication." *IEEE Photonics Journal* 12, no. 3 (2020): 1–5.

19. Bahl, P. and Padmanabhan, V.N., 2000, March. RADAR: An in-building RF-based user location and tracking system. In *Proceedings IEEE INFOCOM 2000. Conference on computer communications. Nineteenth annual joint conference of the IEEE computer and communications societies (Cat. No. 00CH37064)* (Vol. 2, pp. 775-784). IEEE.

20. Bahl, Victor, and Venkat Padmanabhan. "Enhancements to the RADAR user location and tracking system." Technical Report MSR-TR-2000-12. (2000).

21. Youssef, Moustafa A., Ashok Agrawala, and A. Udaya Shankar. "WLAN location determination via clustering and probability distributions." In Proceedings of the First IEEE International Conference on Pervasive Computing and Communications, 2003. (PerCom 2003), pp. 143–150. IEEE, 2003.

22. Youssef, Moustafa, and Ashok Agrawala. "Handling samples correlation in the horus system." In IEEE Infocom 2004, vol. 2, pp. 1023–1031. IEEE, 2004.

23. Duckham, M. and Kulik, L., 2006. Location privacy and location-aware computing. In *Dynamic and mobile GIS* (pp. 63-80). CRC press.

24. Brunato, Mauro, and Roberto Battiti. "Statistical learning theory for location fingerprinting in wireless LANs." *Computer Networks* 47, no. 6 (2005): 825–845.

25. Van Veen, Barry D., and Kevin M. Buckley. "Beamforming: A versatile approach to spatial filtering." *IEEE ASSP Magazine* 5, no. 2 (1988): 4–24.

26. Hightower, Jeffrey, and Gaetano Borriello. "Location systems for ubiquitous computing." *Computer* 34, no. 8 (2001): 57–66.

27. Patwari, Neal, Joshua N. Ash, Spyros Kyperountas, Alfred O. Hero, Randolph L. Moses, and Neiyer S. Correal. "Locating the nodes: Cooperative localization in wireless sensor networks." *IEEE Signal Processing Magazine* 22, no. 4 (2005): 54–69.

28. Teuber, Andreas, Bernd Eissfeller, and Thomas Pany. "A two-stage fuzzy logic approach for wireless LAN indoor positioning." In Proceedings of IEEE/ION PLANS 2006, pp. 730–738. 2006.

29. HP SmartLOCUS. [Online]. Available: http://www.rfidjournal.com/article / articleview/1211/1/50/

30. Stephan R. Sain (1996) The Nature of Statistical Learning Theory, *Technometrics*, 38:4, 409, DOI: 10.1080/00401706.1996.10484565

31. Hightower, Jeffrey, Roy Want, and Gaetano Borriello. "SpotON: An indoor 3D location sensing technology based on RF signal strength. UW CSE Technical Report #2000-02-02" (2000).

32. Ni, Lionel M., Yunhao Liu, Yiu Cho Lau, and Abhishek P. Patil. "LANDMARC: Indoor location sensing using active RFID." In Proceedings of the First IEEE International Conference on Pervasive Computing and Communications, 2003.(PerCom 2003), pp. 407–415. IEEE, 2003.

33. Krim, Hamid, and Mats Viberg. "Two decades of array signal processing research: The parametric approach." *IEEE Signal Processing Magazine* 13, no. 4 (1996): 67–94.

34. Schwaighofer, Anton, Marian Grigoras, Volker Tresp, and Clemens Hoffmann. "GPPS: A Gaussian process positioning system for cellular networks." *Advances in Neural Information Processing Systems* 16 (2003), pp 1–8.

35. Ladd, A.M., K.E. Bekris, G. Marceau, A. Rudys, D.S. Wallach and L.E. Kavraki. "Using wireless ethernet for localization." In IEEE/RSJ International Conference on Intelligent Robots and Systems (Vol. 1, pp. 402–408). IEEE, 2002, September.

36. Haeberlen, Andreas, Eliot Flannery, Andrew M. Ladd, Algis Rudys, Dan S. Wallach, and Lydia E. Kavraki. "Practical robust localization over large-scale 802.11 wireless networks." In Proceedings of the 10th Annual International Conference on Mobile Computing and Networking, pp. 70–84. 2004.

37. Prasithsangaree, Phongsak, Prashant Krishnamurthy, and Panos Chrysanthis. "On indoor position location with wireless LANs." In The 13th IEEE International Symposium on Personal, Indoor and Mobile Radio Communications, vol. 2, pp. 720–724. IEEE, 2002.

38. Gwon, Youngjune, and Ravi Jain. "Error characteristics and calibration-free techniques for wireless LAN-based location estimation." In Proceedings of the Second International Workshop on Mobility Management & Wireless Access Protocols, pp. 2–9. 2004.

39. Werb, Jay, and Colin Lanzl. "Designing a positioning system for finding things and people indoors." *IEEE Spectrum* 35, no. 9 (1998): 71–78.

40. Otsason, V., A. Varshavsky, A. LaMarca and E.D. Lara. "Accurate GSM indoor localization." In International Conference on Ubiquitous Computing (pp. 141–158). Springer, Berlin, Heidelberg, 2005, September.

41. del Campo-Jimenez, Guillermo, Jorge M. Perandones, and Franciso Jose Lopez-Hernandez. "A VLC-based beacon location system for mobile applications." In 2013 International Conference on Localization and GNSS (ICL-GNSS), pp. 1–4. IEEE, 2013.

42. Kim, Hyun-Seung, Deok-Rae Kim, Se-Hoon Yang, Yong-Hwan Son, and Sang-Kook Han. "An indoor visible light communication positioning system using a RF carrier allocation technique." *Journal of Lightwave Technology* 31, no. 1 (2012): 134–144.

43. Wang, Thomas Q., Y. Ahmet Sekercioglu, Adrian Neild, and Jean Armstrong. "Position accuracy of time-of-arrival based ranging using visible light with application in indoor localization systems." *Journal of Lightwave Technology* 31, no. 20 (2013): 3302–3308.

44. Saadi, Muhammad, Yan Zhao, Oumair Naseer, and Lunchakorn Wuttisittikulkij. "A beam scanning-based indoor localization system using light emitting diodes." *Engineering Journal* 20, no. 3 (2016): 197–206.

45. Saadi, Muhammad. "Beam scanning based secure communication using visible light." *Bahria University Journal of Information & Communication Technologies (BUJICT)* 10, no. 2 (2017) pp 1–5.

46. Hosseinianfar, Hamid, and Maite Brandt-Pearce. "Performance limits for fingerprinting-based indoor optical communication positioning systems exploiting multipath reflections." *IEEE Photonics Journal* 12, no. 4 (2020): 1–16.

47. Saadi, Muhammad, Yan Zhao, Lunchakorn Wuttisttikulkij, and Muhammad Tahir Abbas Khan. "A heuristic approach to indoor localization using light emitting diodes." *Journal of Theoretical & Applied Information Technology* 84, no. 3 (2016).

48. Kim, Byung Yeon, Jung-Sik Cho, Youngil Park, and Ki-Doo Kim. "Implementation of indoor positioning using LED and dual PC cameras." In 2012 Fourth International Conference on Ubiquitous and Future Networks (ICUFN), pp. 476–477. IEEE, 2012.

49. Yasir, Muhammad, Siu-Wai Ho, and Badri N. Vellambi. "Indoor positioning system using visible light and accelerometer." *Journal of Lightwave Technology* 32, no. 19 (2014): 3306–3316.

50. Li, Liqun, Pan Hu, Chunyi Peng, Guobin Shen, and Feng Zhao. "Epsilon: A visible light based positioning system." In 11th USENIX Symposium on Networked Systems Design and Implementation (NSDI 14), pp. 331–343. 2014.

51. Saadi, Muhammad, Ambar Bajpai, Yan Zhao, Paramin Sangwongngam, and Lunchakorn Wuttisittikulkij. "Design and implementation of secure and reliable communication using optical wireless communication." *Frequenz* 68, no. 11–12 (2014): 501–509.

52. Rahaim, Michael, Gregary B. Prince, and Thomas DC Little. "State estimation and motion tracking for spatially diverse VLC networks." In 2012 IEEE Globecom Workshops, pp. 1249–1253. IEEE, 2012.

53. Gu, Wenjun, Weizhi Zhang, Jin Wang, MR Amini Kashani, and Mohsen Kavehrad. "Three dimensional indoor positioning based on visible light with Gaussian mixture sigma-point particle filter technique." In Broadband Access Communication Technologies IX, vol. 9387, p. 93870O. International Society for Optics and Photonics, 2015.

54. Chen, Wanming, Tao Mei, Max Q-H Meng, Huawei Liang, Yumei Liu, Yangming Li, and Shuai Li. "Localization algorithm based on a spring model (LASM) for large scale wireless sensor networks." *Sensors* 8, no. 3 (2008): 1797–1818.

55. Russell, Stuart, and Peter Norvig. "Artificial intelligence: A modern approach." *Pearson Education, Inc.* (2002).

56. Kolade, Oluwafemi, Ayokunle Damilola Familua, and Ling Cheng. "Indoor amplify-and-forward power-line and visible light communication channel model based on a semi-hidden Markov model." *AEU-International Journal of Electronics and Communications* 124 (2020): 153108.

57. Huang, Mouxiao, Weipeng Guan, Zhibo Fan, Zenghong Chen, Jingyi Li, and Bangdong Chen. "Improved target signal source tracking and extraction method based on outdoor visible light communication using a cam-shift algorithm and Kalman filter." *Sensors* 18, no. 12 (2018): 4173.

58. Jayaraj, A., T. Venkatesh, and C. Siva Ram Murthy. "Loss classification in optical burst switching networks using machine learning techniques: Improving the performance of TCP." *IEEE Journal on Selected Areas in Communications* 26, no. 6 (2008): 45–54.

59. Cui, W., Dong, A., Cao, Y., Zhang, C., Yu, J. and Li, S., 2021. Deep learning based MIMO transmission with precoding and radio transformer networks. *Procedia Computer Science*, *187*, pp.396–401.

60. Macaluso, Irene, Danny Finn, Baris Ozgul, and Luiz A. DaSilva. "Complexity of spectrum activity and benefits of reinforcement learning for dynamic channel selection." *IEEE journal on Selected Areas in Communications* 31, no. 11 (2013): 2237–2248.

61. Ye, Hao, Geoffrey Ye Li, and Biing-Hwang Juang. "Power of deep learning for channel estimation and signal detection in OFDM systems." *IEEE Wireless Communications Letters* 7, no. 1 (2017): 114–117.

62. Marinescu , Andrei, Irene Macaluso, and Luiz A. DaSilva. "A multi-agent neural network for dynamic frequency reuse in LTE networks." In 2018 IEEE International Conference on Communications Workshops (ICC Workshops), pp. 1–6. IEEE, 2018.

63. Toor, Waqas Tariq, Abdul Basit, Naeem Maroof, Saqib Ali Khan, and Muhammad Saadi. "Evolution of random access process: From Legacy networks to 5G and beyond." *Transactions on Emerging Telecommunications Technologies* (2019): e3776.

64. Silva, Juan Casavílca, Muhammad Saadi, Lunchakorn Wuttisittikulkij, Davi Ribeiro Militani, Renata Lopes Rosa, Demóstenes Zegarra Rodríguez, and Sattam Al Otaibi. (2021) "Light-field imaging reconstruction using deep learning enabling intelligent autonomous transportation system." *IEEE Transactions on Intelligent Transportation Systems* (2021) vol. 23, no. 2: 1587–1595.

65. Bishop, Christopher M., and Nasser M. Nasrabadi. *Pattern Recognition and Machine Learning.* Vol. 4, no. 4. New York: Springer, 2006.

66. Hart, Peter E., David G. Stork, and Richard O. Duda. *Pattern Classification.* Hoboken: Wiley, 2000.

67. Mendonça, Robson V., Arthur AM Teodoro, Renata L. Rosa, Muhammad Saadi, Dick Carrillo Melgarejo, Pedro HJ Nardelli, and Demóstenes Z. Rodríguez. "Intrusion detection system based on fast hierarchical deep convolutional neural network." *IEEE Access* 9 (2021): 61024–61034.

68. Saadi, Muhammad, Zeeshan Saeed, Touqeer Ahmad, M. Kamran Saleem, and Lunchakorn Wuttisittikulkij. "Visible light-based indoor localization using k-means clustering and linear regression." *Transactions on Emerging Telecommunications Technologies* 30, no. 2 (2019): e3480.

69. Ilter, Mehmet C., Alexis A. Dowhuszko, Jyri Hämäläinen, and Risto Wichman. "Visible light communication-based monitoring for indoor environments using unsupervised learning." In 2021 IEEE 93rd Vehicular Technology Conference (VTC2021-Spring), pp. 1–5. IEEE, 2021.

70. Hastie, Trevor, Robert Tibshirani, Jerome H. Friedman, and Jerome H. Friedman. *The Elements of Statistical Learning: Data Mining, Inference, and Prediction.* Vol. 2. New York: Springer, 2009.

71. Tran, Huy Q., and Cheolkeun Ha. "Reducing the burden of data collection in a finger-printing-based VLP system using a hybrid of improved co-training semi-supervised regression and adaptive boosting algorithms." *Optics Communications* 488 (2021): 126857.

72. Thrun, Sebastian, and Michael L. Littman. "Reinforcement learning: An introduction." *AI Magazine* 21, no. 1 (2000): 103–103.

73. Medsker, Larry, and Lakhmi C. Jain, eds. *Recurrent Neural Networks: Design and Applications.* CRC Press, 1999.

74. Wang, Tianqi, Chao-Kai Wen, Hanqing Wang, Feifei Gao, Tao Jiang, and Shi Jin. "Deep learning for wireless physical layer: Opportunities and challenges." *China Communications* 14, no. 11 (2017): 92–111.

75. Zhu, Guangxu, Dongzhu Liu, Yuqing Du, Changsheng You, Jun Zhang, and Kaibin Huang. "Toward an intelligent edge: Wireless communication meets machine learning." *IEEE Communications Magazine* 58, no. 1 (2020): 19–25.

76. Sun, Yaohua, Mugen Peng, Yangcheng Zhou, Yuzhe Huang, and Shiwen Mao. "Application of machine learning in wireless networks: Key techniques and open issues." *IEEE Communications Surveys & Tutorials* 21, no. 4 (2019): 3072–3108.

77. Tran, Huy Quang, and Cheolkeun Ha. "High precision weighted optimum K-nearest neighbors algorithm for indoor visible light positioning applications." *IEEE Access* 8 (2020): 114597–114607.

78. Chen, Yirong, Weipeng Guan, Jingyi Li, and Hongzhan Song. "Indoor real-time 3-D visible light positioning system using fingerprinting and extreme learning machine." *IEEE Access* 8 (2019): 13875–13886.

79. Wang, Xinyi, and Jianhua Shen. "Machine learning and its applications in visible light communication based indoor positioning." In 2019 International Conference on High Performance Big Data and Intelligent Systems (HPBD&IS), pp. 274–277. IEEE, 2019.

80. Zappone, Alessio, Marco Di Renzo, and Mérouane Debbah. "Wireless networks design in the era of deep learning: Model-based, AI-based, or both?." *IEEE Transactions on Communications* 67, no. 10 (2019): 7331–7376.

81. Ye, Hao, Geoffrey Ye Li, and Biing-Hwang Fred Juang. "Deep reinforcement learning based resource allocation for V2V communications." *IEEE Transactions on Vehicular Technology* 68, no. 4 (2019): 3163–3173.

82. Tang, Fengxiao, Bomin Mao, Zubair Md Fadlullah, and Nei Kato. "On a novel deep-learning-based intelligent partially overlapping channel assignment in SDN-IoT." *IEEE Communications Magazine* 56, no. 9 (2018): 80–86.

83. Tang, Fengxiao, Bomin Mao, Zubair Md Fadlullah, Nei Kato, Osamu Akashi, Takeru Inoue, and Kimihiro Mizutani. "On removing routing protocol from future wireless networks: A real-time deep learning approach for intelligent traffic control." *IEEE Wireless Communications* 25, no. 1 (2017): 154–160.

84. Qin, Zhijin, Hao Ye, Geoffrey Ye Li, and Biing-Hwang Fred Juang. "Deep learning in physical layer communications." *IEEE Wireless Communications* 26, no. 2 (2019): 93–99.

85. Arfaoui, Mohamed Amine, Mohammad Dehghani Soltani, Iman Tavakkolnia, Ali Ghrayeb, Chadi M. Assi, Majid Safari, and Harald Haas. "Invoking deep learning for joint estimation of indoor lifi user position and orientation." *IEEE Journal on Selected Areas in Communications* 39, no. 9 (2021): 2890–2905.

86. Van, Manh The, Nguyen Van Tuan, Tran The Son, Hoa Le-Minh, and Andrew Burton. "Weighted k-nearest neighbour model for indoor VLC positioning." *IET Communications* 11, no. 6 (2017): 864–871.

87. Xu, Ming, Weiwei Xia, Ziyan Jia, Yaping Zhu, and Lianfeng Shen. "A VLC-based 3-D indoor positioning system using fingerprinting and K-nearest neighbor." In 2017 IEEE 85th Vehicular Technology Conference (VTC Spring), pp. 1–5. IEEE, 2017.

88. Alam, Fakhrul, Moi Tin Chew, Tapiwanashe Wenge, and Gourab Sen Gupta. "An accurate visible light positioning system using regenerated fingerprint database based on calibrated propagation model." *IEEE Transactions on Instrumentation and Measurement* 68, no. 8 (2018): 2714–2723.

89. Li, Dong, Baoxian Zhang, and Cheng Li. "A feature-scaling-based k-nearest neighbor algorithm for indoor positioning systems." *IEEE Internet of Things Journal* 3, no. 4 (2015): 590–597.

90. Wu, Zheng, Kechang Fu, Esrafil Jedari, Shaeera Rabbanee Shuvra, Rashid Rashidzadeh, and Mehrdad Saif. "A fast and resource efficient method for indoor positioning using received signal strength." *IEEE Transactions on Vehicular Technology* 65, no. 12 (2016): 9747–9758.

91. Van Nguyen, Thang, Youngmin Jeong, Hyundong Shin, and Moe Z. Win. "Machine learning for wideband localization." *IEEE Journal on Selected Areas in Communications* 33, no. 7 (2015): 1357–1380.

92. Wymeersch, Henk, Stefano Maranò, Wesley M. Gifford, and Moe Z. Win. "A machine learning approach to ranging error mitigation for UWB localization." *IEEE Transactions on Communications* 60, no. 6 (2012): 1719–1728.

93. Qiu, Zhirong, Han Zou, Hao Jiang, Lihua Xie, and Yiguang Hong. "Consensus-based parallel extreme learning machine for indoor localization." In 2016 IEEE Global Communications Conference (GLOBECOM), pp. 1–6. IEEE, 2016.

94. Chen, Yirong, Weipeng Guan, Jingyi Li, and Hongzhan Song. "Indoor real-time 3-D visible light positioning system using fingerprinting and extreme learning machine." *IEEE Access* 8 (2019): 13875–13886.

95. Huang, Heqing, Aiying Yang, Lihui Feng, Guoqiang Ni, and Peng Guo. "Artificial neural-network-based visible light positioning algorithm with a diffuse optical channel." *Chinese Optics Letters* 15, no. 5 (2017): 050601.

96. Sharma, Abhishek, Sushank Chaudhary, Jyoteesh Malhotra, Muhammad Saadi, Sattam Al Otaibi, Jamel Nebhen, and Lunchakorn Wuttisittikulkij. "A cost-effective photonic radar under adverse weather conditions for autonomous vehicles by incorporating a frequency-modulated direct detection scheme." *Frontiers in Physics* (2021) vol 9: 467. DOI: https://doi.org/10.3389/fphy.2021.747598

97. Polasek, Martin, and Jiri Nemecek. "Optical positioning using neural network." In 2018 41st International Conference on Telecommunications and Signal Processing (TSP), pp. 1–5. IEEE, 2018.

98. Arfaoui, Mohamed Amine, Mohammad Dehghani Soltani, Iman Tavakkolnia, Ali Ghrayeb, Chadi M. Assi, Majid Safari, and Harald Haas. "Invoking deep learning for joint estimation of indoor lifi user position and orientation." *IEEE Journal on Selected Areas in Communications* 39, no. 9 (2021): 2890–2905.

99. Jiang, Jiajia, Weipeng Guan, Zhounan Chen, and Yirong Chen. "Indoor high-precision three-dimensional positioning algorithm based on visible light communication and fingerprinting using K-means and random forest." *Optical Engineering* 58, no. 1 (2019): 016102.

100. Gradim, André, Pedro Fonseca, Luis Nero Alves, and Reem E. Mohamed. "On the usage of machine learning techniques to improve position accuracy in visible light positioning systems." In 2018 11th International Symposium on Communication Systems, Networks & Digital Signal Processing (CSNDSP), pp. 1–6. IEEE, 2018.

101. Jiang, Jiajia, Weipeng Guan, Zhounan Chen, and Yirong Chen. "Indoor high-precision three-dimensional positioning algorithm based on visible light communication and fingerprinting using K-means and random forest." *Optical Engineering* 58, no. 1 (2019): 016102.

102. Alonso-González, Itziar, David Sánchez-Rodríguez, Carlos Ley-Bosch, and Miguel A. Quintana-Suárez. "Discrete indoor three-dimensional localization system based on neural networks using visible light communication." *Sensors* 18, no. 4 (2018): 1040.

103. Yoo, Jaehyun, Karl Henrik Johansson, and Hyoun Jin Kim. "Indoor localization without a prior map by trajectory learning from crowdsourced measurements." *IEEE Transactions on Instrumentation and Measurement* 66, no. 11 (2017): 2825–2835.

104. Wang, Xuyu, Lingjun Gao, and Shiwen Mao. "CSI phase fingerprinting for indoor localization with a deep learning approach." *IEEE Internet of Things Journal* 3, no. 6 (2016): 1113–1123.

105. Wang, Xuyu, Lingjun Gao, Shiwen Mao, and Santosh Pandey. "CSI-based fingerprinting for indoor localization: A deep learning approach." *IEEE Transactions on Vehicular Technology* 66, no. 1 (2016): 763–776.

106. Wang, Xuyu, Lingjun Gao, and Shiwen Mao. "BiLoc: Bi-modal deep learning for indoor localization with commodity 5GHz WiFi." *IEEE Access* 5 (2017): 4209–4220.

107. Niu, Jianwei, Bowei Wang, Lei Shu, Trung Q. Duong, and Yuanfang Chen. "ZIL: An energy-efficient indoor localization system using ZigBee radio to detect WiFi fingerprints." *IEEE Journal on Selected Areas in Communications* 33, no. 7 (2015): 1431–1442.

108. Xu, Yubin, Mu Zhou, Weixiao Meng, and Lin Ma. "Optimal KNN positioning algorithm via theoretical accuracy criterion in WLAN indoor environment." In 2010 IEEE Global Telecommunications Conference GLOBECOM 2010, pp. 1–5. IEEE, 2010.

109. Ye, Xiaokang, Xuefeng Yin, Xuesong Cai, Antonio Pérez Yuste, and Hongliang Xu. "Neural-network-assisted UE localization using radio-channel fingerprints in LTE networks." *IEEE Access* 5 (2017): 12071–12087.

110. Xiao, Chao, Daiqin Yang, Zhenzhong Chen, and Guang Tan. "3-D BLE indoor localization based on denoising autoencoder." *IEEE Access* 5 (2017): 12751–12760.

111. Guo, Xiansheng, Sihua Shao, Nirwan Ansari, and Abdallah Khreishah. "Indoor localization using visible light via fusion of multiple classifiers." *IEEE Photonics Journal* 9, no. 6 (2017): 1–16.

112. Guo, Xiansheng, Fangzi Hu, Nkrow Raphael Elikplim, and Lin Li. "Indoor localization using visible light via two-layer fusion network." *IEEE Access* 7 (2019): 16421–16430.

113. Xiang, Zhe, Song Song, Jin Chen, Hao Wang, Jian Huang, and Xingxin Gao. "A wireless LAN-based indoor positioning technology." *IBM Journal of Research and Development* 48, no. 5.6 (2004): 617–626.

Index

Printed in the United States
by Baker & Taylor Publisher Services